AN ISLAN

Geert Mak is a journalist and historian, and one of the Netherlands' bestselling writers. His previous books include *Amsterdam*, *The Bridge* and the acclaimed *In Europe: Travels Through the Twentieth Century*.

GEERT MAK

An Island in Time

The Biography of a Village

TRANSLATED FROM THE DUTCH BY
Ann Kelland

NEW PREFACE AND AFTERWORD FOR THE 2010
EDITION TRANSLATED FROM THE DUTCH BY
Sam Garrett

VINTAGE BOOKS
London

Published by Vintage 2010

6 8 10 9 7 5

Copyright © Geert Mak 1996, 2010

English translation copyright © Ann Kelland 2000
English translation of preface and afterword to the 2010
edition copyright © Sam Garrett

First published by Uitgeverij Atlas in 1996 with the title
Hoe God verdween uit Jorwerd

Geert Mak has asserted his right under the Copyright, Designs and
Patents Act 1988 to be identified as the author of this work

First published in Great Britain in 2000 by
The Harvill Press with the title *Jorwerd*

Vintage
Random House, 20 Vauxhall Bridge Road,
London SW1V 2SA

www.vintage-books.co.uk

Addresses for companies within The Random House Group Limited
can be found at: www.randomhouse.co.uk/offices.htm

The Random House Group Limited Reg. No. 954009

A CIP catalogue record for this book
is available from the British Library

This translation has been published with the financial support of the
Foundation for the Production and Translation of Dutch Literature

ISBN 9780099546863

Penguin Random House is committed to a sustainable future for
our business, our readers and our planet. This book is made from
Forest Stewardship Council® certified paper.

Printed and bound in Great Britain by Clays Ltd, St Ives plc

In memory of my mother,

Geertje van der Molen

Contents

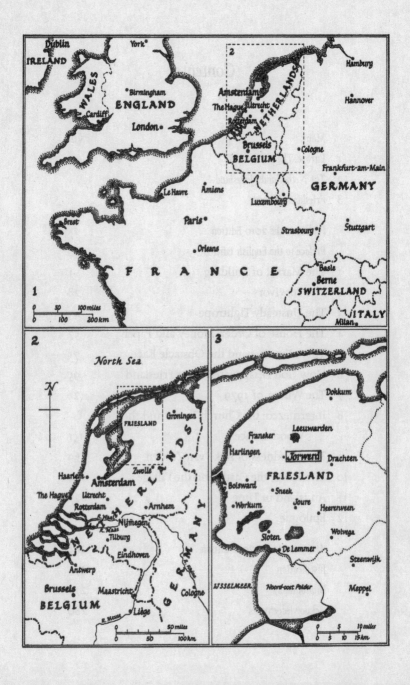

Preface to the 2010 Edition

"YOU SHOULD GET OUT OF TOWN," MY PUBLISHER SAID. "WE CITY FOLK aren't interested in anything but ourselves. I have a feeling that the big change these days is taking place quietly, in the European countryside. What's going to happen to all those farmers, now that one farm after another is shutting down? What will happen to the villages once the baker, the greengrocer and even the local school disappear? The same thing is going on everywhere you look, whether it's the Netherlands, France or England. What's going to become of the people, of that centuries-old rural culture? Try writing a book about that!"

My publisher was right, even more so than he may first have realised. The silent revolution taking place all over Europe and the rest of the world is of historic proportions. In 1960, two-thirds of the world's population still lived in the countryside. Estimates are that by 2025 it will be precisely the other way around: two-thirds of humanity will be living in the city.

This is an historical *volte face* comparable to the abandonment of nomadic hunting and gathering in favour of the static farmer's life. The consequences of this great migration, for those who have eyes to see, are visible everywhere: in the thousands of ruined and almost-vacant villages all over Europe, in the millions of poor factory girls in China, in the young people abandoned to their fate in the suburbs of Paris, in the cigarette vendors on Istanbul's Galata Bridge, in the timid Moroccan village women in their flats in Amsterdam-West, and on and on.

In the autumn of 1993 I took up residence in a Frisian village. Friesland is a typical agrarian province in the northern Netherlands, with lots of water, huge pastures and here and there, like islands in that sea of green, the steeples and trees of hundreds of little villages. The ancestors of Henry and Jane Fonda came from there, as did those of John Updike, and of all Americans and Australians with surnames like Hoekstra, Hofstra and Dijkstra. People of that ilk, in other words. They speak a language of their own there, Frisian, with a vocabulary closer to Old English than to Dutch. Friesland even has its own, thriving, literature, with hundreds of new titles published each year – even though the Frisian-speaking region has no more than half a million inhabitants.

I grew up there, I understand the language, and from my earliest years I wandered the countryside. In the 1950s the pastures were still dotted with innumerable cows of the celebrated black and white Holstein-Friesian breed, the farms, like the villages, were full of day labourers, and in spring the chatter of birds in the field was positively deafening.

With such a background it is hardly surprising that I should choose a Frisian village as the starting point for my rural project. Yet it could also have been a French or Scottish or Bavarian village, for there are essentially few differences between such agricultural communities.

Instead, I opted – somewhat on the off chance – for Jorwert. It is an old-fashioned village built around a central mound, there was a convivial café and a few of my friends lived there – that, to be honest, was the primary reason.

Once I moved in, however, it turned out that I had struck a bulls eye. It had taken me countless discussions to make it clear to my urban acquaintances precisely what I was up to. In the village, they understood right away. "Yes, a lot has changed around here, the last few years," they said. "Yeah, it would be good for you to write about that." Then they began telling stories, and never stopped. That was how this book came to appear in 1996, under the original title *Jorwerd: The Death of the Village in Late Twentieth-century Europe.*

Friesland, after a fashion, is unique. In the church at Jorwert, opposite the pulpit, is the enormous gravestone of Pastor Hotthie Fons, who died on 26 November 1556. It's a lovely stone, carved by mason Peter Dircks in 1558 and covered in motifs familiar to us from the Italian Renaissance. The presence of such a stone in this relatively plain village church indicates once-great wealth, and more than that; specialised stonemasons must have been available for service here, the kind of craftsmen usually found only close to the major cities. The decorations also show that this relatively remote corner of Europe was actually very much in tune with the zeitgeist in the cultural centres of the Continent of the day.

All these things are characteristic for large parts of Friesland. It was something of an island, Friesland, surrounded by the sea to the west and north and vast swamps to the south. But at the same time it was a wealthy agricultural area, connected by myriad ties with the rest of the world, both economically and culturally. In some ways, the network of Frisian villages with their collective wealth and specialisations formed one large, spread-out city.

Before starting this book I had perused a great many international research papers and studies of rural cultures and village societies. In all of them, one element came to the fore: the universality of farming cultures. Or, as the American journalist-anthropologist Richard Critchfield, who studied dozens of farming communities around the world, put it: "The peasant is a recognisable and long-enduring human type."

I realised that a village like Jorwert, in the densely urbanised Netherlands, was in this respect a major exception. Yet beneath all this modernity, or so I hoped, a few of the classic agricultural behavioural patterns might still be discernible. To my surprise I didn't have to dig deeply at all. Even in this modern Frisian village, that classic farming tradition, that "recognisable and long-enduring human type", proved to be alive and kicking.

That may partly be down to the speed with which this revolution took place in the twentieth-century European countryside. There is a photograph of a farmer's yard near Jorwert from 1931. The yard's furnishings – haystack, outbuildings, wooden ladders and tools – differs only marginally from a similar yard sketched by Rembrandt three hundred years earlier. Rembrandt's farmer would probably have been able to work on that farm in 1931 without a hitch. A few decades later, however, farm work had changed beyond recognition. On a farm from, say, 1981, both of those earlier farmers would have been at a complete loss. Yet it was in that world, that farmer's yard from 1931, that many of the village elders had grown up.

The tenacity of farming tradition, however, has to do largely with the toughness of the farming life itself. Farmers, after all, are born survivors, a human type which in the words of British author John Berger "who has continued to live, while others have disappeared or perished." The same applies to village communities: it is amazing to experience how hardy those communities were and are. And it applies to little, modern Jorwert as well. Even today.

This book, ultimately, is not about a forgotten past. On the contrary. It is an ode to the survivors. An ode to perseverance.

Preface to the English Edition

JORWERD IS THE BIOGRAPHY OF A VILLAGE DURING THE SILENT
revolution that swept through Europe between 1945 and 1995. It is the
story of the farmers and the funds, of the small shopkeepers and the
encroaching city, of the church tower that collapsed and the new cows
that no longer had names. It is the story of the publican who wanted
to get on in life; of the attractive Gais Meinsma; of Fedde with his five
cows and muddy acres; of Peet, who died among the cabbages. It is the
story of the small Frisian village of Jorwert, and all the other villages in
Holland, Britain, France and the rest of Europe.

In 1960, two thirds of the world's population lived in the country
and one third in towns. By 2025, according to predictions made by the
United Nations, the opposite will be the case: two thirds of humankind
will be living in towns and one third in the country. The historic moment
itself occurred just before the turn of the century, the turning point at
which for the first time in history there were more people living in
towns than in the country.

The consequences of this enormous cultural shift can be seen and
felt wherever you go. The remnants of the farming culture that has
shaped the continent for thousands of years, and that has apparently
been wiped out during the last few decades, can be found throughout
Europe: the derelict farmsteads in Ireland and Southern Europe, the
dried-up communal washing facilities in French villages, the farmhouse
conversions on the outskirts of London, the overgrown terraces on the
slopes of the Pyrenees, the empty and impoverished villages in Poland
and Portugal. And everywhere you see farmers and their children who
have been cast adrift in all sorts of different ways – in the churches
of Warsaw, in the grey tower-blocks of Bilbao, in the refugee city

of Sarajevo, in the doorways of drab Amsterdam suburbs.

This is not a nostalgic history. Farming as a way of life was often a matter of surviving by the skin of your teeth, and nobody wants a return to that. In Jorwert too, in the north of the Netherlands where I spent my youth, everything has been turned on its head. But at the same time, certain things have remained the same. As far as that is concerned villages seem to be much tougher than people generally imagine. Jorwert is representative of tens of thousands of villages in Europe. To this day it is little more than a small circle of houses and farms grouped around a stumpy church, like so many others on this continent, bearing the marks of time and history. The surrounding countryside is green and wet, the world thereabouts is as flat as a pancake, the clouds and the skies come and go. That is not likely to change. But this story is a different matter, it slips through your fingers before you know it, tomorrow, or perhaps next year, it will all be forgotten.

GEERT MAK

Spring 2000

AN ISLAND IN TIME

What the Poet Should Know

First the marvel of building.
The door of the stall is open; the man lays the stones on top of
    each other.
He builds a wall. On top of the wall go the wooden planks.
Next to him is the toolkit with its powerful tools.
This is how what seemed timeless grew into existence!
Then the boy himself builds too;
He digs holes and tunnels in the earth,
In the sand he builds canals and locks and from stone, towers
    and castles.

Then the marvel of nature's bounty.
The courtyard covered in the big, red, sweet-smelling fruits,
That the wind took from the heavy trees.
Oh the joy of the harvest, stowing the riches of the world in
    the roomy attic!
Then the trailers, piled high, that wobble through the barn door;
And the white fruit of the earth dug from the rich ground!

Will he gain something from growing up in the discernible
Community of the village?
That he knew the cowshed and the barn, the garden and the pasture?
That he was in the corn shed and with the men in the hay meadow?
That he knew the smell of the wood in the pile-driver drilling on
    the dyke,
Of the boat steering past the nets and of the tannery at the back
    of the fisherman's house?
That he knew the houses with stone floors
And the low smoke-blackened attics?

OBE POSTMA

Chapter One

The Marvel of Building

 PEET HAD NEVER LEFT THE VILLAGE. HE LIVED in closed circuits of family, relations, friends and neighbours. On some mornings he would leave a bunch of carrots on the doorstep of someone he liked, or a cauliflower, or a few leeks. He loved the clouds, from which rays of light could stream, the open field, the red sky of dawn, the blue of an autumn morning. And if, then, he turned round, he always saw the same tower, the houses huddled around the church, the roofs white from the first night frost, most of the branches already bare and black.

It was quiet in the village now. Sometimes schoolchildren biked along the road, bent over, peddling furiously, snaking along, bags full of homework on the back. Sometimes you saw a farmer in the distance, hurrying along beside a ditch. Sometimes there was something wrong with a sheep, or a tractor got stuck. Sometimes smoke came out of a chimney.

In Peet's youth you always heard clogs and bicycles in the village street. Mornings, when all the farmhands came back at the same time from milking and went home for breakfast. At midday, when the clock struck twelve for a cooked dinner. Afternoons, when the children swarmed out of school. Evenings, when all the shops were still open, and the women ran to get some last-minute shopping.

Peet and his classmates only had to screw up their eyes to see ghostly forms roaming the streets. The old man who lived at the end of the village just before the open countryside began. The milk bargee. His neighbour, a butcher, who traded in cattle and kept a few for himself in the shed. Old De Groot, with his grocery and his cheese warehouse. The skipper who sold turf and anthracite, brown fuel and black fuel, and who transported manure, sugar beet pulp and potato silage in summer. His wife, who hawked a yoke with two large panniers full of bread and biscuits from farm to farm when times were bad. The small-timers who lived next door. Little people who survived by staying small: a few jobs for the farmer, some trading in petroleum. The workman next door, who also sold coal. Old Jantsje, who had a lodger, a simpleton, that had all been arranged with the family. Evert Beton (Concrete), that was his nickname, because of his stiff, taut muscles. Next door the cowhand who sold rope, carbolic and udder ointment, and his wife who cleaned for the village nabobs.

And then you had Simon Tijssen's café, there on the corner by the bridge, where there is nothing left to see now, where weddings and funerals were held and where even the vicar came to perform the funeral oration. The café was living room, village hall and theatre all in one. When the youngsters gathered there on winter evenings to rehearse the annual play, Tijssen's wife Janke would be sitting by the fire darning socks. And Thijssen himself, in his shirt sleeves, would sit all evening at one of the tables doing the accounts. There were always two performances of the play: on Sunday evening for the young people, on Tuesday evening for the married couples.

Once, a long time ago, Peet had wanted to see the world. There had been stories in the paper about a war in Spain, about bombings and children shot dead, and early one morning he had got his bike out. He had begun to cycle through the flat, green land, from church tower to church tower. He cycled out of the county into the sea, over the long, bare Zuider Zee Afsluit dyke, through the province of North Holland, in the direction of Spain. Then it began to get dark. Somewhere in the vicinity of Hoorn he remembered a distant member of the family. He was warmly received. When he woke up next morning his father was already at his bedside. Peet was back in Jorwert in time for coffee, and he never left again.

At the end of his life, Peet de Groot was a tall, thin man with a pale face and dark glasses. I had sometimes sat talking with him, together with his friend Folkert. They had worked all over the place: for farmers, for the baker, at the grass-dryers, as carpenters; Folkert had laid bricks right up into the top of the tower. "They were strange times but they were good ones," they said, and then they began to talk about the performances of the village amateur dramatics society that always attracted a full house. And about "tilting" (*tippen*), a game that had been played in farmyards for centuries, and in which the players had to knock a ball off part of a cartwheel, by means of the ingenious throwing of a stick. Or about the time

The game of tilting, now only practised in Jorwert, dates back to around 1800.

the tower collapsed and Folkert had gone from village to village with his accordion, thus managing to raise 300 guilders for a new tower – the vicar had not wanted to take the money at first. Or about the difference between manure and dung. Manure that had piss mixed with it, and afterbirths and other rotting substances, and that stank of fire and acid. And the dung, the dung of yesteryear, rich and dry, full of straw. And about the birds and the dung, the birds that flapped around the dung when the muck was spread, all sorts, and about the sounds, ebbing away over the countryside without echo.

But now Peet himself lay among the curly cabbages, dead, face down in his garden, half in a ditch, and afterwards the bells had tolled the required number of times. Folkert had found him.

"He had wanted to pick some leeks, he had the bucket next to him," said Folkert in the café. "But, well, that's the way things happen,"

They had both spent their whole lives in the field, looking for eggs, doing a bit of poaching and dropping a few eel-pots in the river, and every evening they had stood on the bridge with their friends, chatting and chucking cents into the water, until radio arrived, and after that television, and everyone became glued to the box. As boys they had seen the new lighting arrive, the transition from petroleum lamp to electricity, house after house, farm after farm, suddenly illuminated with unprecedented clarity each evening, one after the other. Mothers began to redecorate and clean everything because the new light showed up so much more. All the petroleum lamps were thrown out. "This is really going to be something!" they had said to one another.

They had seen the arrival of the first milking machines in the village, the chug of the single-cylinder engines, the cleaning of the spark-plugs, over and over again. The first cars: the blacksmith's and the solicitor's.

Now Folkert was small and bent, but his eyes still sparkled. In the 1970s he had single-handedly pointed two rows of newly built houses. He and Peet had seen the strangers arrive, with their sunken sitting areas filled with cushions and their wild gardens, they had seen the shops disappear, one after the other, they had seen the farm labourers move away and they themselves had moved with the times.

"When we are dead, yes, then that is the end of it," said Folkert. "Otherwise it would be a fine to-do."

"A young person can die, an old person must die," said Peet.

The bells had tolled for Peet's funeral, just as they had tolled the day he died, and on the day he was born. The big bell that dated from 1354, and the small one that had been recast in 1748, because a crack had appeared during the ringing for the birth of Prince William.

In 1991 the regulations governing bell ringing had been printed once more in the local paper: "In the case of a death, the bell will be rung at nine o'clock or at four o'clock in the afternoon. In the case of a birth, at eleven o'clock in the morning. For a man, the big bell will be sounded and then be joined by the small one, for a woman, the small one will begin, after which the big one will join in." In this way, in Jorwert you always knew who had died, as the codes were clear, and the rest you heard from the neighbours.

The memorial service was held in the village, and Peet was buried by the old tower at Oosterwierum, a few kilometres away. It was small-scale, short and quiet, like his life. A week later I went and had another look in the churchyard; the tower stood lonely in the flat countryside, the rain pattered on the clay of the grave, two bunches of roses and tulips lay wilting on the pile of earth.

Folkert told the story of how he had found Peet at least 30 times afterwards, to his friends from the café. He had placed a separate advertisement in the paper, with the heading: MY BEST FRIEND. It had – as he kept repeating – given him a bit of a jolt. But he was quite at ease with the idea.

The weather was cruel, as they say here, during those last months of the year. The land was of a flatness seldom found anywhere in the world, and every cloud drifted towards you like a battleship. The wind whistled for days around the wet trees surrounding the church, but afterwards all was silent. Daylight appeared slowly, and everything remained enveloped in shades of grey. The birds had left. The sheep lay close together in the field, huddled in a circle, half in a ditch, the strongest on the outside.

The mist amplified every sound, and we heard the distant invisible city, thudding like a ship's engine.

During those months I lived in the house where Folkert was born. After Folkert, a family of nine had lived there for years. A kitchen had been made from one of the tiny bedsteads, and behind that, half under a cupboard, they had built a chicken run. The parents had slept in the remaining bedstead, the rest lay on hay-sacking in the attic.

Later still, Kooistra, the grocer, had had his fryer with oven-ready chips there, until the chip pans caught fire and he gave up on the chip business. And now it was a sort of weekend cottage, hidden away at the back of the village: living room, kitchen, stairs, loft.

Jorwert was situated in the so-called *Greidhoek*, an area of flat pasture-land, roughly in the middle of the triangle: Harlingen, Leeuwarden and

Sneek. One kilometre away lay the hamlet of Funs, where three farmers lived in eternal discord. A bit further along were the villages of Weidum, Baard, Bears and Jellum. And then there was the slightly larger Mantgum, where there was a small supermarket, a shop with pots and pans, iron-mongery and plastic flowers, and a train station to get away. "I wouldn't be seen dead there," said the Jorwerters about Mantgum, for they hated their rival with a passion.

Jorwert itself was not insignificant. The village had a school and a greengrocer's, there were 29 societies, a village hall and a skating rink, there was an elderly solicitor and a young one – Sjoerd Gjalts van der Hem and Gjalt Sjoerd van der Hem – there was a vicar and a school-master (although he officially worked in another village) and there was a pub called The Baarderadeel Arms.

Old postcards of the village were in circulation, but I could only find my own house on them with difficulty. It was tucked away between the high roofs of the farms, the trees of the vicarage garden and the church-yard with the old gable-roof tower. Most of the village houses were clustered around this and from the terp* they spread out and away into a few small neighbourhoods, a total of about 100 houses, if I count the handful of new ones.

In general the pattern of streets, alleys and farms had changed little since the 1950s. But if you talked to the older villagers and you stacked all the stories and all the houses behind one another, then they grew into a multicoloured beaded necklace of light and dark, of experiences and strokes of fate, of celebrations, loves, children, toil, storms, death agonies, of human lives that were totally unrecognisable to us – even though their world had only just become submerged.

Let us try and sketch the village as it would have looked around 1950. We have already mentioned the milk bargee and Simon Tijssen's living-room-cum-café near the bridge. On the other side of the water the painter had his workshop. A bit further along was a carpenter's and a greengrocer's. The greengrocer had a small cart on which he displayed everything, he had his own fruit trees and he also had a barge on which he took cheese and vegetables to Leeuwarden. His son took over

---

* A terp is a flat hillock on which settlements were often built to protect them from high water. [Tr.]

the business, but later went to work for the post office. He sold ice-cream through the kitchen window. Then there was the church vestry, where the verger-cum-cobbler lived. Behind that the smithy. Then a haberdasher's shop, a few small farmers, a potato dealer's, Lamkje's butcher's shop, the railwayman's house and the vicarage.

We now come to the harbour – cut deep so that the peat barge could always moor in the centre of the village. Nearby there was another grocer's-cum-general store. Then a farm, a few workers' cottages, a baker's, and the tiny house belonging to the council worker who collected the rubbish. Next to that was a sweet shop that had biscuits and acid drops and liquorice – each week the shopkeeper called on all the farms in the area carrying a yoke and two baskets full of groceries. Then a shop occupied first by a goldsmith and later by a greengrocer's. Next to that lived another skipper – legend had it that he had paid for his house with winnings from ice-skating races. He sailed, his wife had a small grocer's shop. Then the petroleum man – who also distributed the *Leeuwarder Courant* and later on dealt in pots and pans and china as well. Next, a shop selling underwear, patches of cloth and buttons – these people too, cycled to all the farms each week, with a suitcase full of merchandise. Then the Agricultural bank, the schoolmaster's house, the post office, the big café, the cycle-shop – the bicycle repair man who was also the village huntsman – another baker's, the solicitor's office, then the school, the district nurse's house, next to that a man who stuttered and made clogs, then a woman with cinnamon, herbs and sugar, and lastly, a handful of hovels, the people who lived there were brown with poverty. You see their children in old school photographs, they were obviously suffering from malnutrition; they disappeared in the 1960s and afterwards those sorts of people and their suffering were completely forgotten.

That was what the village looked like when Peet and Folkert were in the prime of life: two butchers', four grocers', two bakers', four skippers and freight carriers, four fuel merchants, two cafés, a painter, a carpenter, a greengrocer's, a cobbler, a bicycle shop, a shop selling pots and pans, two drapery shops and a blacksmith's. There were a few rich people and a few poor, and I am not talking about the usual scrimping and scraping of all those almost-poor: the goings-on with petroleum, the petty dealing in rope and in udder ointment, the hawking of baskets of bread.

At the turn of the century there were about 650 people living in the village. In 1950 there were still 420. By about 1995 there were 330 residents, but most of those had one foot in the town. Within 100 years the village had been almost halved.

The library disappeared in 1953, the post office in 1956. In this same period the harbour was filled in, in 1959; after half a century, the cobbler shut up shop; the last bakery closed in 1970. In that same year, Thijssen and his wife closed their living room-cum-café; in 1972 the bus route was discontinued, street signs arrived and the Reformed church council merged with two nearby villages; the last local skipper stopped work in 1974; the butcher shut in about 1975; in 1979 the last village huntsman died, and in that same year the carpenter's and the voluntary fire brigade disappeared too; the blacksmith stopped in 1986; the last grocer's closed in 1988; and in 1994 the church was bequeathed to an association for the preservation of old buildings.

In the council archives there was a photograph, taken some time during the 1930s, of the big procession that was always held before the annual village competition: two men with a drum and an accordion at the front, behind them half the village, women in pork-pie hats, men in caps, boys in short trousers, children cheering, flags, the proud tilting players with their wooden sticks on their shoulders. Peet and Folkert must have been standing somewhere between them, but I could not find them.

———

On a quiet afternoon, not long after Peet's funeral, I saw a boy with a skateboard practising in front of the café. About 15, he had a denim jacket on and blond, closely cropped hair and he was trying to teach himself some sort of jump. He had already been at it for an hour, and for that whole hour he had been missing the board. But he went on, with the same quiet determination with which his father had probably ploughed through secondary school, and after that perhaps agricultural college, and then on through life. It was a scene unimaginable in a city. In a city you never see boys practising, you only see them achieving.

Success alone is public there, not the long road that leads up to it.

I saw Lamkje driving towards me in her electric invalid car, at once shrunken and sprightly. Eighty two years old, a butcher's wife for 49 years, one son now prepares the meat in a care centre, the other is a chemistry professor and the daughter is married to a doctor.

In the school playground the children were walking on stilts. Two boys were riding around in a cart, welded by their father, with a large round steering wheel. Later on there was the sound of a bell: the milk-man, with bottles of milk – no cartons on principle – and biscuits. The afternoon died away slowly. In the solicitor's office the light came on.

Lamkje had said that I should come to tea. Next to her house was the butcher's, closed for years, but always swept and clean, with the red scales still on the counter and behind it the big slicer.

Lamkje showed me the old premises. Or rather, I walked around and she shouted instructions from her chair. The rails on which the carcasses were hung were attached to the ceiling. Three cows a fortnight, plus a pig. They made use of every part of these animals: the sweetbreads were eaten on bread, just like the dripping, the udders were smoked in the chimney and even the pig's bristles were sold to a buyer who made brushes from them.

"I can still hear the man haggling over 20 or 25 cents!" cried Lamkje. "Money was still worth something then." In the afternoon she had to cycle round the whole district delivering meat. "That was hard going, you know, when it was stormy and pouring with rain."

She spoke of her only outing in the years immediately after the war: a performance by the group Tetman & Jarich; a company that toured the province with all sorts of songs and sketches. The maidservant had heard that they were to perform in a nearby village and suggested they go together. The entry fee was 2.50 guilders – exactly half of her weekly wage.

"Off we went on our bikes. It was a revelation. They sang so beautifully. We had five years of Occupation behind us, no wireless, no going out. I still remember how wonderful we thought that was:

"'Then is the month of May, may-time in the land. When all is joyous, joyous to behold!'

"And I still remember that there was an interval – they did not have decent coffee, but even so. My husband preferred to stay at home. He was always tired, he always had work to do."

He was 70 when he had a heart attack, and that was the end of the village butcher. After his death Lamkje did not want to make any changes to the house, the shop and the surrounding sheds.

"He had all sorts of plans to start something with sheep, and that is why it should remain as it is," she said to me. "It takes a lot of maintenance, it costs a lot of money, but it has to be done. Those were his plans, with the sheep. And that is the way it must stay."

Later, Lamkje was no longer there either. Like an old cat she had fought against the nursing home, and if she had not been so incredibly strong she would have been admitted years ago like any other mere mortal. In the winter of 1995 she had to capitulate.

"What I would not give to be back in Jorwert among my own people," she whispered to visitors. "Neighbour, neighbour, I should so like to live a little longer!"

She died within a month of moving, and after that the house and the butcher's stood quietly, waiting to be bought by wealthy Dutch import.*

Every afternoon, during the calm autumn months, a flyer was put through the door. The residents of Jorwert were seduced into purchasing oven-ready rabbits from J. Hallema, having new tyres fitted at Hoekstra's, the car dealer, and into buying pots of super-glue for fl.5.90, decorative cats for fl. 2.95, silk plants for fl.2.00 and mug racks for fl.2.50 at Frits Smidstra's. The smoked udders, the wind, the rain and the rye bread with dripping seemed as distant as the Middle Ages, but nevertheless it had all happened within one generation.

The transformation of the village had been a lengthy and restrained process, but no less spectacular for all that. Ids Meinsma, the son of the painter and decorator, told me that his ten fellow pupils at the village school between 1965 and 1971 were all without exception the children of farmers, farm labourers or people closely linked with farming – like the solicitor's son. Of those ten, one had remained in farming. The

---

* "Import" is the term used by Frisians to denote their non-Frisian Dutch compatriots. [Tr.]

others had become lab technicians, or worked at the fairground, or were clerks of the court, like him. Of the whole class only one was still living in the village.

In 1995 there was one farmer's son all told at the village school. The fathers now were road-construction workers, office clerks, electricians, computer programmers, schoolmasters, photographers, civil servants. And in at least half the cases the mother, too, now had a paid job, or she was studying – something that was unthinkable 20 years ago.

Agriculture was the raft on which the village economy floated, but since the 1970s the farmers' role was played out. They were no longer the central force around which everything revolved, and their status dropped accordingly.

Take the Casteleins for instance, the farming family that had lived in the heart of the village for decades. In 1950 Tjerk Sakes Castelein, with his 40 cows, was a big farmer. Mornings and afternoons he needed at least four pairs of hands to milk all those cattle: he himself, two farmhands and a boy. It was always busy on the farms. Farm labourers lived all over the village and the surrounding area. No farmer could do without them.

In the early 1950s the milking machine arrived in the village, and all of a sudden the 40 cows could easily be milked by two or three pairs of hands. Shortly afterwards they started to replace the horses with tractors throughout the district.

In 1950, throughout the Netherlands, there were less than 4,000 milking machines. In 1960 there were ten times as many. Within three decades the amount of labour-time spent on the average dairy cow dropped by more than 80 per cent.

At the end of 1995, Tjerk's son, Sake, had about 70 cows and he did the work largely on his own – all 70 cows with one pair of hands and with that tall, scrawny body of his. Of his former farmhands, two became bus drivers in the neighbouring province of North Holland, another found a job in a dockyard in Alblasserdam, still others left for the blast furnaces in IJmuiden or went to work in Leeuwarden at Friesland Dairy Products. Only Sake still sat on his tractor, surrounded by a dozen knobs and gears, dreaming all the while of the Russians that he read in the evening: Chekhov, Tolstoy, Paustovsky.

*

Characteristic of the erosion of farming in the village was the moving of the date of the annual fair, the merke. Traditionally – this fair is mentioned as far back as 1775 – it was a typical harvest festival that always took place in September. After all, no farmer has time during the summer holidays. Every minute is needed then for mowing, haymaking, silage and whatever else there is to do. In 1974 an exception was made to the rule because a large agricultural show was also taking place on that traditional September weekend. This break with tradition suited most of the villagers – except the farmers – much better. And so the merke was permanently transferred to the last weekend in June. It became a festival that heralded the beginning of the school holidays instead of the end of a period of toil and back-breaking work.

Farming became a lonely profession. The scale of the business constantly increased and consequently the reliance upon machines, investment and banks. Most Dutch farmers did not manage to pull it off: more than half disappeared in barely two decades. In the last census in 1971 it transpired that only a quarter of the population of Jorwert still worked in agriculture, with almost half in the service sector. Afterwards this shift continued apace. Towards the end of the twentieth century, an average of two per cent of Dutch farmers gave up annually. This steady decline was reflected in Jorwert: between 1975 and 1990, one in three of the farms in the district ceased to function. Teachers came to live in the old buildings, or retired farmers, or pensioners from the west. That was perhaps the greatest change, the most fundamental. Because if agriculture disappeared, for centuries both driving force and pivot, then what would hold the village community together?

It was not only the world of farmers and farm labourers that was stood on its head. Lamkje recalled a public lecture, sometime in the 1950s, about the future of retailing, in which the speaker warned that within the foreseeable future all the shops would disappear from the village: "I remember coming out of the café that evening and laughing as I told my husband. What nonsense!"

But the motor car appeared; in town, the supermarket introduced the "special offer" and the village grocer's could never offer the range of products a shop in town could with so many different chocolate bars and so many sorts of bread – they would all go mouldy, there were too few people in the village for that; and what did they want all that stuff for anyway? Like everywhere in the Netherlands, Jorwert too grew from being a community founded on mutual need to a miniature consumer society. Things were not usually easy for the classic country family with its bevy of children, but they always had one advantage over city families: they generally had their own vegetables, their own meat, their own milk, butter, cheese, eggs, their own potatoes, and in this way they could more or less support themselves. This is how most families formed an economy within the economy, and it was often the only way they could survive. "We had nine children, but the man from the shop only brought a small box each week," one of the neighbours once told me. "He only came for the things that we really needed, like coffee, tea, sugar, soap and that sort of thing. Just imagine that now!"

Furthermore there was a second change: temptation. Up until the 1960s many farmers rarely went to a shop. The retailers came to peoples' homes.

The same neighbour: "We wrote down what we needed in a note-book, but no more than that. Coffee was coffee, tea was tea, and soap was soap. For the whole week I never had more than about 20 or 30 guilders worth of shopping for the whole family."

Her husband: "We went on in this way until the beginning of the 1970s. Then the roles were reversed and we went to the shop instead of the shop keeper coming to us."

The neighbour: "And we saw this and we saw that, and we had seen a leaflet on those, and 'Oh yes, I better take that as well, and that is really useful, I saw it on television'. The boxes of groceries kept getting bigger. And then we got a car and we drove to the supermarket, and the man from the shop, with his two brands of coffee and his one brand of washing-up liquid, he got left behind."

In the village pub, The Baarderadeel Arms, times were changing too. It was a lovely old place, low beamed, with a tiny bar and a large room upstairs where for the past 100 years all the parties and receptions had been held. When Eef and Jan Dijkstra took over the business, in 1965, the pub hardly ever closed later than 11 p.m. Most customers came at about 8.00, 8.30 – many villagers did not yet have television – and even someone like Folkert had "hit the hay", as he called it, by 11.00. The farm labourers had to rise at 3.30 a.m. for milking, the farmers at 4.00, and the whole rhythm of the village was to a large extent determined by this.

In the 1970s the first customers of the evening sometimes trickled in as late as 10.30 p.m., and the pub never closed before 1.00, and even then there were usually some people left. For this reason, Jan Dijkstra decided to bid farewell to the contracting business, in which he had become quite successful. He could manage to combine the "old" pub with a day that began at 7 a.m., but with the new style of pub this became physically impossible.

Newcomers arrived in the village. In photos from the 1960s and 1970s you can see the clothes changing. The eternal caps disappeared from the village scene, the labourers' Sunday jackets became jumpers and blouson jackets, the women's long skirts became jeans.

I heard Peet complaining that people did not say hello as often. "You used to say hello to everyone." Folkert was of the opinion that the newcomers tended to stick with the newcomers. "They have a different mentality. I do not mean worse. Why, they might even be better people than we are."

The remarkable thing was that the newcomers often launched themselves energetically into village life, learned Frisian, joined the amateur dramatics group. When the farmers' role as economic pivot was played out it seemed as though everybody began to look for new ties: the clubs, the merke, the grand open-air play, the games of tilting and of fives, the language, the traditions. In this way the economic links within village society were gradually replaced by sporting or cultural ones. "I noticed that," said Peet, "all those new blokes playing at tilting."

One evening a few old films that the solicitor had made were shown in the village hall. We saw the village in 1957; boys with close-cropped hair; cows in the meadow; the peat boat; a champion cow; the painter's house with the clothes' line full of washing; the merry-go-round that was erected for the annual village fête; haystacks; caps; clogs. 1959: a tilting competition; fives for women; a girl in shorts who continuously flirts with the camera, she turns around, laughs shyly, turns back, laughs again. A young Folkert, behind the women. 1963: the merry-go-round again; competitions; hunt the clogs in a big pile of straw; prize-winning cows; the solicitor with his pipe in the snow; a skating competition; and in 1995 half the hall still apparently knew which competition it was. 1969: the schoolmaster, grey and distinguished; a wheelbarrow race; bobbing for the cake; a barrel organ in the village; Eef comes out of the pub, she strokes the horse, she is young and looks like a hippy. 1973: the scenery for the annual open-air play; once again the ice rink and the wheelbarrow race; but the haystacks and caps disappear and more and more new faces appear. We saw Peet again briefly, in 1959, when he won a prize for tilting and received a bunch of flowers, and once more in 1963, wearing a large cap, and I thought I caught a brief glimpse of him in 1973. But then he was gone, just like the haystacks were gone, and the farm labourers and the bustle of evening after work, and the blacksmith and the baker and the painter – all gone. And everyone in the hall was amazed at how swiftly and silently all these changes had come over the village.

The quiet transformation of Jorwert at the end of the twentieth century had numerous consequences, large and small. One of the most important concerned the handling of money. Gais Meinsma, the wife of the painter and decorator, once told me that she had begun to collect the payment of bills for her husband. That was during the early 1950s, and at that time there was still a ritual of payment. Accordingly her father-in-law, her husband's predecessor, had always done it himself. He spent entire winter evenings collecting payment personally. "He would drop by, go all through everything again, the whole business. And then he would collect the money, and after that he would depart with a cigar in his mouth," Gais recalled. "I did it very differently. I would drive by for a brief, business-like visit. My father-in-law did not like their briefness one little bit. It was a difference in mentality, and it was the first time I had felt it."

You did not receive or spend money lightly, but this too changed. Money unleashed hitherto unknown forces.

Lies Wiedijk, one of the farmer's wives in the district, was of the opinion that the mess the farmers found themselves in had started when they received their milk money through the bank instead of cash in hand. "When we came here in 1977, almost everything was paid for by cash. The man from the dairy came by on Friday with his linen bag, and in it was your money. The cattle dealer would pay you in 100-guilder notes counted out on the kitchen table. But when people began to receive their money through the bank they started doing other things."

In the case of Eef from the pub however, there was more involved than the thriftiness she had been taught. She wanted to get on, and where she did not succeed, her children would. Her thrift was a sort of saving of strength for the big leap. A few in the village called her haughty. It was something different.

Eef's parents had a small farm in Baard with a dozen cows and some smaller livestock, and in addition her father dealt in livestock. Her mother went round with the "bread basket" — something Eef would do too. "But I felt no less a person because of it," she said. "Through his trading my father went to countries like Germany and Czechoslovakia, he came back with stories, he had seen something of the world, the other village children did not have any of that."

Eef's family had a singular pride. While other fathers objected when their daughters wanted to go to secondary school — "Six years of primary school was good enough for me, and it is good enough for you, too!" — Eef's parents did everything they could to help their children get on in society. "You do not have to follow the same path as us," her mother had always said. "There is more to the world." And to that purpose she was willing to do a great deal — if necessary she would take a second job to finance an extra course for one of the children. "Cannot is buried six feet under," was her motto, "and Willnot is lying next to him."

There were no holidays — one time Eef's mother put her two youngest on the bus for Alkmaar and they were allowed to stay for a few weeks in the house where her eldest daughter was in service, a marvelous experience, comparable to when the tiny tots came to stay in *Afke's Tiental*.*

But thanks to the father's trading interests the family kept the door to the outside world open. "The 'border', the 'border', that word meant so much to me. 'There are problems at the border,' my father would say; it was a sort of mystical wall. Once, when I was twelve, I was allowed to go with him. I crossed the border. It was a tremendous experience."

Eef's parents encouraged their children to better themselves, in every

* *Afke's Tiental* is the title of a classic Dutch children's book. [Tr.]

way. She remembered her father once being abroad and finding himself at a formally laid dinner-table, with all sorts of cutlery that he had absolutely no idea how to use. When he came home he said to his children: "That must never happen to you" – and since then, on that tiny farm, the utmost attention was paid to table manners during meals. If she said "What?" it was immediately corrected: "What did father say?" – once her father had even followed her across the school play-ground because of this. So as to be able to greet guests, the children were taught to shake hands politely.

From their earliest years the children had to help out on the farm. But they were not allowed to do any milking; although Eef, especially, wanted to. "I have been sitting underneath cows since I was nine, you must all learn something different," her mother said. And her father: "Once you *can* do the milking, you will always *have* to do the milking later on. If you cannot, you will never have to."

They were ignored by the farmers in the village. But, as her father impressed upon them, "You are not worth less than them. And not more either. You do your best just like everyone else." When the sons of a very rough family from the edge of the village began to come to the Saturday night dances, her father, after the usual lecture on honour and decency said: "If they ask you to dance you must say 'Yes', because they are people like you and me, but you do not have to bring them home."

Later on, Eef would hang the yoke that had carried the baskets of bread on the wall of the pub, next to the trophies from the fives – and tilting competitions.

In Jorwert, even in the modern Jorwert, much of what the towns had lost still existed. It smelt of grass, smoke, sawdust, hay, manure and earth. The nights were black, and the sky was still full of stars. Everyone had central heating, electronic thermostats and double-glazing, but the weather still managed to force its way into every nook and cranny. A storm here was an adventure the like of which you no longer experienced in a town.

A few days after Peet's funeral, the wind began to roar across the flat countryside, the sheep flattened themselves, bottoms to the wind, and in some places you could barely walk upright. Clouds swept across the heavens like smoke from a factory chimney. Trees and farms stood sharply outlined against the dark-grey sky. In the village the roof tiles rattled, trees and lampposts whistled, plastic wheely-bins rolled across the street. The sky was full of bluster, and when the children came out of school they ran shouting through the streets; their coats half undone they let themselves sail forth on the gusts like leaves.

The next morning it was deathly quiet, and everything that happened in the village was clearly audible: the council workman picking up a broken roof-tile and mowing a verge, the loading of a lorry, a tractor in the grey distance.

Gais Meinsma came out of her door with her dog. "Hey!" Folkert passed by on his bike.

"Mornin'"! Eef got into her car. "Hey!" There is Siesling, the old skipper. "Hey!"

Everyone in the village exchanged greetings. Friends said hello to you, with acquaintances you crooked a finger, to fellow villagers you nodded, but if anything was said it was always: "Hey!" "Mornin'!" was occasionally used, but mainly as a way of bringing a more lengthy exchange to a close. "Hey!" [Hoej!] was the standard greeting, a sigh of air from deep within the vocal cords. The tone of the elderly was often somewhat lower, almost like a soft mooing.

Sometimes a silent conversation occurred, more a mutual appreciation of one another's company than an exchange of information: "Now, now!" (silence) "Now, now!" (silence) "Well, well!" (silence) "A'hem!" (silence) "Well, mornin'!" And often no sound whatsoever was made: the lifting of an outstretched index finger in the direction of a – now usually non-existent – cap sufficed.

Strangers were usually acknowledged with a slight hesitation, at least they were when they took the initiative themselves. With them the greeting functioned as a sort of visitors' pass: they were allowed in, even if it was temporarily.

The import women had developed their own manner of greeting; their "Hey!" contained a hidden melody, from high to low: "He-i-ey!" However it sounded, it was always a tiny ritual of solidarity: she is one of us.

In this way, everything that happened in the village community was governed by the law of small numbers, a law that one is hardly aware of in the city. In a small community the presence of each individual is keenly felt. A row of new housing is barely noticeable in a city area, but in a village, with perhaps 100 households, 20 new families have an enormous impact.

The success of many performances, competitions, get-togethers and other projects is usually due to the efforts of one or two initiative-takers, but the opposite is also true. Village communities have become fragile, now that people no longer work together on the land and with the livestock, and villagers only see one another in the café or at amateur dramatics or passing by in the street. And then, a single individual can destroy a great deal, for a great length of time.

That was the case in Jorwert too. A handful of people had made the village, organised the parties and get-togethers, kept the clubs together, supported the school, throughout the decades. But it only needed one temporary school Head to start drinking – as had happened in a neigh-bouring village – for the school to disappear for good. And when an aggressive loudmouth came to live in one of the new houses, he only needed to spread his poison in the café for a few weeks, for customers to start staying away. Fortunately he soon made himself scarce, otherwise the most important social centre of the village would have been in serious trouble.

Who belonged, and who did not? The young people employed a complex code: there were "natives", and there was "import", and then there was a difference between Frisian import and non-Frisian import, and besides that there was also a difference between active and non-active import. In short, all was not lost in advance for those townspeople who wanted to come and live here.

The older people had stricter standards. When Eef got into a discussion in the café about who was a true Jorwerter, and who was not, Folkert and his friends were most adamant about it. Even though Eef had lived in the village since she was 20, and had run the only café for the last 30 years, the opinion of the men was unanimous and irrevocable: "You are not a true Jorwerter, because you were born in Baard." And when the vicar, in discussion with a number of church councillors, spoke of the very elderly Sije Hogerhuis, one of them had let slip: "Yes, but he is not a true Jorwerter, he only came to live here in 1927."

The import, used to getting on with outsiders, laughed at this. But in a way the older villagers were right. True, there were various elements of conformity and fear of foreigners that surely played a part, but in essence the caution was nothing less than an act of self preservation.

The village community of 1995 may have seemed more stable and wealthier than ever before, but in reality it was pseudo-stable. Together with agriculture, stability disappeared not only from the village economy, but from social life as well. Some village communities were so pseudo-stable that they were prepared to forgo the favourable impulses of the "good" newcomer because, when one let a "bad" newcomer get too far into the community too quickly, the risks were too great.

In the small villages there was a continuous, unconscious weighing-up of the pros and cons. Was this someone who would up-sticks or not? Was this a pleasant family or a group of grousers? Were they old, or would they provide children for the school? Was he going to buy land, even though it was already so scarce? Or, with all that city money in his back pocket, was he going to pay over the odds for that derelict hovel by the canal? And then, if so, would more foreigners come, so that house prices shot up and our own children would be unable to afford to buy anything in the district?

In this way, in a village, the economic remained personal, and the personal was immediately political. Life there, in contrast to the city, was not divided up into segments. It was total.

————

The law of small numbers became relevant for many villages when, in the late 1980s, the builders and developers rediscovered the countryside. The daily papers in the urban belt advertised WATERSIDE RESIDENCES! Adjacent to tiny old villages, next to silted-up streams and tranquil pools, villas suddenly appeared everywhere, with "CAR PORTS AND OWN MOORINGS", in one neighbourhood after another.

This white fungus spread across the province in record time. Small battles were fought between the villages to win the favours of the wealthy newcomers. Planning permission was given for places and projects that would have been unthinkable a decade before. The councils, who saw their income declining, expected the rich pensioners from the urban belt to provide a fresh impulse. The contractors dreamed of extra work. The languishing village schools hoped for new pupils. A developer's Wild West was generated. There was no real policy involved, it was primarily fear that spurred on the councils and villages, fear of times to come.

That is how, in the neighbouring village of Wiewerd, behind a sort of sound-absorbent wall, a cuckoo in the nest developed that, within a very short space of time, grew to be almost as big as the rest of the village. Dotted around in the mud were futuristic constructions, with large aluminium windows, next to them were houses built with high straight Belgian walls of yellow brick, and yet other villas were reminiscent of American outbuildings.

In Mantgum a similar sort of boil had appeared on the face of the village. Living next to water was absolutely essential as far as estate agents were concerned, but because this village was surrounded only by fields the developer had dug the necessary ditches and canals himself. On the banks of the straight, freshly dug stretches of water there were villas everywhere, waiting for their new owners, and in the meantime the "old" villagers drove by of a Sunday afternoon. A little wooden canal bridge had been constructed over one of the ditches. The first few city children plodded through the mud with their colourful plastic bikes. In the gardens, small conifers stood embedded in the heavy, Frisian clay.

One of the houses was built on a sort of terp, under which a garage had been constructed. Another one had broad, rough pointing, with which the developer presumably wanted to achieve a sort of rustic, Brabantian-farmhouse-effect. A third villa was built entirely in the form of a triangle.

Many homes were equipped with antique-German letterboxes and automatic plastic garden lanterns that were – "ENVIRONMENTALLY FRIENDLY!" – solar-powered. The building had been carried out by jerry-builders, and the sunny houses bore only too many traces of this: imposing portals were combined with the cheapest front door from the DIY store, cross frames were fitted between the double glazing instead of on it and due to lack of space the builders had made the steps of the terp slope downwards slightly. "We are coming back here when it is icy," laughed the Jorwerters.

In Weidum, a few kilometres away, the builders were completing work on a greyish-yellow villa that had been pontifically deposited in front of the village. Somehow, the house had managed to wrestle free of the area of new housing in the village, and now blocked the view of at least three of the village cottages. The villa was square shaped, the roof resembled a traditional *stolp*, or dome, right in the middle there was a chimney, and under this a futuristic brick fireplace would undoubtedly be built. On the side of the farmland, the clouds and the horizon the new owners had built a large, semi-circular glass wall. Architect Atsma of Oenkerk had envisaged one of the side walls in wood, with a port-hole window in one corner.

Most remarkable was the structure that was built on the village side: to everyone's amazement, within the space of a few weeks, there rose a monumental grey wall, without a single window. Only the access door and the entrance to the garage faced the village. Apart from this the villagers looked out onto blank walls, executed in wood, sandstone and grey brick.

Only when the building was almost complete did the real significance of this villa become apparent: it was a home that had literally pushed its way to the front of the queue, that had then turned its back on the village and that made it transparently clear that it wanted nothing to do with the community. This new villa sent out a single message: that the owners were rich, that they felt they had earned this spot on the globe and that everyone else could get lost.

Jorwert, miraculously, had managed to avoid this wave of building. Until, that is, a bunch of people at the pub woke up. It occurred to Eef and Jan, together with some of their family and acquaintances, that a home on the banks of the old Jorwert canal would be very desirable. They arranged for plans to be drawn up for about six villas on a plot of land just in front of the old village centre. It would even be feasible to dig out the canal and turn it into a pond. "WATERSIDE RESIDENCES" indeed – although in practice not much more than a canoe could moor at "YOUR OWN PERSONAL LANDING STAGE", because further along the canal was completely blocked.

Each of the participants had their own motives. One lived in a house that was too small, another wanted something smarter, and Eef wanted to get on.

Building them would rob a dozen other residents of their unspoiled view, and that was not the only thing. The classic view of the village, with the trees, the *terp* and the gable-roof tower, a scene that had even graced the Douwe Egberts calendar in the 1960s, that view would be gravely disturbed.

Not surprisingly, behind closed doors, the village was buzzing with rumour and gossip. To begin with, nobody did anything – except for one man who stormed into the café and immediately started on Eef and Jan Dijkstra: how could they even think of building on the canal. "You know that is the loveliest spot in our village. You can't just go building bungalows there, surely?"

Even so, many other Jorwerters were fine about it. "After all we cannot keep walking around in bearskins for ever!" said a man from the council, and a sizeable section of the villagers agreed wholeheartedly with him.

Strangely enough it was primarily the older people and those born in the village who were thoroughly enthusiastic about this sort of thing. And, significantly, it was notably the young and the newcomers who had grave doubts about it. It was a sort of conservatism in reverse, and could be partially explained by the fact that the newcomers were less unsuspecting and knew, from their former life in the city, just what this type of building frenzy could lead to. The anti-builders pointed out that only recently, after an endless palaver, had a rural development plan been approved, and that it was all very well for everyone to say that the canal bank was a lovely spot for building, but that was not what had been agreed on at all.

That was not the only reason for their resistance: the way in which they experienced the village was different too. For the young and the newcomers, the intimacy and aesthetic aspect of the village weighed heavily – it was often the most important reason why they had stayed or come. The older people, in contrast, still experienced the village as an economic entity – even though this had in fact disappeared. For them each new family was still an extra customer, a new face in the pub, a child at school perhaps. They could not get the law of small numbers out of their head, especially when that number was getting ever smaller.

Even so, initially both groups seemed resigned to the building plans. This had everything to do with the interweaving of interests that unavoidably occurs in a small community. That too, is a thing that city dwellers repeatedly underestimate. It takes a great deal more courage

to stick one's neck out in a village than it does in the relatively anonymous world of the city.

I happened to be present at the small, homely meeting at which the
opponents of the plan first put their heads together. One of the women,
who had obtained information from the council, expressed her concern;
having done so, if the others did nothing, would she not then be the
only one in the village to be branded a troublemaker? They did not
dare attack the chairman of the Village Association too much, because
he was the manager of the bank as well and nearly everyone had a current
loan there. One of the farmers was strongly against, but because he
was in the middle of a land consolidation procedure he could not afford
too many problems with the council. Another farmer kept his own
counsel because they could make a lot of trouble for him by demanding
his farm be licensed under the Public Nuisance Act – his farmyard had
smelled of manure for more than 200 years, but all the new rules and
requirements made him extremely vulnerable. His neighbour was
against, but at the same time had his eye on the garage that would
become available if one of the plan-makers did in fact move to a villa
on the canal. A neighbour saw the view from her house being spoilt but
was, at the same time, good friends with one of the plan-makers. And
for their part, the plan-makers realised that it would leave deep scars
if they pressed on with their scheme at any cost.

In short, the law of small numbers paralysed both parties: after all, one
must try and get along together in this life. Harmony, that was still the
first and most significant unwritten commandment of the village.

One Friday evening there was a fight in the pub. The loudmouth from
one of the new houses, who was also one of the plan-makers, had
informed the companion of Willem Osinga, one of the anti-builders,
that she was a "silly cow". The next thing Willem remembers, he was
sitting on top of the man, while the other pub-goers were attempting
to pull him off. Willem himself was the one who was most upset. "Up
till now, in the 60 years that I have been in this life I have always been
able to avoid letting my fists do the talking. Nothing like this has ever
happened to me." But one of the farmers, usually no friend of Willem's,
walked up to him and shook his hand.

A week or so later all the tables in the Baarderadeel Arms were arranged in the form of a large magnet. At the end of the left fork of this U-form sat the import, at the top sat the women, and around the right fork were grouped the farmers and older men. At 7.30 p.m. everyone still thought that 10, perhaps 15 people would attend this special meeting of the Village Association, but by 8.05 it was chock-a-block.

The bank manager-chairman began with a statement: the mayor and the councillors had not yet taken any decision on the planning application and therefore there was no need for a protest action by the village. He feared however, he said, that the evening had been organised out of dissatisfaction with the committee of the Village Association. "That is all very well, but it is a waste of time, and all we are doing is spoiling our weekend, because there is nothing to talk about now."

During the next half an hour he repeatedly tried his utmost to get the building plans removed from the agenda. Little by little the hall began to stir. And when the chairman also wanted to limit the number of speakers, Willem Osinga stormed out of the hall: "If there is not going to be any discussion, then there is no point me being here!"

Somebody stood up: "It is high time we heard something about those plans, but all I keep hearing is the Village Association's committee defending itself. I want to hear from the Association's members."

The bank manager: "But nothing has been decided yet."

A farmer said that that did not fit the facts, that the council had purchased land for the scheme a good while ago, and that even the province had given it the green light.

One of the youngsters: "Let us all just talk about the scheme, otherwise I know what will happen, there will just be a row."

The bank manager: "I will allow you time to do that, but do not ask me how, as I have hardly any information on it. Besides which, we still have to discuss the new bridge."

A general grumbling was now audible at all the tables. Jan, the pub owner, pointed to the pile of paper on the bar: "The chairman says that there is nothing definite, but these are the plans, down to the smallest detail. And we informed the Village Association months ago."

The bank manager made a fresh attempt to get the matter off the agenda, but by now the whole hall was united against him. Bravely and with verve, he took upon himself the role of scapegoat, and in this way a small miracle occurred: within an hour he had succeeded in uniting the builders and anti-builders, real Jorwerters and newcomers, young and old, farmers and import, in short, all the factions within the village, in a single front. Against him.

The interval arrived, and a bizarre upsurge of unanimity swept through the pub. Eef sat joking with one of the most outspoken anti-builders. Gais strode happily from one to the next. Folkert made his corner of the table hoot with laughter. I tried to imagine a Jorwerter heaven, and I realised that it would look something like this: peace, unanimity in the upstairs room of the Baarderadeel Arms, and everybody present: Gais, Folkert, Peet, Lamkje, Sake, the solicitor, the school master, the bank manager, Gijs, Armande, Marieke, the painter and decorator, everybody.

"Private initiative is all very well!" one of the men shouted. "But you will get polarisation in the village. We must keep talking to one another. We Jorwerters rule this village, and not any old project makers."

A woman: "I let it sink in a bit, and I thought: we might get a really attractive skyline!"

One of the older men: "There has to be building, otherwise the school will empty. You already have to go to Mantgum to do your shopping."

Gais: "But the view from the old people's home will disappear, and that, now of all times, during Senior Citizens Year."

Someone else: "The people who want to build have lived here for years. I do not object to that. But I understand that there could be people from Amsterdam coming, and that would create problems."

And then an old, bent farmer stood up: "I would like to say something," he said. "They want to buy my land. But I will not be stampeded into anything by all that pestering – first it's this, then it's that, its enough to give anyone a headache – as far as I am concerned they can forget the whole thing. And you can scowl at me as much as you want, but that is the way it is."

And so the plan for new housing in Jorwert was frozen. It was not abandoned, no noisy dispute developed, no discussion was held, it congealed gradually until it was totally inert. It was preserved, from then on, somewhere in village history, between the memories, the images, the dreams and the vague fears for later.

The next day everything was back to normal. Above the land hung a grey haze that gradually spilled over into the dusk. Just outside the village the man who ran a mobile lending library for magazines was waiting by a driveway, with his car full of back numbers. Behind the windows of the solicitor's office, the light shone, yellow and welcoming. I saw Boonstra the clerk shuffle through the room housing the deeds and the weighty tomes, as he had done for 40 years.

In the village, the street lamps had not yet been switched on. Between the houses the echo of a creaking bicycle saddle could be heard. Folkert. His dynamo slipped a bit, his headlamp searched hesitantly from left to right, but he cycled dourly onwards through the deserted village street. The church stood with all its bulk in the middle of the village, eternal, unchanged, like time petrified. The empty building seemed bigger and more impressive than ever, and everything around it became small and insignificant as twilight fell. In the distance, the noise of the road to Wommels, the road to Grouw, the city, the railway line to Sneek, was carried on the air, and it was as if we lived in a rectangle of sound.

Chapter Two

The Survivors

 THE MOST IMPORTANT EVENT IN FEDDE'S youth was the invention of the "perpetual motion" machine — an engine that worked without any fuel whatsoever. A bachelor near Wolvega had invented it and someone had seen it working at the annual fair in Gorredijk. Everyone was talking about it. Soon all the heavy manual work would be done by the new machines. No more carting milk churns, mowing, pitching hay, wheeling manure, digging and drudgery. Just a little while longer and everything would be different, but it never happened. Later on it was rumoured that a large oil company had bought the inventor's silence, for a million guilders they said. So that explained it.

Fedde was the first farmer I got to know. He lived about 30 kilometres from Jorwert, beyond Heerenveen where the soil was sandy. In the early 1970s I became his nearest neighbour, and within a short time it was coffee and conversation every Sunday, along with his brothers Pieter and Goitsen.

"It was a time of working and dying," said Pieter. His father had gone before he was born, and no one then had heard of widows' pensions or social security. When the farmers cooked potatoes for the pigs the family had a good day too, as all the children ate them as well. "Milk and poverty, that's what we lived on," said Goitsen.

Sietske van der Spoel was their mother's name, and when she was widowed she had ten children: Lipkje, Fedde, Hendrik, Harm, Catrinus, Trijntje (who later became rather muddle-headed), Goitsen, Hylke, Klaas and Pieter. Two did not survive those years. Hendrik contracted Spanish flu when he was 18 and Catrinus died of an obscure infection when he was 13 – but he had never been strong anyway.

The others had to start earning their keep as quickly as possible. Pieter started at the grocer's when he was 14, delivering shopping; he came home at midnight and by seven in the morning he was off again. Goitsen had been with a farm since the age of twelve. Fedde too, he set up shop for himself later on, with a handful of cows and some small-scale trading in calves: four animals in a cart behind his delivery bike and two more in an enormous wicker basket in front, which he lugged along the muddy cart tracks, from farm to farm. "You didn't know any better," said Pieter.

During the 1930s most of the children left home. Only Fedde and Pieter stayed with their mother Sietske. They lived behind the Meibos coppice on a tiny farm with a shed, a yard and a muckheap, in the middle of nowhere, far from the world. Nearby was a similar farmstead where Minne and his mother lived. They were surrounded on all sides by land – although, in the teeming rains of autumn and winter, it was usually little more than an overgrown mudflat as far as the eye could see.

For Minne, too, it was hard going. He had a few cows and in addition rented himself out to other farmers as a cowhand. Only his brother Lammert seemed determined, with all the might and rage he possessed, to break free of the mud. He saw a future in that new means of transport, the bus, and started his own business. One day the bus ended up in the canal and after that it was back to the old way of life.

There was the odd festive occasion. Fedde sometimes told us about that wedding reception at which he got terribly drunk, and then there was something vague to do with a girl and a mill. The memory had not been obliterated by many later events and had remained intact, and Fedde talked about it as though it had happened last month rather than 50 years ago.

In the summer when they were making hay, they occasionally saw people on holiday cycling by: "A holiday!" said Pieter. "We didn't even know what that was. A cycling holiday! It was a different world."

They knew straightaway that war had started. Pieter: "It was in May 1940. By five o'clock Fedde had already gone to market with his calves. I was at the water-butt having a wash, but suddenly Fedde was standing next

to me again. He said: 'The market is closed, as war has broken out.'
I was 23."

The next day they saw their first Germans, on horseback, en route to
the Zuider Zee Afsluit dyke. "They all rode horses, there were horses
everywhere – yes, it was scandalous, but we paid more attention to the
horses. They were beautiful animals!"

The countryside changed only when the shadow of the clouds passed
across it. Fedde had started to collect potato peelings and vegetable
waste from the houses, and by these means he was able to keep a few
extra cows without having to rent any more land. Only in September did
they learn that Rotterdam had been bombed. One and a half years later
the butcher in Gorredijk appeared behind his counter wearing a yellow
star. A few months after that he disappeared, never to be seen again.

The neighbours, in their poverty, had pinned all their hopes on the
New Order. Minne and his mother became enthusiastic members of
the National Socialists and Lammert had even joined the blackshirts.
He was so ferocious that he became known as "the terror of Wolvega".

One day the vet dropped in on Sietske, Fedde and Pieter. Would
Sietske give shelter to a few Jewish refugees hiding from the Germans?
They were in a bit of a fix. Sietske wiped her hands on her apron and
nodded: "Well all right, bring them along. It is a bit of a worry for
them, after all."

They were the first of many. Fedde planted willow and elder trees
all along the edge of the property to prevent people looking in. Every
evening they sat and played cards with the refugees, who, if there
were unexpected visitors, would dive under the bedstead. Pieter: "We
didn't always see eye to eye, but, when all is said and done, we had a
lot of fun."

Eighteen months later, things went wrong. An elderly neighbour, the
mother of Minne and Lammert, came by unexpectedly for a spoonful
of sugar. The refugees could not slip under the bedstead quickly enough,
and when the neighbour stepped into the room there was still a pair of
legs sticking out from the wooden panelling. Next day they were taken
to another address. A raid never took place.

After the war there were medals for Sietske, Fedde and Pieter, and
commemorative trees in an Israeli "Forest of Heroes". Lammert was

sentenced to death, later on his sentence was commuted. His mother died soon afterwards. Sietske fell ill in 1951. She had survived everything, but not liver cancer. She died at home, in great pain. After the funeral there was tea and a biscuit.

The two little farmsteads in the backwoods remained. Fedde now lived alone in one, Minne in the other. Minne threw himself into motorbikes and mopeds. He was fascinated by machines, and in and around his house were scattered cogwheels, pinions and old cylinders. Fedde kept five cows and an old bull – "a farmer without a bull is no farmer"– a billy goat, a donkey, two cats – one of which had a limp – 14 chickens and 18 cockerels. Apart from the cows everything roamed free. He still cycled with calves and potato peelings.

They both went grey, and their bodies were tough, wrinkled and calloused. Minne retained his fervent demeanour. One day he saw in the *Leeuwarder Courant* that an old teenage love of his had been widowed after 40 years. He cut out the newspaper announcement. A few weeks later, on a Sunday afternoon, he started his motorbike. "I ought to drop by and see how the land lies," he said to Fedde. He had not spoken to her since he was 18. Two hours later he was back: "She has grown fat."

With the passing of the years Fedde turned into a sort of Dr Doolittle, a sweet-natured man who always wore the same cap and the same corduroy jacket, and who rose with the dawn and went to bed when it got dark. He was in charge of the stock of Beerenburg liqueur that he and Minne had managed to acquire when a nearby café had closed down – first of all they had emptied the enormous demi-john into a milk churn and then, together, they had carted their booty home on the motorbike, Minne in front, then the milk churn, then Fedde. They always drank at Fedde's, under the petroleum lamp. Every now and then they both went outside for a pee and to look at the stars.

Late in the evening, Minne would stagger home across country and clamber up the ladder to the hayloft where he slept because the beds were covered with gearboxes, mudguards and piston-rods. There he lay with eyes wide open, because, he said, his house had been haunted since the war.

*

During their conversations they usually skipped those years. "Oh, well," said Fedde, if you asked him about that strange period, "you still have to get along together, don't you?"

They only fell out once, about a vague matter that nobody else was clear about. They did not speak to each other for a year. After that, Minne was again to be found every Sunday morning at his neighbour's drinking coffee, and Fedde cut him slices of sponge cake with his big hands – cellophane and all, "because that is more hygienic".

In 1972 Fedde became ill. A swig of petroleum – since his youth a proven method against all ills – did not help this time. They took away a piece of his stomach, but the wound did not heal properly. While he was in hospital Minne looked after his animals, and as soon as he was back home he started all over again with calves and chickens. With his ailing body he lugged the delivery bike with milk churns along the muddy Meibos path to the road, twice a day, come rain or shine.

Meanwhile Minne had given up his farming business. He had had a new house built a bit further along the road, with water and gas, electricity and television. The first few weeks he went there in the evening to switch on the lights and watch *Peyton Place*. Only later on did he move house.

That summer, Fedde often sat quietly watching the evening from within the hay barn, surrounded by his animals. The lame cat on his lap, the donkey and the billy goat by his side, the chickens like plugs of wadding on the supporting beams.

Then autumn came and everything started to go wrong. A cow died. A man from the dairy came to say that everybody had to change over to cooling tanks, and that small-scale milk transport and old-fashioned milk churns would soon be a thing of the past. On a stormy night the biggest tree blew down, blocked the whole yard and almost flattened the house. A few weeks later the donkey lay dead in front of the door. Fedde himself was so weak that, soon after, he had to get rid of the bull.

Fourteen days later it was all over. On a wet and windy December day he got stuck in the mud with his delivery bike and could no longer pull it free. A few weeks later he was dead.

*

That is what happened. Sietske is dead. Fedde is dead. Lammert is dead. Minne is dead. Now there is a yacht stowed away in Fedde's hay barn, his old muddy path is a nature trail, and the pasture that Minne mowed year after year has been planted full of oaks, birch, larch and other flora by the Forestry Commission. But the survivors are dead, and no one has taken their place.

————————

At the end of the twentieth century we experienced the final years of a culture the like of which we had known for centuries, but that within a few decades was slipping through our fingers.

A good 100 years ago, farming everywhere still played the role it had played for 10,000 years: that of nourisher, begetter and instructor. In the greater part of Europe, agriculture was the most important means of existence, the central engine that determined all aspects of human activity, the framework within which the laws of life and death were enshrined.

Most townspeople only have to go back a few generations before they come across a grandfather, a great-uncle or a great-grandfather who tried to scrape a living by farming.

In 1849, 44 per cent of Dutch households kept themselves alive with cattle, arable land, vegetables, or a combination of all of these. A hundred years later, by 1950, it was only 20 per cent. In 1995 the Netherlands had the most intensive agriculture in Europe, but the farming population had been literally decimated during the previous half century: from 750,000 in 1950 to 75,000 in 1995. By the turn of the century, less than two per cent of the Dutch still had anything to do with farming.

Worldwide a similar pattern began to appear. Until long after the Second World War the vast majority of people were farmers. In 1960 two thirds of the world's population lived in the country. In 2025, according to the latest United Nations forecast, only a third of the population will earn their living by farming.

In 1950, there were a mere two metropolises with more than eight million inhabitants: London and New York. In the year 2015 there will be 33, plus another 500 cities with a population of more than a million.

The critical juncture then, will occur around the turn of the century, the historic moment when, for the first time in human history, more people will live in the towns than in the countryside.

Even so, when I lived in Jorwert half of the world's population still consisted of farmers. And that farmers are a different breed to towns-people is abundantly clear to anyone who has ever set foot in the cattle market at Purmerend, or an auction near Woerden, or the cross-country rally in Bontebok, or the Whit Sunday market at Oudeschoot.

A country market like that has everything an ordinary market in town would have, only the accents are different: there is an excess of tools, spades, forks and the rougher type of working clothes to be found; the pot plants are cheaper but less varied; the tradespeople selling miraculous polish, sensational lemon-squeezers and American string laces that never have to be retied are still present in all their glory; and of course there are all sorts of livestock on sale: horses, chickens, geese, sheep, goats, ducks, canaries, pigeons, rabbits, even a tame crow.

And then there is the unbelievable amount of alcohol: in tents and old sheds, standing or sitting at rough-hewn tables and benches, talking stiltedly or swaying gently to the music, we down it until we are sloshed. The girls have short blond hair or greasy, tight curls, the boys wear blue denim suits or plaid shirts; they hold a thin cane in their hand and, in 1995, small sunglasses were the height of fashion. "We men cannot accept that," I hear someone next to me say, and I see a 16-year-old carry out a quasi-attack on his neighbour, while his girlfriend, half screaming with laughter, snuggles against him. Both are fresh, ruddy complexioned, with close-cropped hair and hard as nails, and in the eyes of a town dweller they might have come from another planet.

At country markets you see faces you will never see in town, and you see them in their thousands. They are red and furrowed – due to constant exposure to the open air. They are fat – due to the kilos of grease they consume at such markets in the form of hamburgers, sausages, fried fish and deep-fried chops. They are strong – the young men especially, because of the work they do, are generally as strong as oxen. They are marked, quite often covered with scars and lumps – farmwork remains risky, and frequently the older ones especially treat themselves little better than their livestock: each doctor's visit costs money and they are rarely insured.

And they are as old as the hills – they bear the traces of generations, they are indifferent to fashions and trends.

Peet, Folkert, Lampkje, Fedde and Minne had one thing in common, despite all their differences: their lives, but also the way they thought and behaved, and even their very "being" would have been unthinkable in a town. While borders disappeared and distances got ever smaller, at the close of the twentieth century there was still a deep cultural gulf running through every country; a fault line visible to everyone, but about which you rarely heard: it was the difference between towns-people and farmers, consumers and survivors.

That difference, surpassing languages, cultures and religions, had always been there. Plato wrote about the contrast between the "inflamed society" of the town and the "simple society" of the country village. In the nineteenth century the difference between town and country formed an important element in public debate. For Tolstoy, country life and city life were almost synonymous with good and evil – he even constructed *Anna Karenina* completely around it. Karl Marx talked about the "insular city type" as opposed to the "insular country type". And when, after the nineteenth century, political interest in this antithesis disappeared, it engaged the continued interest of sociologists and anthropologists.

One of the most important researchers, the American Robert Redfield, even developed the theory of continuous movement, whereby the more "civilised" cities repeatedly gather might and riches, but pay a high price for this in alienation, delinquency and personal isolation, and eventually disintegrate once again.

That same theme – put into words by the Russian poet Nicolai Nekrasov 150 years ago – recurred again and again:

> In the principal cities fierce orators lash out
> at slavery, untruthfulness and evil.
> Still, in distant regions of the country,
> a confounding silence hangs, as before,
> Above the endless plains.

In the twentieth century, the relationship was no longer such a simple one. It had ceased to be a case of the self-contained, reserved city versus the naïve, open-hearted countryside a long time ago. In all sorts of ways the city had, during recent decades, infiltrated the countryside with commuters and rich pensioners, money, cars and hundreds of thousands of cable TV connections. But at the same time the countryside continually stirred within the city's unconscious. City dwellers too, were far more influenced by country traditions than they realised.

When politicians spoke of a return to "family values", it was – rightly or wrongly – a throwback to the village, to a nostalgia for the outside life that still slumbered in the hearts of many city dwellers.

When, in the huge high-rise districts, a Moroccan teenager came into conflict with the strict authority of his father, the argument in many cases could be traced to a clash between the norms of the countryside and the norms of the city.

When, in a respectable suburb, a Dutch mother flew into a rage when her daughter came home with a coloured wedding dress instead of a white one, each spoke a different language: the daughter the language of the city with its pleasure and beauty, the mother the language of the village with its tradition of honour and disgrace.

When, in a modern apartment in Moscow, a grandmother ran her daughter's household, when Parisians phoned their family every day, these facts simply illustrated one thing: often, even in a big city, the village often still set the standard.

When, in the Balkans, mountain villagers deliberately shot to pieces libraries, mosques and ancient art treasures, it signified not indifference but hate, the hatred of the farmer towards the complex world of the city. And when one spoke, in that same context, of the wildness that formed the darker side of our civilisation, then it was the city dweller's eternal fear of the untamed strengths of the ever silent countryside that lay behind it.

The tension between town and country was one of the most suppressed, and yet at the same time one of the most sensitive focuses of conflict within twentieth-century culture.

There were a few typical characteristics that applied to almost all farmers, wherever they lived. Farmers, for instance, almost always lived in small communities, with all that this implied. There existed a certain amount of autonomy – most farmers were essentially self-employed, and they attached great value to this. Nevertheless everything was almost always governed by outsiders: landowners, suppliers, key buyers, the bank, the auctions, the Organic Products Association, the government.

Fathers, sons, mothers, daughters, grandparents and grandchildren spent most of the day in one another's presence, and they did most of the work together. Because there were never enough hands to do all the labour, the children were put to work at a young age, and in doing so they learned, in an almost playful fashion, the most important practical aspects of the craft of farming: weeding, mowing, harvesting, milking. Almost all the farmers' children in Jorwert to whom I spoke had been given small chores to do by the time they were six or seven years old – driving livestock from one field to another for example. They all learned to milk when they were about ten. At the same time, even in the most modern businesses, I often saw a grandfather pottering around in the cowshed, performing small tasks and giving a lot of good advice, because, when all is said and done, a cow is still a cow, a living and complex creature.

All this gave rise to another peculiar characteristic of the craft of farming: for most farmers, when it came down to it, the continuity of the business was paramount, rather than achieving the maximum profit. The professional goal of the average farmer was still, primarily, the survival of the group. He was concerned with creating security for his family, for his relations and for future generations, and everything else was secondary to this.

So in many ways the differences between Jorwert and Amsterdam were far greater than between Jorwert and any village in England or Germany.

A great many villages have been studied in the course of the last century, and one thing is noticeable in almost all the research: the "universality" of village life. Villages, wherever they are in the world, in some respects bear an amazing resemblance to each other. Did they not get all worked up in Jorwert about keeping the school open? In a research project on an American village I came across exactly the same worries. Was everyone migrating to the towns and was agricultural land reverting to wilderness again? In France, that was the way it had been for decades. Did it not all come down to the family in the end, for many Jorwerter businesses? Polish, Indonesian and South American studies revealed precisely the same social patterns.

Robert Redfield analysed three rural societies. One from *Works and Days* by the Greek poet Hesiod (800 BC). Next, a village in Surrey, England, around 1900, as described by George Bourne. And lastly a Mayan Indian village in Yucatan, where he lived for a few years.

He saw that all three communities were governed by the same cluster of convictions: an intermingling of the work of farming with an almost reverential attitude towards the soil; the linking of labour with personal values; the training of the young boys in tenacity and hard work, rather than risk-taking and the pursuit of personal gain; the acceptance of heavy labour, even regarding it as the norm, and at the same time being very happy when it is over.

Redfield's conclusion: "If a peasant from one of these three widely separate villages could have been transported by some convenient genie to any one of the others and equipped with a knowledge of the language in the village to which he had been moved, he would very quickly come to feel at home. And this would be because the fundamental orientations of his life would be unchanged."

The English essayist John Berger, who, in the 1980s, described a French mountain village, emphasised the continuity and toughness of agricultural life. He drew a picture of an existence that was still totally focused on survival. "The word 'survivor' has two meanings," he writes. "It denotes somebody who has survived an ordeal. And it also denotes a person who has continued to live when others have disappeared or perished."

It was in the second sense that he applied this word to farmers. They were the ones who tenaciously carried on working, in contrast to the unknown number who died young, emigrated or became paupers. Survivors, therefore, in contrast to survival.

Richard Critchfield, the American journalist-anthropologist who studied dozens of villages all over the world, also had the feeling that everything repeated itself, and in one way or another was the same. "The peasant is a recognisable and long-enduring human type," he wrote, and he even wondered whether the farmer was not actually the only archetype, "in other words, the common cultural ancestor of us all".

Nevertheless, there were great differences behind the surface similarities. There was, for instance, a fundamental division between "peasants" and "farmers", or, to put it a different way, between "smallholders", farmers who produced primarily for themselves and their immediate surroundings, and "commercial farmers" who concentrated on the market in the towns and specialised in market gardening, livestock or arable farming, who plied the town and let the town ply them. In the Netherlands by now even the smallest farmer was "commercial", but there were also countries where the "smallholders" still formed the majority.

In addition many farmers were not true farmers but rather jacks of all trades. We should, then, imagine the original undertaking primarily as a hybrid of survival techniques.

For example it is apparent from one of the first Dutch population surveys, the "Informacie" of 1514, that the women in the village of Ransdorp in North Holland, kept "a bantam or two", but that the men spent most of their time at sea. In Nieuwkoop the farmers earned extra by scything reeds, cutting peat and digging irrigation trenches. In Alphen on the Rhine, besides arable farming and cattle-breeding they fished and caught birds.

Hardly anyone in all those villages appeared to specialise in anything. Both men and women were highly adaptable and profited from every chance opportunity that came their way. They milked a few cows, did a bit of trading, kept their eyes open, they seized the day, and survived by means of their ingenuity and flexibility.

It is, then, too easy to generalise about "the" farming culture. The near-serfdom of the Russian farmer in relation to the town dweller and landowner had little to do with the individualism of the French mountain farmer. The Greek farmer, who for generations had produced primarily for his own island, had a very different attitude towards the market than the German cereal farmer on the Baltic. And the extreme poverty of the farmers in Brabant and Gelderland brought with it an entirely different attitude to that of the commercial spirit of the farmers in the coastal provinces of Holland, Zeeland, Friesland and Groningen, who had lived for centuries under the influence of the larger towns.

It was the same with the villages. The phenomenon "town" is barely a few thousand years old, and only after the Middle Ages do towns begin to occur on a larger scale. Almost all nation states are barely a few hundred years old, while many villages already existed thousands of years ago. The village community is the commonest form of coexistence throughout history, and it is one of the most enduring human institutions known to us.

At the same time, even within the Netherlands, the differences between villages are enormous. There are parts of the country where primarily large villages are to be found – like the sandy regions of Gelderland, Overijssel and Brabant – and areas where small villages are strewn all over the landscape – such as Friesland, North Holland, Zeeland and South Limburg. There are villages, like Jorwert, with their own individual character, usually with their own church, a café and / or a few shops. And there are even smaller hamlets and settlements, like Funs for example, that rely on a nearby village and have barely any identity of their own.

There are commuter villages, residential villages, villages the town has eaten into, tourist villages, civil-servant villages, rich-people villages and farming villages. There are boring and beautiful villages. There are busy villages with lots of shops and villages where the last grocer retired half a century ago. There are villages where local societies bloom and flourish and villages where the community spirit is as dead as a doornail. There are villages next to the motorway, villages on the river, villages where the seawater sprays over the dyke, villages where the Civic Guards march and villages by a desolate canal in the fens. There is no such thing as a "standard village", and that is one thing Jorwert certainly is not.

That too, belongs to the phenomenon of the village. All over the world villages have words by which they characterize nearby villages: those people there are "rough and dangerous", that village there is more "open and friendly", and the Jorwert lot are "notorious drunkards, dolts and rascals".

Those feelings of oneness and of being distinct from other villages are experienced by everyone who has grown up in a village. The word "we" – which almost every villager uses at some time – accentuates the distinction between their village and the others. And it goes even further: the more the life of those involved is restricted to the village, the more the village community comes to represent the cycle of life itself for the inhabitants, like a tiny independent cosmos.

*

As far as villages and rural cultures are concerned, the Netherlands is a special case. Holland was highly urbanised very early on. In the seventeenth century Amsterdam was one of the largest cities in the world, and that fact exerted a strong influence on the rest of the country. In addition, because of the flatness of the terrain and the amount of water, the connections between town and country had traditionally been easy and intensive. Even a close community like Jorwert cannot, with the best will in the world, be compared to a Russian hamlet or a French mountain village, as it has been part of a semi-urbanised region for so long.

There are authors who, as far as the Netherlands is concerned, dismiss all differences between town and countryside. They are of the opinion that this country is one big cultural system within which, in diverse ways, a constant exchange of people, images and ideas is taking place. Our way of living, working and recreation has, according to them, become a general one; a way of life embraced in equal fashion by townspeople and villagers. Moreover, within this single cultural area, people are constantly moving back and forth between town and country. There are countless people who live in a town but who do not come from the town and, correspondingly, countless others who do come from a town but no longer live there. According to this notion, the country has become such a hotchpotch that you really cannot do anything with it. The countryside in their eyes is now merely something negative: it is non-town and nothing else.

The non-town however is only the surface. What makes the Dutch situation so interesting is that the countryside has preserved its own character. Villages and landscapes may for centuries have been colonised by the towns, but they have not completely lost themselves.

You would have to be blind not to see that the way work is carried out, the history, the rituals, the relationship between public and private, the family ties and friendships, the handling of money and goods, the attitude towards nature and religion, the identification with where one lives, in short, everything that determines a culture is still, in a village, composed differently to how it is in a town. Even in the Netherlands. And whoever argues the contrary, gives neither the phenomenon of the village, nor that of the town their proper due.

An average Dutch/Frisian village like Jorwert, despite its proximity to a town such as Leeuwarden, is still home to the countless opinions and customs that make such a community different to those within the commuter belt.

They are the remains of the earlier village culture, now lying more or less dormant. Often they are fragments of old survival techniques, and not infrequently these philosophies of life have continued to exist quite simply because working with weather, soil and nature does bring with it a different attitude to life in a town.

Villages have survived for hundreds – sometimes thousands – of years; villages have faces, they have stories, they have wrinkles and lines that cannot be smoothed over.

But their sounds have become muted, and their colours grey, and their perpetual motion machine appears, at times, to stall.

Chapter Three

The Unsteady Tightrope

 WHOEVER CROSSES THE BRIDGE NEAR THE OLD painter's shop early on an autumn morning and then slowly walks out of Jorwert, whoever does that for the first time is overwhelmed by light, hundreds of different sorts of light. The light above this flatness determines everything. It is eternal and ever changing, it sets the colour of each day, it threatens and consoles, it frightens and pleases.

During the months that I took my morning walks, the world around the village was one of bewitching landscapes and white mist, in which you could just make out the faint colours of a farm, a church tower or a village. When autumn came to an end and it began to freeze at night the village was surrounded by utter flatness, and everything that stood out above it had been placed there temporarily and could be removed again at any time.

Only the colour of the sky was ever changing. There were mornings full of dark purple clouds against a blue background. The sun rose behind the church tower, she shone her big yellow rays beneath the clouds. A day later the land was again enveloped by a cold, whitish mist, a flurry of snow occasionally drifting across the frozen fields. At twelve o'clock the clear ringing of a distant bell.

And then there were the first warm days after the winter. The trees around the church that had a hint of green about them again. The mornings and the evenings that were full of birds. Daffodils sprouting in all the village front gardens. People spring-cleaned, painted, hammered, and Gijs was using a large compressor to construct a new shed wall, together with Wiebe, Frans and strongman Ype: – "Hey," shouted Ype, "drilling with the compressor! I love doing that most of all. Can I have a go?"

And the grass began to grow rich and green again, the first cuckoo flowers blossomed, cow parsley grew on the verges and the fields were full of sheep and lambs. In the evening, spring mist rose off the water in the ditches, covering the countryside in a thin veil, a dreamy white by the light of the full moon. Later in the night, rain- and thunderclouds drifted across and the moon shone high and red behind the church tower, half-masked by the clouds that were arranged about her in a strange curve, as though a real live artist had been at work.

As well as the light, there was the land. People have lived for thousands of years in Jorwert; a location older than Amsterdam and Rotterdam combined. It lies in one of the oldest landscapes in the Netherlands, an area of former marshland, flat and green, with here and there a raised part suitable for living on, a so-called terp.

When the Icelandic Viking, Egil, journeyed through the coastal provinces of the Low Countries in 960, he described the area as a flat country where ditches had been dug that were full of water and formed the boundaries of the fields and meadows. The inhabitants used to cross the ditches by means of wooden beams, noted Egil. This area must have looked like that too, and it still looked broadly the same in the twentieth century.

If you walked around the village and you knew what you were looking for, you could still see traces of the country that Egil saw. There were faint grooves in the pastureland, the remains of a prehistoric river, the Boorn; a few meandering waterways, probably at one time natural creeks and brooks; streams that zigzagged in a strange way, like an old-fashioned brace and bit. Such indentations were often freaks of nature, but sometimes they were the remains of a medieval dispute between neighbours: one neighbour did not apparently want the ditch dug on his land, and if his neighbour insisted on drainage, then, according to the rules of the time, the ditch would have to be dug on someone else's land. There were the so-called "green ditches", like trenches, only deeper; the remnants of the natural drainage system used in the early Middle Ages until the first windmills appeared in the sixteenth century.

Then there were the raised pieces of ground in the surrounding countryside. Near the hamlets of Battens, Funs and Tsjeintgum, the farms were on slightly higher ground, even though the older terps had been largely levelled off. They were reminders of the first farmers here, pioneers who made the trek from the high sandy regions to the dried-up salt marshes of the Middle Sea 2,000 years ago.* They tended their livestock, laid out the first fields and established their huts on marshy ridges and riverbanks, to avoid being caught by the tide.

Later on they constructed larger peat mounds in the surrounding countryside. Sometimes there was only one farm on one of these terps, sometimes more, arranged in a ring around a water hole for the livestock – the place where later the church would often be built. This is also how Jorwert's large terp must have looked in earlier times; larger than it is now, as sizeable chunks were levelled off in the nineteenth century.

A description of those first terp-dwellers has been preserved, penned by a Roman soldier, Gaius Plinius Secundus, who toured the Northern Netherlands in about 50 BC.

"When the water covers the surrounding land they look just like seafarers on a ship," he wrote, "but when the water recedes they seem more like castaways, the way they go hunting about their hovels for the fish that retreat with the sea."

He felt sorry for them. "They pick up mud with their hands, dry it, more in the wind than in the sun, and they use this earth as fuel to heat their food and themselves, half frozen as they are by the northern cold. They only have rainwater to drink, which they keep in pits near the entrance to their dwellings. And these peoples say that being conquered by Rome is tantamount to slavery!"

Yet this area of terps soon became a comparatively prosperous agricultural region. The settlements spread out from the terps in a star formation over the outlying area, the narrowest part (the arable land), near the farm, the broadest (the hay meadows), behind. The farm buildings themselves were made from planks of wood, sods of turf, wattle and daub. The roofs were made from reed and straw, and for a chimney there was, at best, a hole – often not even that. They were long, primitive buildings, with the living quarters at the front, a cowshed behind,

---

* The Middle Sea was an inlet of the North Sea in Friesland during the Middle Ages. [Tr.]

and a separate haystack, a construction that would develop into the well-known "head-neck-rump" style in the seventeenth century.*

And lastly there was wealth and power. A stone's throw from Jorwert, at the end of the Hesens ride, near the farm that was known as Groot Hesens (Big Hesens) the road suddenly rose. This too was a remnant of an old terp.

And to the left of this, in the pasture, was another strange piece of raised ground. This was the site of the Jorwerter stins or fortified farm. There used to be a castle there, people said. You can still see this by the ditches surrounding the land, they formed the old castle moat.

But when I arrived in Jorwert there was not much to see besides a bump and a deserted worker's cottage where the sheep sheltered when the cold wind blew.

What colour was the countryside? It was green, brownish and grey, but there used to be more. There was arable farming and cattle farming mixed together, and many of the agricultural crops popular then have practically disappeared: barley, flax, madder, hops, oats, spurry, bearded wheat, buckwheat, their colours and forms have long ceased to make the landscape what it is.

Even the meadows looked very different. Whereas now pasture-land consists purely of the eternally green English rye-grass, in earlier times the colour of the meadows changed with the seasons: white with daisies, yellow with buttercups, lilac with cuckoo flowers, red with sorrel, and the countryside changed along with it.

The livestock had their own individual tints. The pigs were bristly, yellowish-white or dark, often also spotted. The horses were grey-brown, grey-black and red-blazed. The cows were originally reddish, but in later times they became progressively more variegated: black, red, white, grey, brown or grey-blue.

A good illustration of the colourful nature of the original livestock is an entry that Rienck Hemmema, a local farmer, made in his rekenboeck (farm accounts book) in 1572. In drawing up his annual balance-sheet he wrote that the following had been born in his cowshed: a

---

* A type of traditional farm architecture: kop-hals-romp translates literally as "head-neck-rump". These types of farm were massive, solid buildings with a narrow "neck"(hals) in the middle. [Tr.]

mousey-coloured calf from a black cow, a mousey-coloured bull calf with a white head from a yellow cow, a mousey-coloured speckled calf from a mousey-coloured speckled cow, a black calf from a small red cow and a black calf with a white head from a cow with a black back. The standard green grass and black-and-white cattle was nowhere to be found until 100 years ago.

In addition almost all animals were smaller than their present counterparts, and that meant that they had a lot of hide and little meat. That corresponded nicely with the proportional economic value. The hides were at least as important as the meat, because leather, clothing and parchment could be made from them.

The average milk yield of the cows was low, about 800 or 900 litres a year. The more than 1,300 litres recorded by Rienck Hemmema in that same *rekenboeck*, was exceptional – it can only mean that he must have been a really good farmer.

Little is known about the first Jorwerters. Last century when the terp was levelled off, a handful of their humble possessions came to light, and this is all the information we have. They include a mysterious, blackish-green translucent glass, with three human figures with pointed beards – one of them is looking at the other two and they are holding one another by the hand. Apart from this there are the usual bits and pieces: a clay pot, a bone comb decorated with little circles, an amphora, a Roman coin, a spindle made from a stag's antler, typical remnants of the smallholders' way of life.

As far as we can ascertain, the farmers in these Frisian lowlands practised mixed farming, just like they did elsewhere, with arable land, pasture and hay meadows, and coppices and vegetable gardens. In those days their work was scarcely profitable. It was the rule that a third of the earnings was used to buy seed for sowing, a third disappeared in the form of rent to one landlord or another, and one third was left to provide for the farmer and his family.

Farming had always been a self sufficient way of life, in this village just as it was elsewhere, and that meant that families made their own clothes, baked their own bread, prepared leather and built houses, sheds and stabling. The average stock of cows probably varied between four and six, and many small farmers often only had two. One got by in life by means of all sorts of other work.

Some specialised in specific skills. There had been independent blacksmiths in Friesland since the Great Migrations, and after that others began to apply themselves to the curing of leather or the baking of bread. Carpenters and potters appeared, millers to grind the corn, and weávers with special looms – although weaving and spinning was still practised on many farms for a long time to come. There was a gradual redistribution of the time available, especially between that allotted to agricultural activities and the rest.

Nature, however, remained unpredictable, sometimes friend, sometimes foe. Dykes were regularly breached, the land mass shrank and subsided – during the last thousand years the ground level in Friesland and Groningen has dropped by two metres – and the windmills were quite unable to deal with the amount of rain water.

Jorwert (then known as Everwerth) is mentioned by Thomas Groningensis in his monastic chronicle of 1220, which makes mention of how desolate the countryside was due to flooding by sea water, leaving it unusable. In Het Bildt in May 1607 a farmer noted in his diary that the roads were so inundated with water that people were moving around his village by barge. A few years later, when his wife was buried, it needed four horses to pull the hearse through the mud, "because it had rained so heavily everywhere". And on 16 February 1825, Doeke Wijgers Hellema of Wiergum wrote that he had climbed the tower and that the "whole surface" of the country "shone like glass, from east to west, as far as the eye could see there was nothing but water".

Until well into the nineteenth century large areas of Friesland, Groningen and Holland were regularly flooded during the winter – it is no accident that the word for "dyke" is synonymous with "road" in the Frisian language. A great deal of land could only be used for a few months a year. Many villages were isolated during the long wet winters, until the frost came, and it was possible to skate. Until the nineteenth century even a town like Leeuwarden was "often cut off from all contact in the winter". There were lakes and marshes everywhere, monuments to a battle for survival fought and lost, just like the deserted villages in France.

*

Until one and a half centuries ago emptiness was the characteristic of the countryside, and this was so in the Netherlands too.

From 1763 onwards, according to old church accounts, Jorwert possessed five street lamps each with one candle. Later on a few oil lamps were added. Futile, almost useless sources of light, but as the historian Auke van der Woud points out in his excellent book on the Dutch landscape, the essential thing with this type of lamp was not the light but something else: "A little flame on a pole three-metres high – a magical sign, comforting evidence of a measure of order in the far-reaching silent darkness."

Up to the beginning of the nineteenth century some two million people lived in this country, and the majority of the population was concentrated in urbanised Holland. That meant that the rest of the country was exceptionally sparsely populated. Besides intensively farmed agricultural areas like the Greidhoek, Friesland had extensive fens and marshes. There were still endless heaths and wastelands in Gelderland and Brabant, inaccessible regions that could only be cultivated at the edges. Three quarters of Drenthe consisted of wilderness. The Peel was one huge bog measuring about 400 square kilometres.

In addition there were enormous tracts of ground that could only be used for a decade, after which they had to lie fallow for some 20 to 30 years. Few people lived in regions like these because there was hardly a penny to be made and besides, whole families, complete with farmhands and maid-servants, usually all lived together on the one farm – it was not without good reason that a nineteenth-century traveller in Twente spoke of "certain islands in the middle of this sea of desolation".

In this emptiness, the darkness after sunset was colossal, a blackness unimaginable for the present-day Dutch. Outside the towns there was no light beyond that of the moon and the stars, and there was hardly any from inside the houses either. People were economical with their light, took the lamp or candle with them if they moved around the house and the outbuildings, and lived and worked by the light of day, from sunrise to sunset.

When Leeuwarden changed over to gas lighting in 1845, and the lamps were lit for the first time, Doeke Hellema wrote in his diary that "the town was so lit up that people elsewhere in the land, including Wirdum, thought there was a fire". When people got used to it, the bright light of the town served as a beacon for the whole district. The Jorwerters saw a large, vague patch of light on the horizon, and they knew: that is the artificial light of Leeuwarden, and that is Franeker.

That mysterious darkness was peopled by mysterious inhabitants. In the empty, flat countryside stories have been told for centuries – and sometimes written down too – about white shrouds in female form floating over the fields, giants who suddenly bent over the unwitting traveller from behind so that their face was seen upside down, cats who accompanied you and grew bigger along the way, headless rogues who made the byways unsafe, shades who followed a lonely skater, ghostlike masses of people who stood on the water wailing, desperate paupers who rose up out of the fen, infants who suddenly appeared at a skipper's helm in the evening, begging for a shroud.

In 1842 the *Friesche Volksalmanak* (Frisian People's Almanac) informed its readers that it was no longer the custom to talk about this sort of mysterious business. "Mark you: there are many who do not believe in ghosts – as long as they are sitting by the fire, or who ridicule witches and exorcists as long as they are talking to the vicar or the schoolmaster or chatting at evening class. But if the butter will not churn, they still quietly draw a cross on the ground at the threshold of their house, and if the old mare is in pain, they try to dispel it with a 'formula'."

All the fears of a life permanently balanced on the edge, were concentrated in magic and ghost stories. People could live off their farm, they could even achieve a mite of prosperity, but as soon as there was a particular setback to contend with – illness, war, flooding, a plague of mice – the family could be plunged into bitter poverty in a moment. Disaster followed disaster. From a failed harvest came hunger, from hunger came illness, through illness a shortage of labour occurred, so that fields and dykes could no longer be maintained. Nature was one big lottery, and the only thing a farming family could do was play safe, and moreover be extremely prudent, generation after generation.

The first farmer from the vicinity of Jorwert of whom we know a little more is the previously mentioned Rienck Hemmema, the owner of all the mousy-coloured calves. He lived in Hitzum, a small village to the south west of Franeker. A series of his business jottings covering the years 1569 to 1573 has been preserved. He was probably not a typical farmer – the fact that he kept a special *rekenboeck ofte memoriael* (accounts book and diary) is in itself unusual – but his notes do, nevertheless, give a fairly good impression of the ins and outs of a sixteenth-century farmer's life in these parts.

Hemmema had four horses, roughly 15 dairy cows and a good 19 acres of arable land, as well as some pasture. From his notes it appears that the making of butter and cheese was already his most important source of income – he had even taken on a separate maidservant to deal with all the milk he produced. But in some years he earned almost half by the production of grain.

In those days manure was an extremely scarce and costly product: it is evident from Hemmema's *rekenboeck* that he had to buy large supplementary amounts for his arable land, from the citizens of the town of Franeker who often kept a few cows themselves, as was customary then.

What is most interesting is that Hemmema was no longer, in any sense, a "peasant". From the "Informacie's" of 1494 and 1514 it can be deduced that, round about 1500, most farmers were still typical "peasants". To a large extent they were farmers who provided for their own needs and did not produce for the market. Half a century later Hemmema's business was completely geared to the market. He even went so far as to save hardly any of his barley and wheat for personal consumption. It is apparent from his accounts that he took almost all of his expensive bread grain to market where he bought the far cheaper rye in exchange, to bake bread for his farmhands and maidservants. And this presumably came directly from the Baltic. Hemmema's prosperity was already interwoven with the currents of European trade, and with the destiny of the towns.

In the vicinity of Jorwert too, from the end of the sixteenth century onwards, the farmers probably began to lose their "peasant-like" characteristics. Just like elsewhere in Friesland and Holland they began to develop into farmers proper, specialised farmers who sold their cheese, meat and other products at market, or had them sold.

There are statistics that show how many farmers in the district around Jorwert had a plough, the characteristic tool of the arable farmer. That number began to drop significantly around 1600 – which meant that more and more farmers here were giving up growing corn and concentrating solely on breeding, rearing cattle and making butter. And a cattle farmer does not need a plough.

This minor turn-around had everything to do with the changes in the towns. While nine out of ten people still lived in the countryside in the rest of Europe, in southern England and the coastal provinces of the Netherlands sizeable urban areas had developed. In the province of South Holland more than half the population already lived in a town at the start of the sixteenth century, in Flanders, Brabant and the province of North Holland it was roughly a third, in Friesland a quarter. In addition these townspeople had more and more money to spend on "luxury" products like meat, butter and cheese. From that moment on, the cow began her advance.

When the towns prospered the villages did not lag behind. The worn tombstones with which the church in Jorwert is paved give a good illustration of that initial urbanisation of the village.

There lie, for example, Eelke Sipkes Banga, County Alderman of the "Five Areas behind the Dijk", died on 13 December 1665; Hottie Fons, vicar of Jorwert, died on 26 November 1566; Elisabeth Hendriks Hemstra, died on 9 September 1772 – she lived on Sake Castelein's farm; Rienck van Hettinga, Captain of the Frisian Nassau regiments, died on 14 March 1602; Wattie van Hania, gentleman, murdered in his sleep on the night of 2 December 1569 at Castle Groot Hesens in Jorwert – the scene of the murder, in all its gory detail, is chiselled into the slab of stone. And there are 20 more like this.

They are definitely no longer the graves of a small, isolated farming village.

That same process of refinement appears in property inventories from the seventeenth and eighteenth centuries: tin and wooden table-ware was replaced by earthenware plates, cups and saucers; rude benches and chests were superceded by large cupboards and fine furniture; shutters were replaced by curtains.

From the first Frisian tax registers, the "Aanbreng" (Collection) of 1511, it is possible to deduce that in the sixteenth century about 85 per cent of the rural population still consisted of farmers. But little more than 200 years later, in 1749, it is clear from those same registers that the farmers were only just in the majority. The village populations had increased significantly, and now tradesmen, labourers, skippers, carpenters, tailors, cobblers, schoolmasters, vicars, alehouse keepers, shopkeepers, bakers and blacksmiths, lived in the villages too.

That also applied to Jorwert. Since the beginning of the seventeenth century there had always been two or three bakers in the village, a few alehouse keepers, a blacksmith, a carpenter, a cooper and a surgeon. We know from a municipal list that in 1850 there were as many as five shopkeepers, a smith, two dyers, a copper-beater, four alehouse keepers, two bakers, three carpentry firms, two coopers, a butcher, a doctor, three pedlars, a merchant and a silversmith.

In short, like significant areas of the countryside in the Netherlands, little Jorwert was highly capable of providing a wide variety of goods and services. It had absolutely no need of the town for that.

In the nineteenth century this independence would lead to a new division between town and country, but now it was chiefly a state of mind. The more romantic townspeople began to idealise the rural community, and the farmers themselves began to consciously differentiate between themselves and the town.

In Friesland and elsewhere a movement to promote the native language developed, and everywhere national dress and the old ways were held in high regard (up until the 1950s, each Sunday morning the Jorwerter church would be full of gleaming eighteenth-century *oorijzers*, or ear-clasps).* In the manner in which they furnished their houses too, the farmers emphasised their group awareness, with certain pieces of furniture, specific colours and patterns, and various status symbols.

In the Netherlands down through the centuries the relationship between town and country was less static than one is often led to believe. And there was probably a fairly extensive period in which the differences

* A brace or cap of precious metal worn by women under their bonnets, with decorative extensions at ear-level. [Tr.]

between towns and villages were even smaller than they are now, partly because the dimensions of the towns were more "village-like", and partly because people in the villages lived lives more akin to those of the towns.

Now it has to be said that the skippers, transporters and cattle-drivers played an important role in all this too. Friesland and Holland were low-lying, flat regions and that meant it was relatively quick and easy to travel through them. Early on, an excellent system of waterways and local services existed by which farmers could bring their produce to market quickly. Even isolated Drenthe was part of all sorts of trading networks. Drenthe farmers produced wool for the Dutch blanket industry, bred horses for the town and were important suppliers of partially fattened oxen for slaughter, to the tune of an estimated three to five thousand a year. There are indications that cattle from Drenthe were even driven as far as the cattle markets of Flanders.

It is no coincidence that in sixteenth- and seventeenth-century oil paintings herds of cows appear everywhere, highways full of them, usually driven by a young lad wearing a hat and carrying a stick in his hand. That scene was no idyllic figment of the painter's imagination. Those roads full of cattle must have been the daily reality.

Although rural life still seemed as uncomplicated as ever, appearances were deceptive. A sort of European agricultural industry already existed by about 1600. The Baltic countries produced enormous quantities of grain for the Low Countries and Southern Europe. Friesland made butter and cheese for England and Holland. And Denmark produced thousands of beef cattle for the towns of Holland.

In his *Geschiedenis van de Landbouw in Nederland* (History of Agriculture in the Netherlands) the agricultural historian Jan Bieleman provides impressive statistics on the size of that seventeenth-century trading network. From Jutland and the Danish islands for example, an average of 50,000 oxen a year were driven via Northern Germany to the south, in herds of 40 to 100 beasts. The animals were bred in Denmark, then fattened in special units during the winter and prepared for the long journey to the regions where they were consumed. The exodus of these partially-fattened oxen began in February, which meant that they could be delivered to their destination in the springtime, when the grass was just beginning to sprout. In the summer they were fattened up some more, in the vicinity of the Dutch towns, and finally sold for slaughter in the autumn. Besides this, a further eight to ten thousand oxen were imported by ship. And we have not even mentioned the vast numbers of beef cattle exported to Holland from other places.

Only the more isolated parts of the Netherlands remained outside this intensive system of trade, transport and increasing specialisation.

For example, by comparing the registers of the professions in Overijssel with those of the province of North Holland, circa 1800, it transpires that, relatively speaking, there were three times more bakers in the province of North Holland than there were in Overijssel, where the bread was apparently still baked by the farmers themselves from their own grain.

It is a known fact that, circa 1820, farmers in the district of Hoogeveen were in such a bad way, that they had no money to buy manure from nearby Zwolle, to improve their poor peaty soil. They had no money for anything apart from the purchasing of seed.

And when P. A. Barentsen, a general practitioner in Brabant, described country life in the Kempen area at the beginning of this century, most of the people who lived there still built their own houses, just like the turf huts in Drenthe and in the Frisian forests. The furniture too, was handmade. Oil-pressing, match-making and the baking of bread had been discontinued only shortly before. A period of specialisation (that most farmers in Holland, Friesland and Groningen had already gone through three centuries before) was clearly still taking place there.

In Bergeyk, the local vet once told me, people still kept cows in 1950, just like they did in Rienck Hemmema's Franeker in 1572. The blacksmith had one, as did the grocer, and the baker even had two.

In Limburg too, where entry to the surrounding markets was blocked by all sorts of trade barriers, farming continued for a long time to be practised in almost medieval fashion. Around the year 1800, three quarters of Limburg soil was still reserved for products intended solely for consumption within the family. Or, as a citizen of Limburg described the situation in about 1790: "One ate and drank what the farm provided. Because very little could be sold, the farmer had ample to eat." In the

isolated world of the small-holders it was apparently possible to develop
an epicurean lifestyle – and perhaps this lifestyle flourished precisely
because of their isolation.

As a result, the villages in these remote regions remained separate
worlds, complete in themselves. People had nothing, but they did not
need anything either, except clothing, food and a roof over their heads.
In earlier times almost all country people danced upon that unsteady
tightrope, but some went on dancing generations longer than others.

In the rest of the country, agriculture arranged itself around the towns
like so many stones being dropped into a pond. In the immediate
vicinity of Amsterdam a ring of farmers developed that specialised
in vegetables, beef cattle and milk, products that had to reach the city
quickly. A bit further away, in Utrecht and the Veluwe district, there was
a ring of commercial growers – of crops like hemp and flax. Then there
was a ring where the cheese and butter came from, and where cattle
were, so to speak, semi-reared for the areas of intensive farming in the
vicinity of the towns. Jorwert belonged to this ring. And a bit further still,
on the heavy clay soil of Groningen and northern Friesland, lay the
extensive areas where the bulk products were cultivated that could easily
be transported over longer distances: grain, beet and potatoes.

The process of separation that took place within farming towards the
end of the sixteenth century was an operation which, to this day, has
determined the light, the colours and the face of the Frisian landscape:
the grain corner in the north, the water in the lower middle, mixed
farming in the Frisian forests, and in the southwest, the broad expanses
of flat, green pasture dotted about with villages. In this district the cow
became the leading player. And the slow conversion of grass into meat
and milk would determine life for centuries.

Chapter Four

The House of Order, Money and Paper

 ONE OF THE OLDEST BUILDINGS IN JORWERD WAS
the house of order, money and paper.

It was the house at the top of the street where the
solicitor lived and where he had his office. A low, honest
house, with two sturdy old-fashioned chimneys, a solid
front door with two panels of stained glass on the left
and three on the right, and with strange, crooked railings around the
doorstep. I gathered that the stained glass and the railings had, at one
time, been added to protect the solicitor's privacy, because half the village
used to hang around, or sit on, his fence.

In the sixteenth century the solicitor's house was home to the most
important local worthies. The *grietman* – a sort of mayor – lived there,
as did the parish secretary and the public notary. Around 1800, the
house was demolished and rebuilt and has been the home of the village
solicitor since 1835. After all, Jorwert was not just any village. For
centuries it had been the district capital of the parish of Baarderadeel;
the "court" had been situated in the café; there was even a gallows;
during the French Occupation the village was a *mairie*; and though all
these honours and titles were a thing of the past, Jorwert had remained
the official solicitor's residence.

The solicitor was a dignified man with greying hair, who cycled regally
through the village street each day. He walked with a stick, but no one
noticed that. Whoever visited him was led to the back of the house, to
a large room that stuck out like a fortress into the old notary-garden,
surrounded by ancient trees and shrubs and dark-green ivy. Not that
the solicitor could enjoy his garden very much. For more than 40 years

the so-called Iepenloftspul had been held there, a series of open-air performances for which the village was known throughout the whole region.

The hammering and banging of the scenery builders could be heard throughout the summer, and between-times a special Iepenloftspul for children was held, and it had gradually become tradition for the vicar to hold a "garden sermon" on stage and lead the parishioners in song, accompanied by the brass band from Weidum.

"You can't really refuse them, can you?" said the elderly solicitor. Each year an official delegation from the village came to ask whether they might use the garden, and when the performances took place he went to watch every evening, in the special chair that was always reserved for him in the front row. He had never been bored. "I have seen Myn Leave Lyske (My Fair Lady) at least 13 times, and I saw something new every evening."

The first time the solicitor gave permission was in 1954, when a few people wanted to collect money for the restoration of the church tower. That year 500 people came to watch. By about 1995 the spectacle in the solicitor's garden was drawing more than 7,000 people a year. They had put on A Midsummer Night's Dream, and My Fair Lady, with large choirs and the schoolmaster in the leading role, and Anatevka with hundreds of extra's and a cowshed with real cows, and each time it took place half the village and the surrounding area joined in.

Organising the props and scenery was something that occupied a few villagers throughout the year: the décor from the previous production would have only just been dismantled before it was time to drum up actors for next year, and once winter was over the scenery builders began, once more, to erect enormous and bizarre constructions in the solicitor's garden: medieval castles, haunted houses, Victorian streets and Russian villages, anything was possible.

Everybody worked for free. "Oh, we like doing it, we enjoy it," said the retired farmers and those on invalidity benefit who hammered and painted, week after week, for a handful of performances. "I have always enjoyed it," said the solicitor. "Only, it does mean I lose my garden for the whole summer, and that has been the case for the past 40 years."

*

The elderly solicitor had started work in Jorwert as a locum in June 1951, and the first deed of purchase that he had conveyed was a tenant farm of 98 acres. The purchase price was 100,000 guilders. "In those days that was paid in cash here in the office, a wad of thousand guilders notes handed across the table. Nowadays, that would be regarded as extremely suspicious, but we did not give it a thought then".

The solicitor had not expected to stay long in Jorwert, "because it was so dreadfully windy there". Nevertheless, since then he had become part of village life in a uniquely wonderful way. You always saw him in the street – either walking or cycling. He knew everybody – if he needed a witness to a deed, he would always go and fetch the cobbler and later on Oebele van Zuiden took over that honourable task, for 2.50 guilders a time. And he was prominent among the leading citizens of the village – he kept in close contact with the retired vicar, who lived directly opposite him, because they were both "night" people. "He would appear on my doorstep at midnight and say: 'I saw the light was still on so I thought I'd pop over.' And then we would drink a glass of cognac together."

The village spoke very highly of his interventions. When the council started to favour the nearby village of Mantgum, it became policy to condemn as many dilapidated properties as possible in the surrounding villages, and replace them with new houses that were then incorporated into Mantgum.

However, thanks to the solicitor's shielding hand nothing like this ever happened in Jorwert. This is how the schoolmaster obtained his first house: late one evening he was invited to the solicitor's home, and while they were both watching television the solicitor pushed a piece of paper towards him: "Just sign this." It was a house for 1,000 guilders, grandmother Sjouke's old place, she was nearly 100 when she died, and out of respect the council had never dared to nail a CONDEMNED sign to her door.

The schoolmaster added his signature, the solicitor leaned back satisfied, rolled a cigarette and afterwards the deed of purchase went missing for a year. By the time the council had sorted matters out the house had been completely renovated by the schoolmaster, the painter and decorator and a few other friends. That was in the early 1970s.

Ten years before he had saved the pub in the same way when it was for sale and could have fallen into the hands of anyone with enough cash. On his insistence the carpenter took it over, once again in the middle of the night. According to family legend, he returned home, his wife asked: "Did you have a good time?" and he said; "Yes, and I have also bought the pub".

It was possible to trace countless village histories in the archives at the solicitor's house. "Traditionally the Church had control of the public purse," he explained. During the Reformation in 1570 the Reformed Church had taken over the monastic properties, the consequences of which had been felt even by him. "Land, roads, streets, everything was owned by the Church. If something happened in the village, if a street lantern was needed or a bridge had to be built, it was the church wardens who paid for it. As late as 1970 I was still transferring sections of road from the Church to the council."

He told me about the building of the drawbridge in 1911, the bridge that the council had subsequently donated to an open-air museum, without having consulted the village – still a very sore point decades later. "In the council archives they have never been able discover any payments or other traces of the construction. Well, that is right, because the bridge was not paid for by the council, but by the Church. Even then. But nobody was aware of that any more, when the council used our bridge to show off to that museum".

A great deal of historical information on Jorwert was collected by the former baker, Klaas de Jong, and by Jolt Oostra, a nephew of the Casteleins, who wrote a whole book on it.

It transpired from their research, for example, that whatever changes had occurred in Jorwert, the places where the farmers lived and worked had always remained the same. In 1995 Hendrik Kundersma still had his farm on exactly the same spot where Tjeerd Jans had lived, in 1755. There had been a record of Bonne Hijlkema's farm since 1640. Cor and Lies Wiedijk's business had once been known as "Fondensera State", and in 1511 it was in the hands of a certain "Katryn of Fondens", otherwise known as Funs. And in that same year Sake Castelein's place was being exploited by a certain "Jacob of the neighbours". "Jorwert lies in a region where traditionally farmers have been tenants, not owners," said the solicitor. "And that meant there was a lot of moving around. Even so, you can see from the documents that farms sometimes stayed in the same family for generations". For example Groot Hesens, the largest farm in the village, had been occupied for almost 150 years by one family, the Kundersmas. And Sake's farming business, which had been home to three generations of Casteleins already, had been run for 117 years, from 1795 to 1912, by a single family; father to son-in-law, brother to widow, a long chain of 13 successors.

The solicitor talked about the durability of the farming community in the village where he came from – his father farmed in Poppenwier – and it was the same everywhere in Europe.

The working methods and way of life were durable too. In essence, until the end of the eighteenth century, farmers continued to use the same means – plough, manure, irrigation and the strength of the horse and the ox – as they used at the beginning of recorded time, they still travelled by foot or on horseback, and they still depended on wood and iron for their tools. That lasted until about 1800. Then all at once everything started to shift.

In the first place, after centuries of stability, the population began to increase dramatically throughout Europe. People were getting married at a far younger age so they had more children, added to which those children often lived longer because they were better cared for; so, by the nineteenth century, the population of the Netherlands increased from slightly more than two million to almost ten million – all people who relied on that same patch of ground for their food. This fact alone had enormous consequences for agriculture.

The second big change was transportation. Transatlantic shipping expanded enormously after 1840; railway tracks were laid everywhere and inexpensive produce could suddenly be transported over long distances in large quantities.

Between 1838 and 1864, less than 30 years, there was a twenty-fold increase in the export of cattle from the Netherlands. The price of butter at the market in Leeuwarden almost doubled. Those years of growth, the prosperity, the feeling of self-respect, manifested itself in Friesland in, the countless proud "head-neck-rump" farmhouses, in the *stjelp* farmhouses* with their many windows, in the decorative gigs, in Frisian national dress, in the broad gold *oorijzers*, in the thousand curlicues on the vicarage at Jorwert, in that single great explosion of rural culture that characterised the middle of the nineteenth century.

The third fundamental change concerned mechanisation. In one of the old deeds at the solicitor's, it said that on 14 April 1864, Oene Sijbes Kundersma, one of the most prosperous farmers, had held a public auction. He owned no fewer than 44 cows and the auction inventory included everything a farmer could possibly need: a bull, a brown mare, a covered carriage, a hooded gig, four haycarts, two wheelbarrows, six chickens and a cockerel; a total of more than 100 items but, as yet, no sign of any machinery. It could, with slight exaggeration, have been the auction inventory of Rienck Hemmema, 300 years earlier.

Of course, the farmers had not been sitting on their hands. Since the Middle Ages a number of important agricultural improvements had been made. The introduction of the windmill in the fifteenth century made it much easier than before to control the water table. The soil was improved through excavation and the dumping of rubbish from the towns. At the corn harvest the sickle was replaced by the scythe, which enabled the work to be done more quickly. Butter-making was made easier by the invention of the horse-drawn churning machine. Better ploughs had arrived, and better ways of sowing. In 1571, our Rienck Hemmema had a proper cowshed built in order to increase the manure yield – the beginning of a separate storage facility for manure. And after 1800 all sorts of authorities and charitable institutions began to show more and more interest in the enormous stretches of wasteland that were then available in the Netherlands.

However, most seventeenth- and eighteenth-century agricultural innovations were deficient in one respect: they scarcely addressed the lessening of the workload of farmer and farmhand, but were solely concerned with increasing productivity: "I sow this much grain, this much beet, this much seed. How much more will I get back: four times more, seven times more or ten times more?" These were the calculations made by

---

* A stjelp farmhouse is a more or less square building with a high pyramid-shaped roof under which there is room for living quarters and/or a cowshed. [Tr.]

the average farmer, and everything else was secondary to that, including the work involved and his own health and that of his family. Labour did not count. Because most of the work took place within a family context, it was readily available and cost nothing.

Agriculture was extraordinarily inefficient in dealing with the labour factor, especially when seen from a present-day perspective. According to an estimate by the eighteenth-century French agriculturist Lavoisier, the average casual labourer spent roughly 12 days a year ploughing and sowing, 28 days harvesting grain and 24 days mowing and haymaking. The rest of the time was primarily spent threshing with the flail. It took up no less than 63 per cent of a casual labourer's time, for 130 days a year. Extraordinarily dusty, unhealthy work, threshing often went on throughout the winter, from November until March, in between looking after the animals during the day and then for a while longer in the evening, after supper.

Interviewed at the beginning of the century by the writer Emile Guillaumin, the old French farmer Tiennon still remembered how, as a boy, he had had to thresh until 10 p.m. every evening, by the light of a lantern. "I do not know of any work that is more nerve-racking than this," he said. "Having to constantly swing the flail at the same regular pace in order to keep in time, because you must do that; never having a second to blow your nose or remove a piece of chaff that is itching your neck – when you are still awkward and lacking in stamina. It is enough to drive you mad!"

In among all those old Jorwerter deeds at the solicitors, there were scarcely any to be found that indicated investment, the systematic lending of money, coming to grips with other methods, the taking of a degree of professional risk, the lessening of the workload.

For example as early as 1893 the *Leeuwarder Courant* published an article about the possibility of milking by machine. Not far from Ijlst, a Danish inventor was experimenting with a "sort of milking machine", and, according to the experts, he had satisfactorily demonstrated the useful-ness of "this deceptively simple, but nevertheless extremely ingenious invention". They had used it to milk cows "with large thick teats and with small teats, all with the same favorable results, even cows with sore teats allowed themselves to be milked in this way without difficulty". In spite of this, it was some 20 years later, in 1912, that the first milking machine made its debut in Jorwert, at Wiepke Algera's farm, Groot Battens. His was also the first in Friesland. And it was only in the 1950s that this "extremely ingenious" invention became commonplace.

There was usually a long delay between the invention itself and its application in the case of other agricultural machinery too. Threshing machines, for example, were in existence by the end of the eighteenth century, but only came into use in the Netherlands from the middle of the nineteenth century onwards. There are certainly bound to have been teething troubles and other technical problems, but there was undoubtedly another factor involved: the phenomenon previously touched upon – money.

Machines cost money, while in the eyes of most farmers labour was free – for he did not count his own toil and that of his wife and children as costs.

There was often little money in circulation, especially in the more isolated farming areas. In principle each family supported itself, and there was little to be bought and sold. In the wealthier regions the farmers did have "best" rooms and gigs or they "hung their money on their wives", as they put it, but even the jewelry and other excesses were regulated by tradition and ritual.

The miserly nature of farmers was in fact not miserliness, but mistrust; a mistrust of the phenomenon of money in general. After all, the basic principle of every farmer was the continuity of the family business and the avoidance of risk, not the accumulation of capital.

In this connection, P. A. Barentsen, the general practitioner from Kempen, described in great detail how reverently farmers and their families treated a new piece of machinery, once they had finally taken the plunge and bought it. A farmer tried to keep going with the old tool for as long as possible, tied together with string if need be, and also if need be at the cost of a lot of extra work and inconvenience. Sometimes the respect for property and a reluctance to throw anything away went so far that old rubbish was stored up all over the place, in the hope of using it for one's own business – Minne's spare motorcycle parts, for instance. Sometimes that eternal prioritising in favour of the business led to frankly bizarre situations – for example, when farms were finally connected to the water-mains, in some cases a tap was only installed in the cowshed. In a world where labour was so plentiful and money so scarce, production always took priority over consumption. In the words of the old farmer, things were there "to be useful, not enjoyable".

One of the first machines to be so potentially "useful" that even the thriftiest farmers were convinced, was the threshing machine. The first American version came onto the market in Groningen in 1846. It reduced the labour time to a quarter of what it was before. The larger machines were powered by treadmills, a rattling belt of wooden staves on which one or two horses trod purposefully forward. A decade later there were a few hundred in use, and by 1885 almost 6,000 horse-powered threshers, 900 manual threshers and 170 threshers driven by "steam-traction engine", were turning in the Netherlands.

And the farmers needed these labour-saving devices. Thanks to the new agricultural methods the yield from land and livestock had increased to such an extent that the farmer's wife, children, farmhands and family could not possibly deal unaided with the amount of milk and grain produced.

The first horse-drawn hayrake for haymaking was introduced around 1850 – an implement that until recently could still be seen everywhere in the hay meadows. On 11 July 1875, Frisian farmers read in the *Leeuwarder Courant* that several reapers had been tried out during a congress in Heereveen. "In general the result was extremely satisfactory and expectations were exceeded," the newspaper reported. "As a consequence, a few agriculturists have already purchased one of these machines, and it is to be expected that these implements, once perfected, will quickly become commonplace."

The *terp* at Jorwert was partially levelled to obtain the fertile soil it contained, a fate shared by many other *terps*. More mills and steam-pumping stations appeared, which meant that the land no longer turned into a marshy bog each winter.

In the year 1858, the Frisian Society for History, Archaeology and Language asked all village schoolmasters to record for future generations their impressions of the village where they worked. This is what Heerke Alberts Jonghoff, the Jorwerter schoolmaster, wrote:

> The village of Jorwert lies practically in the middle of the parish district of Baarderdaal. It is a pleasantly situated village, arranged more or less in a circle. The church with its tower is situated on high ground, and the houses are grouped around it. [. . .] The village is in a good state, the inhabitants have neat and well-constructed houses and buildings that have been greatly improved and embellished during the past few years. This place contains about 1,900 acres of clay ground, including five acres of built-up area, but the rest consists of pastureland and hay meadow, for the most part in good condition, due to the fact that the farmers have made many improvements in the past few years.

Looking back, Jorwert was quite possibly at its peak in that ancient year of 1858 – as a classic village community, at any rate. At that time it had more than 600 residents; there were shops, bakers and cafés and it was a focal point for everyone who lived less than half an hour's walk from the village.

However, in 1878 the agricultural heyday of that period came to an abrupt end. The construction of new railways meant that the enormous cornfields of the Ukraine and the American heartland became accessible too, and suddenly the European market was deluged with cheap Russian and American grain. There was a sharp fall in the price of wheat, followed by wholesale diversion to other products by crop farmers, whereupon those markets collapsed as well.

The cattle farmers also ran into trouble. Cattle exports to England began to decline. The invention of margarine, the so-called butter substitute, led to the collapse of the exceptionally lucrative butter market.*

Countless farm labourers left the villages during this crisis that lasted until roughly 1895. They tried their luck in the large towns where one factory after another was springing up during that same period. More than 130,000 country dwellers migrated to the urban regions between

---

* Margarine was invented in 1870 by a Frenchman – Hippolyte Mège-Mouriez – in response to an offer by the Emperor Louis Napoleon III for the production of a satisfactory substitute for butter. [Tr.]

1880 and 1900. Fifty thousand people left from Friesland alone, a quarter of the population of the day.

The exodus continued for years afterwards. In Folkert's class at school, in 1925, there were a few farmer's sons, a handful of labourer's children and the solicitor's three children. A certain Johan has become a tramp, and most of the others have left too. "We never saw them again."

The crisis served to heighten the modernisation of the countryside, rather than holding it up. The Cooperative Agricultural Bank came to Jorwert, making it possible to invest larger amounts in spite of the crisis – initially business was carried out on the farm of one of its founders. Between 1883 and 1885 the Leeuwarden–Stavoren railway track was laid. Jorwert was granted a station too, and suddenly everyone could be at the market in Leeuwarden within half an hour, or standing on Dam Square in Amsterdam within half a day.

With the invention of artificial fertiliser it became possible to keep far more cattle on the same amount of land. For the first time the size of a farming business was no longer linked to the amount of land farmed. Thanks to fertiliser it became possible for small farmers like Fedde and Minne to milk a number of cows, despite having little land.

By the start of the new century, the chimneys of the dairy factories were seen all over the countryside, sticking out above the trees. In 1894 one was built in Weidum too, and from then on the farmers of Jorwert were able to put their butter- and cheese-making out to contract. This led to a totally different division of labour between men and women on the farms. Tjerk Castelein bought the first tractor in the village: a converted model T-Ford.

The history of the solicitor, the archives and the deeds, was getting closer and closer to the present village. I came across about 20 photographs of Jorwerters from the beginning of the century in the council archives, presumably duplicates that they had had to provide for a passport; a small cross-section of the population of the day. Most of them were standing in front of the camera looking stiff and formal in their Sunday best, after all having one's photograph taken and going on a journey would not have been everyday occurrences.

The faces that regarded me from within the faded files were

roughened by wind and weather, faces on which the toil was deeply etched: Atse Leistra, born in 1895, farm labourer; Auke Romkema, b.1918, cowhand; Jan Veenbaas, b.1909, farmhand; Auke Sierdsma, b.1876, stockman; Hiltje Idema, b.1918, no profession; Petrus de Groot, b.1918, farmhand; Albert Heslinga, b.1867, retired; Anne van der Hoek, b.1890, farm labourer; Albert Hoeksma, b.1914, farmhand.

Among them were men like Fedde and Minne, small farmers who had made a conscious decision to remain in the countryside. For them the piece of land they owned was their only certainty in life, and the greater the problems, the more they clung to it. This often resulted in an accumulation of disasters: poverty; extreme hard work to try and escape from it; physical neglect; and finally illness and even greater poverty. Some gave up the fight, lapsed into what was referred to as "listlessness", and lived from hand to mouth. Others supplemented their farms with odd jobs or some small-scale dealings.

"Oh, when I was a boy the people were so poor," said the solicitor. "There was no dole and you could see everyone attempting to sell something or other. A man who had six cows, started a sideline in coffee and tea as well. I can still remember them buying a pig from my father, and it dying soon afterwards. That was a disaster. Those people paid off that pig with ounces of tea, year after year. That is how poor they were."

"Our parents didn't have a farthing, so we couldn't do anything either," said Folkert. "It was dreadful."

Many young people, who watched it happen in front of their eyes, tried to escape the same fate. "I was good at school," said Folkert, "but there was no way I could have gone to college. That was only possible if you had some money, but my parents earned perhaps twelve guilders a week." So the farm-labourers' children in his class had all become farm labourers themselves.

This was the manner in which a number of people were forced to remain in Jorwert. Added to which migration to the urban regions stopped during the crisis years of the 1930s, because the absorption capacity of the towns had been practically reduced to zero. Unemployment was so high that there was no room at all for immigrants.

So a generation of "reluctant residents" came into existence in the village. Folkert was one of them, and Peet, too, might well have moved to town, and Riemer de Groot, the grocer, would have liked to have seen a bit more of the world. And we have not even mentioned the dozens of small-timers, the sidelines and petty dealings that the village was full of in those years; the desperate attempts of little people just to get by now there was no chance of them making the move to town. As far as they were concerned, staying in the village was not a choice, but a permanently postponed departure.

"When I started here in 1951," said the elderly solicitor, "Jorwert was one of the largest country practices in Friesland. We did nothing but deeds of purchase, mortgages, wills and testaments and marriage contracts. Now we do a lot of company law and partnership contracts for people living together. Things we had never heard of years ago. Mankind has become mean-spirited, and solicitors nowadays really have their work cut out."

When the solicitor started in 1951, he did not own the large solicitor's house, all he had was a moped on which he rode through the village each morning, with his face turned towards the tower, and towards the hands of the clock. The solicitor was one of the last to learn to live by the rhythm of the village and the striking of the clock in the tower – a measure of time, but a different time to ours.

Village life had been governed by this for centuries – ancient deeds even use the phrase "residing under the stroke of the clock in Jorwert". People went to work at sunrise – the craftsmen and the shopkeepers a little later – the bells of the clock were rung at midday to signal that it was time for a "hot meal", and after that they worked on until the clock struck six. During the harvest they worked until the dew fell. This is how the days passed in the village, including those of the solicitor's early years.

There had been domestic clocks everywhere for centuries, of course, but people's interaction with time lacked the exactness we are used to now. It was a more fluid system, without accurate numbers, merely indications such as "later", "early tomorrow morning", "towards evening", "before supper-time".

It is questionable whether country folk really used to have so much more time and peace of mind. They probably had just as much patience as us, the only difference being that they simply had to accept events, methods of transport, and the vagaries of nature, for what they were. Or as Auke van der Woud points out: "People only lose time when they know that the transaction could have been carried out quicker or better, or that a more productive transaction could have been effected."

Until 1885, a journey from Jorwert to Amsterdam took at least a couple of days, and if the weather was bad it could sometimes take even longer. However, this slowness only became unbearable when the railway track was extended to Stavoren, and everyone knew that the same journey could also be made in just over half a day, via the boat from Enkhuizen. When the bicycle arrived, shortly afterwards, and later the bus and the car, this awareness grew stronger. In Jorwert, too, time became scarce, because quicker and easier alternatives arrived, and being conscious of this created a state of permanent dissatisfaction as well.

The same thing happened with the conception of space. In the past this was restricted and closed-off, and this restriction also facilitated a clear-cut social order. But now, distances suddenly turned out to be flexible, borders no longer mattered, the close-knit inside world flowed over into the loosely-woven fabric of the mysterious outside world where everything was possible, everything was permissible and everything was available.

The Jorwerters were gradually liberated from a constraint that had determined their lives for centuries. The omnipotence of nature had ended, but at the same time, along with this, a certain psychological harmony had been disturbed.

Chapter Five

Three Farmers and the Obstacle Race

 **WHEN BIG CHANGES ARE IN THE OFFING THERE** is occasionally someone who senses it, who is gripped by an almost missionary zeal and who, like one possessed, attempts to capture the current situation before it is lost for good. The painter Ids Wiersma was just such a person, a labourer's son from the village of Brantgum who, with great accuracy, recorded Frisian country life at the turn of the century for future generations.

He painted the last turf huts (the same constructions the *terps* had been covered in during the Middle Ages); the tools of the village carpenter and the blacksmith; the last seventeenth-century cowshed; the German harvesters; the scythes, the sickles, the pitchforks, the buckets, the earthenware. On the farms, he painted the cowsheds; the dairy where butter and cheese were made; the milk cellars; the churning, the scrubbing and cleaning outside.

He recorded all the activity of the flax harvest and the tilting matches; he drew the gathering of sheaves of corn; the threshing with the manual threshing machine; but also the silversmith making precious metal *oorijzers* – a craft that was in the process of dying out, and therefore had to be documented.

Ids Wiersma made most of his drawings in the 1920s. By then all the Jorwerter farmers had already contracted out their butter- and cheese-making and the mowing took place mostly with reapers, but apart from this the farms where Sake Castelein, Bonne Hijlkema, Oebele van Zuiden and Gais Meinsma grew up looked just like they did in his drawings. Even so, it was their generation that would experience the greatest revolution.

Gais Meinsma was one of Kees Greijdanus and Trijntje Kundersma's brood. Trijntje was a daughter of the Kundersma's of Groot Hesens. She started helping in the cowshed when she was five; by the time she was seven she was walking behind the cows with a stick when they had to cross the road; she learned to milk when she was nine; she wanted to do everything her father did.

Her grandfather taught her the basics. That you had different sorts of cows, light-milkers and tough-milkers, and then there were the nasty pieces of work. The nasty ones kicked out or started to walk around during milking. She was taught that you first had to secure the back legs with a hobble, before you sat on the stool with a bucket between your legs — she was allowed to try the hobble on her grandfather's legs first, to get the hang of it.

And then she learned to make the milk foam: first pulling and squeezing with the right hand, then the same with the left, but you always had to make sure that the milk landed on the same spot in the bucket. If you could milk well then you squirted it right to the bottom of the bucket. And then you got foam. When you had milking lessons that was your first success, a decimetre of foam. Without foam it did not count as milk, it was just dishwater.

She learned that cows had to be milked in the same order each time, otherwise you got confused. She learned how to find cows in the field, early in the morning, in the autumn, when everything was blotted out by mist and you had to listen for a quarter of an hour first — because there was always one who would cough or chew in her sleep. And then you slipped underneath, leaning against that big, warm body, and there was the abiding sensuality of the milking, those eight minutes of peace between man and beast, that strange intimacy. "You made sure you had a little foam, and then you carried on milking, you just carried on milking," said Gais. "And then you let your thoughts wander. You thought about the new day, the weather, the birds. Your thoughts skipped from one thing to the other. What is happening in the world? Why do things turn out the way they do?"

In Jorwert the chug-chugging of the first milking machine was heard in 1912. The owner, Wiepke Algera, was mad about the machine, even though the thing did have everlastingly greasy spark plugs.

"I have only ever had one farmhand who was better," he always said.

For Sake Castelijn, the initial shock of mechanisation came later, in the early 1950s, when Algera's milking machine had finally been perfected. For him, the abolition of hand milking was the biggest turnaround he had ever experienced – because then the people disappeared. "It used to be so busy around the cowshed at milking time. The good-fellowship around the yard; within a few years that became a thing of the past."

For Bonne Hijlkema, one of the farmers from the neighbouring terp of Funs, it had all started with the tractor: "Our first tractor arrived in 1960, and it made all the difference in the world. In the beginning when I was mowing with it and it stalled, I didn't press down the clutch, I called out 'Whoa!' – that is how used to the horses I was."

And for Cor Wiedijk, his neighbour, it was the first loose box cowshed that he saw, in 1972, when he was still at school: "It was just not on, we thought it was useless, it was nonsense. But ten years later, there they were, dotted all over the countryside".

The 1950s were the years of reconstruction; they were also the years of "never again". No more Great Depressions, no more war, no more famine-winters like that of 1944–5, ever again. In Leeuwarden a large sculpture of a cow was unveiled, christened "Us Mem" (Our Mother) by the Frisians. The cow was the crowning glory of Dutch agriculture: black and white, ideally proportioned and with more milk in the udder each year, the result of a breeding tradition going back to the mousy-coloured calves of Rienck Hemmema. The Shah of Persia, on a state visit, went with Queen Juliana to see the cattle breeder Jan Wassenaar in Jelsum, in order to look at the wonderful cows. It was a legendary visit – Wassenaar is supposed to have shouted: "Your Majesty, mind you don't step in the muck!" – and, in retrospect, it was the culmination of a new heyday.

Agriculture had become a question of politics. Prices were kept artificially high by all sorts of European subsidies. At the same time levies and tariff walls protected domestic farmers from cheaper goods produced by the rest of the world. For the farmers themselves all this meant only one thing: produce as much as possible at the lowest cost.

On the Jorwerter farms the first machines were warmly welcomed as the start of better times. Bonne Hilkema's face would acquire a bony, weather-beaten aspect later on, but as a boy he had seen the effects of endless toil manifested a hundred times more strongly. Take the German harvesters who used to work at Funs during each hay harvest. They were masters of their craft, and some of them could manage single-handedly almost two-and-a-half acres in one day. But every year that they sat at the Hijlkemas' dining table they looked more exhausted, and most of them were finished by the time they were 50. "From the humane point of view alone," Bonne often said, "the reaper was a godsend."

According to him we should be careful not to get too sentimental: the tractor was an enormous improvement. "You always hear how good it was in the past," he said, "with all those horses, but I can assure you, it was not so good at all, especially for the horses. If the grass would not mow properly it was 'Whoa, and back!' the whole day long with those horses. You lay in bed at night, and it was still 'Whoa, and back!' Now you sit warm and dry on your tractor with the radio on. Long live progress!"

The milking machine appeared in 1954 on the Hilkemas' farm, and in the beginning it meant that Bonne could stay in bed longer. His grandfather still got up at 3.30 a.m., but when the milking machine arrived this soon became 5 a.m.

The apparatus was a godsend in other ways too. Not only were more and more farm labourers being sent away from the farms, the labourers themselves were also no longer prepared to be at the farmer's beck and call, day and night.

First of all the labourers from their own village disappeared from the Hijlkemas' farmyard. The young Jorwerters no longer wanted to do the heavy farm work, especially now they realised that they could make more and easier money in town.

Following this, for a while during the mid-1950s, the Jorwerter farmers recruited labourers from the Frisian forests, a poorer region: men of between 40 and 50 already bent over from hard work. Making the move to tractor and milking machine proved too much for most of these labourers. "They were real livestock types, not tractor types," said Bonne Hijlkema. "They could do anything with cows and horses and they were excellent at milking. But they had absolutely no feeling for machinery." The last regular farm labourer left the Hijlkemas' in 1961.

After that there came a period when the farmers did most of the work alone. And subsequently there was the farm-help – a sort of employment agency for farmers – and the contracting company. But it got very quiet in the cowshed, and in the farmyard too.

Between 1947 and 1960 the total number of farm labourers in the Netherlands dropped by more than a third, from more than 200,000 to 124,000, according to successive censuses. Of all the women who worked on a farm in 1947, there was only a quarter left by 1960 – after all, milkmaids were no longer needed. Even more noticeable was the exodus of the children who had formerly worked alongside their parents. Their number had almost halved since 1947. Less than one in three farming businesses still had a potential successor working on the farm. The young had already drawn their own conclusions.

––––––––

Those years saw the start of a development among the Jorwerter farmers that we would now term "The Big Decline" but that, as is often the way, was initially not taken seriously by anyone. For those who experienced it, it was no more than a number of unconnected incidents, and only years later would they say: "Hey, but that's when it all started." The process was comparable to an obstacle race in which more and more people kept having to drop out. The only thing was that the first obstacle was so low that no one had noticed it.

It was in the early 1960s that the elderly solicitor suddenly had to conduct a noticeable number of public auctions. Normally there were about three each spring, but then all at once there were ten. Looking back on it later he saw that this had been the prelude. "It was all very unspectacular," he recalled. "Every one of them concerned older farmers, 'little people', both literally and metaphorically, who had doggedly kept their businesses going for years, and who had enough go in them to be active in the Church and community politics besides, but who, when a successor was lacking or had deserted, quietly divested themselves of the whole lot."

It was the period when many planners were talking about the "problem of the small farmers". The sector was on the eve of a period of unfettered land mergers. All over the country the landscape was reallocated; it was reorganised for large-scale agriculture and not infrequently changed out of all recognition – in Friesland alone, 26 land consolidations took place between 1955 and 1975 – and the small farmers were no longer players in the game.

It was also during this period that the inflation of the cow began. When Gais Meinsma, Bonne Hijlkema and Sake Castelein had started milking they worked in cowsheds with 20 or 30 dairy cattle plus some calves and yearlings – whoever had more than this counted as a big farmer. This type of farmer worked himself, had a farm labourer, a farmhand, a maidservant, and another family member often working alongside as well. It was a question of necessity. As even a good cowhand or milkmaid could only milk approximately eight or nine cows an hour and the milking had to be completed in about an hour and a quarter, this meant that roughly speaking you needed one labourer for each nine cows. The muck-spreading, mowing and haymaking was also very time consuming. A farm of this sort provided at least four incomes.

Just how much standards were changing could be gleaned from what people regarded as a "large" or a "small" business. For example, in 1755 Tjeerd Jans of Groot Hesens with 20 cows, 5 heifers and 5 horses was the biggest farmer in Jorwert. Almost 200 years later, in 1945, that would still have been a sizeable business. Less than 30 years later, a farmer with 20 cows was regarded as a smallholder.

Just after the war, at the five-yearly inspection of bulls for the *Pedigree Frisian Herdbook*, a herd of 15 or fewer cattle was classified as a "small business". Fifty dairy cattle, that was big to very big. Then the standard for "small" was changed to 20, then to 30, and finally every business with fewer than 50 cows was regarded as "small".

That tendency to enlargement was closely connected to changes in the work itself. In 1755, Tjeerd Jans of Groot Hesens would have spent an average of over 300 hours a year on each cow, and just after the war this still applied to most farmers. A farmer who was alone could not manage more than eight to ten cows. The arrival of the milking machine, the tractor and the baler meant a saving of some 70 hours a year on each cow for the farmer. By the late 1950s he could manage about 14 cows without help.

In the 1960s the after-milking chores and the muck removal were also mechanised. The number of hours of work each cow took dropped to 80 a year; one dairy farmer could now keep 40 cows. Next came the cyclo-reapers, milk tanks, loose box cowsheds with milk-wells and the computers. Forty years after the arrival of the milk machine a big farmer could milk 80, if not 100, cows on his own, and indeed he had little choice if he was ever to recover his investment.

Hardly anywhere in the postwar Netherlands was the shift from physical strength towards financial might more visible than in agriculture.

On 12 May 1975, the last regular farm labourer in Jorwert was fired. Hilbrand Medemblik was 58 years old and he had worked on the land for 33 years, searched for the cattle in the early morning mist, sat up at night with the cows when they were calving, but his boss said he could no longer afford to pay him. "I shall be busy doing nothing," he informed the journalist from the *Leeuwarder Courant* who had dropped by on this special occasion. He had worked for the same farmer for 22 years, had always drunk his coffee and tea at the farmhouse, no, he had no complaints. He said he did not want to work for a farmer any more. "It has become too monotonous nowadays, too rushed, and they have too many cattle. They are drowning in them." He was going to look for something else, perhaps with the parks department.

———————

The second obstacle – still hardly felt by large businesses, but fatal for some small farmers – was the arrival of the cooling tank.

In the autumn of 1969, the 75th anniversary of the dairy factory at Weidum was celebrated with an exuberant revue. "See you in 75 years!" they sang at the end, and everyone had clapped along. Less than a year later the factory had closed and all the milk was sent to Dronrijp. The farmers had to purchase a big cooling tank. The old-fashioned milk churns that were placed by the side of the road mornings and evenings, the milkman who came to collect them, the clamour and the clatter in many small dairy factories, were all things of the past.

Oebele van Zuiden was the only farmer in Jorwert who stopped because of the cooling tank – but there were more elsewhere in the province. For cow-milkers like Fedde and Minne it was an insurmountable barrier. It

meant installing new vacuum plumbing, sometimes even the electricity
had yet to be connected, and money had to be borrowed for
an investment on which they would never recoup.

The effect of the cooling tank and further mechanisation on the bigger
farmers was one of a hasty retreat forwards. Prices remained low
and their only chance of survival consisted of three words: "more" and
"increased efficiency". That meant continuous new investment – in
machinery, livestock, land, fertiliser, pesticides, new outbuildings – so
that a third obstacle was created for the farmers: capital.

"We were always vulnerable financially," said Bonne Hijlkema. "We
were always dependent on the weather. The quality of the hay could
have enormous financial consequences. If you had a disappointing
summer you were left with a barn full of poor hay, and that meant
supplementary feeding and what's more the cows gave less milk. Then
you sometimes had hardly any income. But you also had the opposite.
In a single season you could suddenly have a really good harvest and
make a fantastic amount. So you always had to have something in reserve,
and most important of all, not incur any debts."

In a world that was in principle self-supporting, for many farmers a
bank loan was irrefutable proof that they had hit rock bottom. It meant
the start of poverty, and was usually followed by more borrowing and
exorbitant rates of interest, and they were afraid of it.

The most important thing was land ownership, not money. "Land
never leaves you, money does," the Frisian farmers said. " If you wanted
to buy something then you saved up for it, and if it was really urgent then
your parents usually had something tucked away at the bottom of the
linen cupboard," was how Cor Wiedijk saw it. "That is how you used to
solve things. And if a farmer bought land he usually did it with ready
money. Borrowing from the bank was not something you did."

Somewhere around the 1960s the attitude of the Jorwerter farmers
towards incurring debts changed, though exactly when this happened
remains unclear. For some, the road to the bank started in the late
1950s, with the purchase of their first tractor. Most farmers though,
were still able to pay for that in cash.

But more and more money was required: for machinery, for

outbuildings, for one new investment after the other. And in about 1975, when the money from the dairy factory was no longer spread out on the kitchen table by the milkman – the poor chap kept having to set off on his rounds with thousands of guilders in his jacket pocket – the bank became a permanent fixture of farming life.

"I still remember my father buying his first tractor," said Cor Wiedijk. "Where he got the money from was not something you thought about as a child. But when I was putting his papers in order after his death I came across an old bank statement that showed he had indeed borrowed money for it. That must have had quite a psychological effect on him, that our father had had to borrow money."

So the money factor became more and more important for the farmer. This is well illustrated by the amount the solicitor at Jorwert recorded for that 98-acre tenant farm in 1951: 100,000 guilders. In 1995 one would have had to fork out at least two million, if not more, for a similar business, including milk quota.

Something also began to go awry with regard to the price of land, especially in the vicinity of the larger towns. There, the building constructors and developers were sometimes prepared to fork out ten times the agricultural value for a piece of grassland. It made economic sense, but for the farmers themselves it meant that things got totally out of proportion. In business terms, taking over a farm was sometimes sheer folly.

The consequences of all this differed according to the farmer. The larger businesses became trapped in a vicious circle, a continual spiral of more investment, more production, more subsidies, more profit, and more investment again – because otherwise it all went to the taxman. The sheds filled up with tractors, combine harvesters, beet-lifters, water-spraying systems, pickup trucks, crop-sprayers, top-dressers, reapers, low-loaders, hydraulic shakers, silage wagons, feeders, cultivators, coulters, maize-cutters, crushers and whatever else had been thought up in the way of machinery.

Other farmers were up to their ears in debt in an effort to keep pace with developments, debts that their grandchildren would still be paying off. The government encouraged this in every possible way by subsidies and an army of agricultural advisers. Later on that same government would change its tune, to one of moderation and calm, but by then many farmers had already fallen into the trap.

Exactly the opposite happened to the small farmers: unlike their bigger brethren they could not invest much because the business was too small, which meant fewer subsidies and less business capital. As a result there was even less room for investment, and it was not uncommon for all this to end in debt and bankruptcy. The majority, though, did not let it get that far.

Oebele van Zuiden still remembered a conversation in a café when his colleague, Cor Jellema, with his twelve cows, stopped farming. "I said to Jellema: 'It is your turn now, but me with my 30 cows and Algera with his 40 cows, our time will come too.' Algera, my neighbour, would not hear of it. But I said: 'No, we cannot turn things around. We are all going to go under. There are still three working men sitting here now, but in a few years there will not be a single one left.' He did not believe me."

The utter peace and quiet of Jorwert was lost in the 1950s. A horse does not make any noise. Even after the war the flat countryside around the village was still largely engineless. Almost all the older people whom I spoke to could recall the time when the hammering of the blacksmith, the tinkling of a reaper, a bucket that fell over somewhere, a cow, an occasional car, could be heard for miles across the fields, disembodied sounds against a backdrop of silence.

"Early in the morning you harnessed a horse – the beginning of the day had a really peaceful feel to it – and then you rode out to the fields to do the milking," recalled Bonne Hijlkema. "With a horse you heard everything: the birds, the cattle, the village sounds. After that there was only the din of the tractor."

During the 1960s the colours of the village began to alter in the same subtle way. The yellow haystacks of the small farmers disappeared. Unnoticed, the colourful summer scene of haycarts and families hay-making became a thing of the past. Extraordinarily useful machines arrived to mow the grass, to shake and transport, red-and-green noise-makers, and all over the place silage mounds of black plastic appeared next to the farms, as you were far less dependent on the vagaries of the weather with pre-dried and chopped silage grass.

"These days it is silage, silage, silage," said Bonne Hijlkema. "For hay you needed at least week of good weather, and a regiment of young men to gather it in. Now a single day is often sufficient. And you can do it on your own."

But I heard old reapers like Folkert and Peet complain that it was a dead loss nowadays. Haymaking was hard work, but you did it together, they told me. "At about nine in the morning you went and sat on a haycock, the maidservant came by with coffee and bowls wrapped in a cloth, you sat for half an hour, chatting quietly and then you carried on. Nowadays there is just some beer or lemonade for the man who operates the baling machine: gulp, gulp, and on with the job."

The march of progress was reflected in the numbers. If you had 300 chickens in the 1950s, you had 30,000 in the 1980s. Through improved feeding and breeding techniques, milk production was increased to previously undreamed of heights. Butter mountains and milk lakes were created, fruit and vegetables were dumped and destroyed. Whereas an average cow in the 1960s managed some 3,500 litres a year, 8,000 to 10,000 was not abnormal by the close of the century; and in 1995 the most productive cow, the eleven-year-old Julia 16 of Sint Nicolaasga, even managed 16,000 litres.

And in some areas, particularly in Brabant, Gelderland and the Achterhoek, the new techniques that made it possible to farm with practically no land were enthusiastically taken up. You laid a few thousand square metres of concrete, constructed some pigsties, the animal-feed factory supplied piglets and feed on credit, every now and then a truck arrived to fill up the feed silo, every now and then a tanker arrived to pump out the muck, every now and then a lorry arrived to take away the fully grown pigs, and you raked in the money.

They were quick and easy cycles, those pigs and chickens, three to five times a year, and the money you took in was quickly and easily made. The pig farmers' children were viewed with a jealous eye by the offspring of the dairy farmers: they went to agricultural college in a Mercedes; the others did not. But nobody loved pigs, and nobody loved chickens.

*

A farming couple I know once showed me their rekenboeck covering the period 1965–75. His father had bought his first cow in 1930, at the Whitsun market in Oudeschoot, and had led her home on a rope, all of 20 kilometres away. In 1950 he had a dozen cows, and when they took over the business in 1965 there were 18 cows, 5 horses and some breeding sows.

They lived in a house at the crossroads of four canals and the amounts in their rekenboeck during that first year did not differ much from those of Rienck Hemmema. But just after this couple had taken over the farm the production figures in the book shot up. "'Feed them more and more will come out' was my motto," he told me. "My parents didn't dare do that, and they didn't dare spread fertiliser either. If there was a bill to be paid they simply got rid of another cow. But I had been to agricultural college."

In 1970 they had 30 cows and they were able to buy a tractor. She: "We did everything together. How we rushed around in those years. We had very little, but even so, they were good times. We were young, and we knew we were working towards something."

In 1974 a new canal was dug and plans were laid to construct a harbour in their vegetable garden. When they moved to a bigger farm they had 38 cows.

In 1978 they had 68 cows. They were on the point of building an entirely new farm, but during a game of tug-of-war at the Union of Farmers and Market Gardeners' annual get-together he smashed up his knees, the cattle had to go, and after that it was all over.

They grazed some beef cattle, he took up pigeon racing and the horses – and still being breeders through and through they were soon taking one prize after another – and they answered advertisements in De Boerderij (The Farm) that promised the world if you went into breeding worms in big plastic containers. But that market had been spoilt too.

———————————

After the sounds and the colours, the smells round about Jorwert finally began to alter too. The dung used to have a warm smell, often not at all unpleasant. But from the 1970s onwards, the muck that came out of the loose box sheds smelled rank due to the feed concentrate with which the production of the cows was further increased, sour because of the slops that had got into it, vicious because of the placentas that had been hoofed away through the concrete grids, and sometimes it could get pretty smelly round about Jorwert.

The combination of subsidies, scaling up and expert breeding had pushed production levels so high that the milk lakes had become milk seas. Everyone saw that the market had outgrown its strength, but on the other hand the politicians, under pressure from the farming lobby, were prepared to pay whatever it took to maintain this situation for as long as possible. In the early 1980s more than a million tons of powdered milk and 600,000 tons of butter was stored in European warehouses, and the subsidies had run into millions. One way or another milk production had to be curbed.

This was how the fourth obstacle in the farmers' knockout competition arose, one on which the crossbar was suddenly raised higher: the so-called super-levy.

"It was a totally different way of thinking," Cor Wiedijk told me. "That you could actually produce too much milk was something that had never occurred to you as a farmer. It was an enormous shock."

In the spring of 1984 the European ministers of agriculture decided to take drastic action to end the over-production: from then on, all farmers were only allowed to produce a certain quota, a set quantity of milk, based on their production during the previous year. For every excess litre that they milked they received a hefty fine rather than a subsidy. Those who had produced a sizeable milk lake in 1983 were therefore home and dry. Those who had only got as far as planning to expand could forget it. That was the super-levy.

Bonne Hijlkema lost quite a lot of milk. "Things had always ticked along nicely here. That is why we were so late with land consolidation and that sort of thing. If we had modernised earlier we would have had a lot more milk. It is always the way: as soon as you think that things are fine as they are, your business is in fact going downhill. And it all grinds to a halt."

"The quota system had one big advantage," said Cor Wiedijk. "The farmers knew where they stood again. Things calmed down. But the measure also divided the farming community. Those who had expanded their businesses during the 1970s had lots of opportunities later on. But the smaller farmers could scarcely expand at all, and the smallest could barely manage to keep their heads above water. Their land and their quotas went to the big farmers, their farms went to outsiders, and they perished like rats."

The number of cows grazing in the Frisian pasture declined by more than a third between 1984 and 1994. From then on you hardly ever saw a full cowshed. The super-levy was also a heavy blow for the provincial economy that had revolved for centuries around milk, butter and cattle-breeding. Besides which a drawbridge effect was created: the bigger farmers kept getting bigger, the small smaller; the rich richer, the poor poorer. Bonne Hijlkema: "That's what was most unjust about the super-levy. But that's the way they wanted it in the Netherlands. And that's because they don't like farmers in the Netherlands."

And then there was the great temptation. The farmers began to trade in milk quotas, and it soon grew into a lucrative business. You could easily pay four guilders for the right to produce one more litre of milk a year. Those who wanted to milk an extra cow had to pay out 24,000 guilders, ten times what the animal itself was worth.

Thanks to the super-levy the remaining Dutch dairy farmers seemed all of a sudden to have won the lottery. An average business with a quota of 250,000 litres was suddenly worth a million guilders more. And in addition there were the amazing sums being paid for land in the vicinity of the towns. So the emergency exit was thrown wide open for the small farmer who was getting older and had no successor: you could easily stop, there were all sorts of decent benefits and you received a golden handshake to boot. The only difference was that it was no longer your own milk on the kitchen table of a morning, but a carton from the Frico-Domo factory.

Looking out of his window in 1995, Bonne Hijlkema had no trouble pointing out a handful of farms where work had ceased. They were occupied, they looked well kept, there was nothing wrong with the land or the fencing, but the farmyard was frighteningly tidy, and light no longer shone from the cowshed windows early in the morning. He recited their names effortlessly: Van Zuiden in 1978, Siderius in 1981, Ringnalda in 1991, De Vries in 1989, Jellema in 1977, Fopma in 1986, Sipkes in 1988. In 1980 there were four farming concerns around the Hegedyk (hedge dyke). When I spoke to Hijkema there was only one left.

In the Netherlands in the mid-1990s an average of six dairy farmers a day were winding up their businesses like this. Twenty per cent of the smaller farmers gave up between 1990 and 1995 alone. The owners embarked upon a life of leisure; they often remained on their farms and kept a few sheep and goats and sometimes a horse, as a hobby. They gave themselves up, without feeling that they had surrendered. The survivors did not perish, they simply retired.

There was only one problem, although it was no longer theirs: the trading in milk quotas had always been and remained a speculative one, speculation on vague future prospects; speculation on a right that might tomorrow be a favour; a speculative trade that did not yield anything tangible. By dint of the buying out of the older farmers, millions of guilders flowed out of the agricultural sector each year. It was spent on cars, newly built villas, holidays for pensioners and at the DIY store, but agriculture did not recoup any of it.

What's more, it became practically impossible for young farmers to start a dairy farm. The business had become so expensive due to the large quotas that the interest on a mortgage was more or less prohibitive. Even if the family farm could be taken over, usually enormous amounts of money had to be found – since the other brothers and sisters still had to be bought out. "You can no longer become a farmer unless you have a million in the bank," said Sake Castelein. "Although there are those that still try. But that's vocation for you."

So for the most part, cattle farming round about Jorwert died a luxurious death. And it would be the following generations that would pay the price.

———————————

There was a new obstacle looming for the farmers, a problem that spread out over the land like a brown apocalypse, slowly, from south to north: the 83 million tons of slurry produced each year by the 4½ million cattle, 15 million pigs, and 84 million Dutch chickens. What Rienck Hemmema and his contemporaries had regarded as a valuable waste product had grown into an enormous problem because of immense overproduction.

Regarding the manure problem, farmers became the victims of the omnipotence their own pressure groups had once possessed. Far more manure was being produced than the environment could cope with, especially in the intensive pig-farming sector, and this had been well known since the beginning of the 1970s. Nevertheless, the lobby of animal-feed factories, pig-breeders, meat-processors and farming organisations – the so-called Green Front – succeeded for years in keeping the overproduction of manure off the political agenda.

It was only in the mid-1990s that the influence of this power block reached its limits. Calculations of the damage to society had exceeded the billion mark, and finally things could go no further. The farmers were more or less put on probation concerning the manure. They were not allowed to store it in the old-fashioned way, they were only allowed to spread it over the land in a special way, during a limited period, and a manure quota was introduced as it had been for milk. The bigger users had to keep a record in a so-called "minerals account book", and if they were unable to get rid of the excess manure in an acceptable way they faced crippling financial sanctions.

The consequences of all this for Jorwert and its surroundings were not too bad. Thanks to constantly improving breeding techniques the vast majority of the dairy farmers were able to produce ever greater amounts of milk with ever fewer cows, and consequently most of them stayed well under the limits stipulated by the Ministry of Agriculture. But Sake Castelein did have to double his manure storage facilities, and Cor Wiedijk had to invest heavily as well – and that was without taking into account the cost of the contractors, who from now on drilled the manure into the ground by means of a coulter-muck spreader. "That costs each business at least 100,000 guilders, if not more," said Sake. "And what do you get in return? A manure silo. And what does it get filled up with? Manure. And what does that earn you? Nothing."

"We always reasoned: if you want to keep livestock you have to have land as well," said Bonne Hijlkema. "Those pig-breeders didn't respect that. But we are the ones who have to pay the consequences!" According to him the same thing happened with the manure as had happened with the super-levy: once again, those who were made to feel the pinch the most were not the ones who had contributed to the excesses. "The small farmers were absolutely not the polluters, never ever, most of them were very precise. But in spite of this they were the ones who had sleepless nights".

For the really big farmers this sort of investment was not an insurmountable problem, but it was a headache for a medium-sized farmer like Cor Wiedijk. He really needed to invest 400,000 guilders, but he wondered whether there was still any point in doing so, especially when the prospects for the future were not particularly rosy. "Then it is time to ask yourself just how much of a farmer you still are," he said.

One evening he had gone to listen to the minister of agriculture at a meeting in Oranjewoud. A small farmer had stood up and said, "I am going to have to stop, because I just cannot make ends meet."

"That is good", the minister had replied. "That will give us more space. Next question".

Every form of repression conjures up its own illegality. Anyone who lives in the country knows all the night sounds, as they are still easily identified: the boy next door arriving home from his girlfriend's on his moped; the neighbours opposite who have friends over; the postman or the milkman early in the morning. But sometimes, in the spring and autumn, there were sounds that nobody could place, that you registered even though you were half-asleep because they were different from usual, and that made you restless, although you did not know why. That was the White Horse.

The White Horse – it was revealed to me one evening by friends – was a car with a trailer for two horses. What was actually in the trailer was a cooling tank, in which some farmers transported their milk surplus to colleagues who had milked under their quota for one reason or another. Thousands of litres of milk trundled from farm to farm in this way each night, illegally, along the dark provincial roads, sent on its way by an extensive and unprecedented network. That was the illegality of the milk quota.

The manure quota brought with it its own temptations. Pig farmers from the south were all too happy to drive up north with their manure, and were prepared to pay generously for the privilege of dumping their muck on Castelein's, Hijlkema's or Wiedijk's land. "They are handing it to me on a plate," said Bonne Hijlkema. "If I let them cover my land in manure and I lease out my milk quota as well, that will give me 100,000 guilders a year, without me having to do a thing for it. It is all legal, but ridiculous of course. I will not do it. I would not have that stuff spread all over my land for all the tea in China. But the State has no morals."

Some farmers thought differently. Those were the sounds heard by the half-asleep.

The decline of the farming community around Jorwert was not accompanied by the sort of tragedy that it was in the south, where some pig breeders simply locked the doors of their sties behind them and literally left hundreds of their animals to rot, insofar as they did not devour each other. There were no suicides, no divorces, no insurance fires, no riots, no bankruptcies. But the social and economic consequences were the same as everywhere else.

At the end of the twentieth century, for the first time in living memory, there were more people than cattle living around the church tower of Jorwert. The importance of agriculture for the rural economy was being eroded. During the 1971 census it transpired that two thirds of Jorwerters no longer worked in agriculture. Whereas, in the 1960s, it had been the farmers who had set the pace in and around the village, 30 years later it was garages, retailers, banks and tourist organisations. In 1995, according to provincial statistics they contributed one-and-a-half times more money to the rural economy than the farmers.

The status of the farmer declined. Castelein, Kundersma, Hijlkema, the traditional farming aristocracy of the village, had become Sake, Hendrik and Bonne, still valued as people but no longer looked upon as gentlemen.

The Dutch agricultural sector could still blow its own trumpet where productivity was concerned. In the mid-1990s the dairy farmers still extracted some 10 million litres of milk a year from their cows, enough to fill a fleet of 10,000 tankers. Although only a few per cent of the population were employed in agriculture, the farmers were responsible for a quarter of Dutch export earnings. Eight of the Top Ten Dutch export commodities came from the agricultural sector. The annual turnover in cattle farming, dairy farming, the beef-processing industry and associated trades sectors was 16 billion guilders, and provided work for 200,000 people. The pig-breeders, calf-fatteners and chicken farmers were good for a total of ten billion, with work for 100,000 people.

Nevertheless, during the period that I lived in the village, the trade journals and the local papers were full of doom and foreboding.

In 1995, according to the annual report of the Agricultural Institute, generally regarded as the annual report on the Dutch farming community, the average family income of a dairy farmer was back at the level it had been twelve years earlier. Each 80 guilders of income had to be set against 100 guilders in costs. In that same year, two out of every three pig-breeders had an income lower than their expenditure. Forty per cent of businesses were struggling with liquidity problems.

After a series of disastrous years, things had improved for the crop farmers, and that could easily happen to the cattle farmers and market gardeners in the near future. But most of them had hardly any reserves left with which to ward off fresh blows.

Each year, 12 to 15 thousand agricultural employees lost their jobs, and we have not even mentioned the thousands of redundancies in the supply industry.

The number of farmers knocking on the door of the Social Security office for unemployment benefit – a route that farmers had been loathe to make up until then – practically doubled each year. And that was where "our weaker brethren" belonged, according to the Minister of Agriculture. "The farmers need to operate in accordance with market conditions. If that does not happen, there is always the Department of Social Security," he said literally.

By the waterside, on the road to Weidum, someone had opened a campsite, with cups of tea and hot food. There were a few goats and chickens, some canoes and a plastic tractor, and the children from town adored the place. By the mid-1990s, half the Dutch farms had a second income from some sort of sideline or other, which varied from part-time teaching to fish farming or a wind turbine for electricity. "Shouldn't we all become park keepers?" they asked each other, down the pub.

*

According to the statistics, of the 91,560 dairy farming businesses in the Netherlands on 1 January 1975, there were only 38,938 left by 1 January 1995. The struggle for survival in the countryside had entered a rough phase.

In 1995, the worldwide free-trade agreement became operative, and that meant another new obstacle for the farmers. The protection of subsidies and tariff walls would gradually disappear and, like their grandfathers in the previous century, Bonne Hijlkema and Sake Castelijn would have to start competing with American cattle and New Zealand sheep.

Many dairy farmers feared for their livelihood. In 1995 they received 75 cents for a litre of milk, but that included a sizeable amount of subsidy. Without that government support they would be no match for the cheaper producers like the United States (cost price 50 cents a litre), Australia (40 cents), and New Zealand (25 cents). And nowhere else in Europe were the most important factors in production – land and milk quota – so costly as in the Netherlands. The land in 1995: an average of 22,000 guilders an acre, as opposed to Germany's 17,000, and England's 5,000. The milk quota: 3½ guilders a litre, compared, for example, to Belgium's 2 guilders, and Germany's 90 cents. There was bound to be trouble.

And furthermore, the sky-high subsidies on agricultural products were becoming an ever-increasing burden on the national budget. The accountants began to grumble. "The average dairy farmer in the Netherlands has a disposable income of 90,000 guilders, and 47,000 guilders of that amount consists of subsidy", a well-known economist wrote in one of the big national newspapers at end of 1995. "A concert musician in the Netherlands will earn roughly 80,000 guilders, of which the taxpayer contributes about 60,000 guilders. So there are more extreme cases, but there are many more dairy farmers than orchestra musicians and, what is more, behind every cow there is a cowpat."

The problems were further intensified for Dutch farmers by the so-called "law of diminishing returns". Cost-cutting by more efficient working practices was almost impossible in the Dutch agricultural sector, because it was already so efficient. While it was possible, with all sorts of new techniques, to further increase agricultural production in other European countries, the Dutch farmers had reached their limits years before. The only solution was to build and farm on an even larger scale. That was the disadvantage of a super-advanced agricultural sector: it left so little room for manoeuvre.

The problems within agriculture were unique in character. For the first time a crisis arose not out of backwardness, but out of large-scale development and the continuous drive towards innovation. Many farmers hardly dared look beyond the magical boundary of the next century. The experts had no such qualms. According to forecasts by the Ministry of Agriculture, of the 47,000 dairy farmers in 1990, there would only be 25,000 left by the year 2005; but the production per business would almost double. Some were of the opinion that farmers would only be able to turn back the tide of reorganisation by concentrating on landscape conservation and recreation. Others saw increasing possibilities for smaller, specialist concerns, like organic growers.

According to the experts, more growth was completely out of the question. It was estimated that by that same year, 2005, an area the size of the Noordoost polder would have been withdrawn from agriculture in the north of the Netherlands. Almost half the cattle would disappear – but that would be compensated for by the fact that the average milk yield of each cow would increase still further. The researchers predicted the emergence of a different type of farmer. "Not a 'tractor-farmer' but a 'computer-farmer'," they wrote, " someone who spends his whole day fine-tuning his business and the health of his cows. A real manager in fact."

But Bonne Hijlkema thought differently. "The only farmer who will survive is the old jack of all trades," he said. "That is the man who can repair his own machines, who does not have many debts, where nothing is too costly, who is flexible, and who knows how to treat a cow. That man will survive."

The solicitor had invited Teun Siderius to sit beside him on his bench at the open-air performance because, he said, "You are one of the last real farmers here in the district."

———

Sometimes I could still see Fedde's ghost stumbling through the Meibos coppice with his delivery bike, that one rattling milkchurn upfront. Strange times were dawning. The climate began to change, figuratively and even literally, and agriculture had to adapt.

A survey by the magazine *De Boerderij* (*The Farm*) in spring 1994 found that the majority of farmers regarded the end of the century as a time of deep crisis – albeit a luxurious one, as more than half had nothing to complain about as far as income was concerned. Only two thirds of those questioned expected their own business still to exist in ten years time. Forty per cent thought they really ought to emigrate so as to be able to farm properly. Less than one in five saw any future in large-scale businesses. "We are all becoming so damned vulnerable," said Cor Wiedijk.

The majority of Dutch farmers no longer had a successor, and the number of businesses that were being taken over by one of the children was decreasing by leaps and bounds. The prospects were too poor, the cost of the takeover and the buying out of the other children too high, the expense too great. So modern times had managed to destroy that last bastion of farming: the family, the handing on from generation to generation, the continuity of the business that was more important than anything.

Bonne Hijlkema did have a successor, but none of Sake Castelein's children felt any calling. Cor and Lies Wiedijk's offspring were still too small – while we were discussing it they were just being sent to bed. While the little ones capered about in their pyjamas, Cor said: "They are the reason you do what you do. If it weren't for the children I would be far more inclined to think: 'I am going to let things wind down'." But Lies forbade him to carry on talking in this vein.

"No", she said, "you must not think like that. It is a cycle."

From friends living locally I heard the story of their great-aunt and -uncle, Granny Teatske and Grandpa Romke.

Teatske and Romke lived together on a farm and both had one finger missing, they had been amputated because of whitlows, a nasty inflammation of the nail.

Teatske had once been married to a brother of Romke's, but he soon died of consumption. In order to save the farm, both families suggested that Teatske should marry Romke. She did not want to and he did not want to, but it happened nevertheless.

They spent their whole lives together, willy-nilly, on account of the business. They never had any children.

When they were old and worn out, their nephew, Freek, inherited the place. He toiled until he too was broken and bent.

His son, Jelmer, took over the business in the 1990s. Within a year he had sold the old farm to a doctor from the city.

Most of the farmers I spoke to were wrestling with an emotional and intellectual conflict.

Sake Castelein was fighting on: "You work twelve hours a day. Its true, the income is not bad, but you still won't make it."

Oebele van Zuiden was glad he had stopped. "We have had a good life," he said. "We had a splendid business, we enjoyed our work, we bred excellent cattle, we had a good auction day, we earned a fair bit of money, but I would not want to be a farmer these days. Because they are up to their eyes in it, the farmers. And they will never get out".

Bonne Hijlkema was not thinking of giving up, not by a long chalk. "Farming is a way of life. You won't become rich, but you carry on as long as you can. Sore fingers, sore toes, you stumble on anyway. Only when your body gives up do you give up. Then there is no point any more."

Cor Wiedijk felt that a good farmer would never go bankrupt. "He gradually eats into his capital reserves; he re-mortgages; he uses his land, his property and his quota as a life-jacket. Discreet poverty, you can keep that up for a long time."

Those who got out in time were not the worst farmers, almost everyone acknowledged that. A good farmer knows what is possible, but also his limits. Even so, almost every farmer who stopped felt that he had failed. In the eyes of his parents and grandparents, his children and his successors; in the eyes of the world. And that was also the reason why many farmers kept going for so unbelievably long.

Only Cor and Lies Wiedijk had mixed feelings about it all. For them stopping was tantamount to desertion. It was different for the older farmers, but someone of their own age? "Well, he could never have been a real farmer," Cor felt. "Get in cheap, make a quick profit, find an excuse and call it a day. That sort."

He raked up the case of a neighbour who had stopped when the super-levy arrived. "He wanted to treat all his children equally. He had an enormous house built."

"But he had a son who wanted to carry on," said Lies. "And that boy didn't get a chance. And *he* was given that chance by *his* father. I just think – you ought to pass it on."

He: "But that is not always possible any more. When we started there were 100,000 farmers, now there are only 40,000; those are the times we live in and you can't turn back the clock."

She: "It also has to do with those girls from the towns. More and more, country boys are taking up with girls from towns, and they want to be free. That never occurred to us; that is how we were brought up."

He: "It's the same everywhere, people are spreading their wings."

She: "It depends whether your feet are firmly planted in the new world or more at home in the old one."

He: "But the youth of today keeps its eyes peeled; it sees what else the world has to offer."

She: "I would like to shout it from the rooftops: 'Give the young farmers a chance! To get to know nature, the land, the livestock.' But they are being robbed of that chance."

He: "You're not a farmer any more, you're a producer."

She: "It's such a crying shame."

Chapter Six

How God Disappeared from Jorwert

 SLOWLY THE DAYS GOT SHORTER, AND SOMETIMES in the morning the cold woke me up. I could get round my Jorwerter house in 20 paces. It consisted of a tiny hall, one large room, a small kitchen, a staircase and an attic room. That is where I slept, just under the roof-tiles, and each night fresh gusts of wind came storming in from the flat countryside and whistled round my bed.

In the morning I put more wood in the stove, I made tea, I moved a chair near the fire, I looked outside and asked myself what I should write about. About this silence? About the emptiness? About the wind last night?

I wrote: *The sky will cover this village like a dome, for all eternity, and above it nature rages* – then crossed it all out again.

Meanwhile the leaves were falling from the trees of their own accord, slowly spiralling down; there was no longer even a breath of wind to blame, they were doing it all on their own. In the crown of the old beech in front of the rectory – the beech that had seen poets and vicars' daughters – the rooks sat, stiff and silent.

The street remained the domain of the cats. They patrolled the pavements, zigzagged over the cobbles, kept watch on car roofs.

I turned on Radio Friesland. Four pairs of precious metal *oorijzers* had been stolen from the museum in Heerenveen. A factory in Wolvega was planning to transfer the production of electric blankets to Czechia. A brass band, De Sterrekijkers (The Stargazers) was disbanding because it was becoming more and more difficult to get all the players together. In Dokkum, a woman in a wheelchair had fallen into a canal. In Sint Annaparochie an asylum seeker from Somalia was interviewed. For four years he had lived on this flat patch of clay and it suited him just fine. "At weekend have fun shouting in pub," he said to the reporter. "When they have drink, they very generous, the Frisians."

A white delivery van drove up the street. Once a week the fishmonger made his rounds. The sound of a bell. Then a megaphone voice: "Fresh fish! Lovely Dutch herrings! Freshly caught herrings!" The houses were silent. A solitary figure in a red jumper crossed the street to the trailer and the whole village now knew that Sake would be having fried cod this evening. The fishmonger started his car.

The village fell silent again. And beneath the hushed surface the other news flowed slowly through the village, the stories which were passed around by word of mouth, Jorwert's age-old talking newspaper: Lamkje suddenly had to go to hospital yesterday evening; Eef and Jan had a new car; new people had come to live in Pastorijfinne street; in Oostwierum a birth had gone badly wrong but the baby was alive; a new purchase; another illness; a sheep in a ditch.

To begin with I experienced what all aspirant villagers experience: peace and quiet was immediately converted into restlessness, movement, the radio on, then off; every impulse was tangible, there were so few of them; but Mantgum, Leeuwarden and Grouw were nearby: fetch the paper, biscuits, flyers on the doormat, sit down, look outside, then pace around again; walking off the city's restlessness.

A flock of geese flew over. In the summer they were not there, in the winter you saw them throughout the brief hours of daylight. I heard about a man who had looked into where they came from. It turned out to be somewhere in distant Siberia. He had talked to the Siberians. Whereas here people asked themselves "Where are our geese during the summer?", in Siberia they asked themselves "Where are our geese during the winter?"

Just outside the village cattle were being loaded up for the butcher's shop. The farmer in a brown coat, the purchaser and his wife on a tractor, behind it an open trailer. The gates are opened, three calves and the cow that is to be slaughtered are driven towards the trailer and forced in, the farmer and the purchaser shouting, ankle-deep in mud, then the flap is shut, the engine starts and the cow looks over the edge of the trailer, confused and placid at the same time, and too surprised to be afraid.

I know: on such a Sunday as this
Conceived wistfully by wind through rain
She knows not the roads to happiness
And sits by the window reading
In the early morning.

At ten o'clock the church tolls its time,
She puts on a shawl, she goes
Languidly, her face withdrawn,
Along the short path that leads towards the church:
Their garden backs on to the churchyard.

Her father pronounces his Amen.
In the garden she shivers
By the dark and narrow paths.
Through her thin garments
The wind transgresses her. Her small feet wade
Through the crushed flowers.

In the afternoon no outlet other than a walk
Through the meadow. She is bound to meet
Swarms of country folk, who greet her,
In hallowed fashion:
The daughter of their shepherd.

And then it was afternoon, a good afternoon for reading Jan Slauerhoff.

Throughout the centuries Jorwert has only managed to achieve one footnote in history: a famous poet and ship's doctor came a cropper with the vicar's daughter. This pastoral idyll must have taken place in about 1916. The poet, Jan Slauerhoff, was still at secondary school in Leeuwarden, and it concerned one of the daughters of Hille Ris Lambers, the vicar.

It was actually more complicated: first of all the poet fell in love with Annie, one of the vicar's daughters, and later on with her sister, Heleen. One suspects that more than anything else he was smitten by the family itself, where the children sang Mahler and the father wrote books on Brahmanism, spirituality and Chinese philosophy.

Meanwhile a veil of thin, white mist spread over the countryside behind my house, and within it you could just make out the faint colours

of a handful of farms and a church tower. The horizon was blue and red
where the veil touched it. Every now and then the sun broke through
above this enchanted landscape.

> I have found it all again,
> Beguilingly neglected as of old:
> The green path overgrown with sparse grass,
> The sunflowers, that were shorter then;
>
> The stillness of the garden and the greyish blonde
> Of the sun lately shining through tarnished glass.
> At the bottom of the garden a shallow pool began,
> Where we found one another of an evening under
>   branches.
>
> Everything: not the sweet, half-rustic, half-worldly,
> Precarious enchantment that has buried itself
> In England, as a governess I believe.
>
> I filled my pipe and pondered and said: "Enfin . . ."
> But was silent when I found her room, sad
> As a recently deserted chapel of rest.

———————

The following night it was freezing cold. The first ground frost. The
fields, white with hoarfrost, glistened in the early morning light.
My neighbour wore a woolly hat and looked half-frozen; the whole
neighbourhood was scraping at car windscreens. The beech in front
of the vicarage had now lost all its leaves, its bare branches pointing
up, but the trees around the churchyard still had a fair amount of foliage.
The children, on their half-term holidays, were wandering up and
down the street.

At nine o'clock the bells of the church clock began to toll. This meant
someone had died. From the resonance of the sound I could tell it was
a man – the big bell dominated. I thought of old Sije Hoogerhuis, now
almost 100, who lay in a tiny room somewhere being nursed by a
neighbour. But, standing at the baker's trailer, I heard that it was someone
else: Tjitse Tijssen, who, with his horse and cart, used to operate the

parcel delivery service with Leeuwarden. He had died last night in hospital people said; but it had not been much of a life; his wife had already passed on; all he did was walk his dog.

A fighter jet roared across the horizon.

That afternoon I visited the vicar, the eleventh to succeed Hille Ris Lambers and his lovely daughters. On the doorstep the children had made a huge pile of yellow leaves from the vicarage trees, a fort in which they played throughout the long, grey day. I opened the gate, went through the big garden; rang the bell; the front door; a hall; old rooms with high ceilings, large windows.

The vicar cherished his vicarage like a small museum. In later years he had had extensive contact with Heleen Hille Ris Lambers – the "precarious enchantment" – and she had presented him with her complete collection of Frisian photographs. We walked through the house, hardly altered since 1917, with doors, fireplaces and dressers, still completely the world of the domestic servant of that time.

> Where does she go?
> In the middle of the attic
> They have screened off a small space,
> Called it her room;
> Faded cloth serves as decoration,
> The creaking door cannot be closed
> And the wallpaper is floral patterned.

And sure enough, there was the tiny servant's quarters in the attic, and the wallpaper was floral patterned, and the door still did not shut. The vicar drew me to a spot at the bottom of the garden. He had brought the collections of poetry with him and, blue with cold, we read one verse after the other, and everything was clear and undistorted by time.

> At the bottom of the garden a shallow pool began
> Where we found one another of an evening under branches.

I was shown the photograph albums, and in the afternoon half-light of the vicarage we sat leafing through it: the beautiful Heleen Hille Ris Lambers as an old woman – she only died in 1991, when she was 92 – but still quite distinguished. A photograph of all the daughters in a dinghy, the village and father Siesling's sailing ship in the background.

Annie and Heleen: Annie blonde, sprightly and square-built; Heleen slightly older, dark hair gathered into a tight bun, "half-rustic, half-worldly", attractive, thoughtful eyes.

"I never realised it had affected him like that," she had written to the vicar in an outpouring of feeling about her old friend. "Oh come now, Jan is no match for you," her brother Marius had said and, yes, she wrote, "that was true of course. I soon realised it myself, and then I quickly ended it."

> She lives in the far-off, misty country
> That I left to travel the world;
> She resides there still, I am sure, as
> Hers was a powerful contentment.

Later she would go to Italy where, for 19 years, she nursed a man who was an invalid.

When I walked home the silence was overwhelming. Even in the centre of Leeuwarden, where I had been a few days earlier, you heard the rain pattering in the gutters, and the sound of my footsteps rebounded off the stately gable roofs of Great Church street. But here I was becoming accustomed to the silence, because it was a silence full of small sounds: the starlings around the church tower, the ducks in the field, a sheep, the geese that flew in a V-formation over the village. In Leeuwarden the silence had a nineteenth-century quality. Here, the silence was older.

The vicar was a slightly stooped, thoughtful man with a beard and glasses. He was neither old nor young. He had told me about the glass house that you lived in as village vicar; the fact that you always had to set an example; you lived in the village but never really belonged. "Everyone here can get drunk at the merke except the solicitor, the schoolmaster, and the vicar," he said, as we looked outside at the quiet street and the children in the leaves.

He spoke of the 150 members of the congregation of his Jorwert church, and about the fact that every church tower hereabouts always had its own creed. Hiljaard was strictly Reformed; Weidum, Beers and Jellum were traditionally socialist; Oostwierum was catholic.

Jorwert was Broad Church. The village was considered evangelical, but its people were not inflexible. Vicar Hille Ris Lambers was allowed to experiment with spiritualism and Brahminism as much as he liked; his parish councillors concerned themselves with the Scriptures and their application to daily life.

The church had been full every Sunday until after the war, he told me. Then God gradually began to disappear from village life.

The older churchgoers had died, others had moved away and most of the newcomers had no affinity whatsoever with the House of God. In Jorwert, on an average Sunday during the 1990s, 40 people at most listened to the sermon. His parish now included no less than four former churches: Jorwert, Weidum, Beers and Jellum. There was also more and more collaboration with other denominations – after all, what was the alternative?

"Nowadays we are all small churches in a large, non-churchgoing area," he said. What the vicar described was a decline that had already taken place in towns. Fate seemed no longer to exist in the modern welfare state. Medical techniques and social security had provided people with the means by which death, disaster and misfortune could be banished, controlled or at least removed to the margins of existence. This led eventually to a different attitude towards uncertainty in general, and towards the concept of personal fate in particular. The awareness of tragedy, the recognition that in a life certain inescapable events could take place, seemed to have been replaced by the idea that everything was tractable, or repairable, or could at least be compensated with money.

Along with this, something in people's attitude to nature changed too – though far more subtly. In Jorwert it could only really be measured by the constantly diminishing number of people who attended the services of prayer and thanksgiving for the crops that were traditionally held in the church every spring and autumn. Thanks to modern techniques, farmers gained the impression they had more and more control over nature. This lessened their fears, but at the same time it reduced their respect for the Almighty. They no longer needed to glance up anxiously at every thundercloud during haymaking. Now there was silage and that could stand a shower or two. There was no more fear of plagues of mice. Now there were pesticides. The old prayers and songs of thanksgiving for the crops were no longer so vital. More and more

often the livestock remained inside summer and winter, and the feed
was supplied from outside, whatever the weather.

> It did not sadden her that the pasturelands
> Were green, in spring, summer, autumn and winter.
> She worked, and was always able to find something
> That conjured dull reality into pure wonder.

When a town-dweller ends up in the country it is difficult for him not to
be struck by the part played by religion. At the end of the century religion
played hardly any part in city life anymore whereas in Jorwert, despite
the enormous decline, a significant percentage of the population still
went to church every Sunday. And this was true of most villages.

To a certain extent this marked contrast between town and country
was determined by the make-up of the population: families with a
traditional lifestyle often preferred to remain in the country, whereas
people looking for something different were keen to move to the towns.
In this way, over the years, a sort of process of selection according to
religious inclination had taken place in the Netherlands.

But the part played by religion also had to do with rural life itself: the
daily confrontation with birth and death, the mystery of nature, the cycle
of existence, the taking up of the work of the parents by the children.

While country dwellers throughout the world might differ from one
another in all sorts of specific details, most of them were in no doubt
that they were a part of a universal order that justified their life.

Scepticism as to the existence of a divine order was common enough,
but it did engage people's interest: they thought about it, talked or
philosophised about it. The really fanatical atheists were chiefly to be
found in the countryside. And that had everything to do with nature's
overwhelming influence that permeated the whole of existence, day after
day, each season anew, a rhythm and a force that nobody could ignore.

A farmer saw life as an intermezzo. His ideals lay in the past, his
responsibilities in the future, but he would not see the outcome in
his own lifetime. He would always be dependent on forces beyond
the reach of human beings and over which he had only a partial control.
An arable farmer could plough, sow and do any amount of arithmetic,
but if the sun shone at the wrong moment or the rain poured down at
the wrong moment he could lose everything.

Those who work with wind and weather and life and death every day are aware of their own limitations. But this changed with the passing of the years. As it became increasingly possible to combat the forces of weather and mortality through one's own strength, God too slowly began to disappear from sight in Jorwert.

A few times I went with Jan Koopmans, the vet, on his rounds. Early morning surgery; coffee; on with the overalls, body-warmer; and then off in his four-wheel jeep, with half a dispensary's worth of bottles, drips and injection needles in the boot.

The practice had changed considerably since he started in 1978. In those first years, two out of three farmers still had the communal type of cowshed where the cows stood in a row with a runnel behind them for the dung. Now there was only one old-fashioned cowshed in the whole practice, the rest were all loose box sheds, enormous constructions with clanking railings and cattle roaming around. He used to be responsible for 12,000 cattle, now it was 9,000. The amount of medicine used had increased by a third during the same period.

"Everything is far more strictly controlled," he said. "If you have too many pathogens in the milk you will be penalised. But nowadays farmers do nearly all the inoculating themselves. We're just too expensive. A single visit by the vet to attend a sick cow and a farmer's profit margin is completely wiped out."

The first time I accompanied him it was a freezing cold morning, the sort of day when the mist just will not disperse, and every now and then there was a light flurry of snow. We drove into a farmyard. A dead lamb lay against the muckheap, its frozen legs sticking up stiffly in the air, its tongue hanging out of its mouth, and instead of eyes there were two big holes in its head, for the crows had done their work well.

We walked into the shed. There were cats all over the place, in the hay, on the beams, in the straw. The railings rattled, there were about 100 cows snorting and chewing, everywhere soft noses protruded between the metal bars. There were two patients: a cow with a badly inflamed udder and another with milk fever. The udder of the cow in question was extremely swollen and angry looking. Her back was hunched, her ribs stuck out, she was running a temperature and shivering, so many hundred kilos of sickness was all she was.

"I should be able get her up and about," mumbled Jan Koopmans, "but I'm afraid this beast will give hardly any milk this year. And I don't know whether the farmer will think it worth it." The farmer, also dressed in a worn body warmer, nodded.

In the next shed lay a cow that had just calved. A radio stood on a mucky beam, its tuning knob permanently stuck on the golden-oldie station Radio 10 Gold. The cow could no longer stand up, the calf lay shivering next to her. Over in a corner one of the cats was chewing on the afterbirth. The concerned farmer had covered the animals with sacking and was arranging bundles of straw under the udders. He knew all of his 100 cows by name, he said, and also their mothers and fathers, and he also knew their habits, and when he stood in the milk-pit he could tell by the shape of the udders who he had in front of him.

"Calcium deficiency and too little magnesium," said Jan Koopmans from behind the cow with milk fever, and he juggled with pills and hypodermics. The cow groaned, she rolled her big eyes in fear when she felt the needle, and her mouth opened wide and soundlessly.

We walked back into the farmyard, passing the lamb. "A runt," said the farmer. Nothing to be done about that. "I think I could have done something," said Jan Koopmans when we were sitting in the car. "But if they had got me out it would have cost twice as much as the price of the whole lamb. No lamb will ever see a vet." Or, as a pig farmer once said to me – because pigs share the same misfortune – "After all, it's not a dog."

The next farmer was a conference farmer: a farmer who was hardly ever there because he sat on 101 committees. The farmhand took us to a freezing cold cowshed where a skinny cow stood shivering, with blood on her hooves and sharply protruding withers.

Jan Koopmans took its temperature, palpated and listened, donned a large plastic glove, wetted his hand, wiped the cow's backside clean, applied pressure and then inserted his whole arm into the animals rectum. The cow mooed softly.

"I am feeling whether the fourth stomach is in the right place, and what the kidneys are like." Then he slowly withdrew his arm. In his hand he held some dung, and he brought out some thin liquid along with it. "It's gritty, that is odd."

Meanwhile the cow's backside was steaming like a volcano. It produced one fart after another, and all the while the thin liquid kept on coming. "A typical diarrhoea-cow," said Jan Koopmans.

He grumbled a bit in the car. "They tried far too long to cure that animal themselves. She probably had a gastric haemorrhage first of all. Then she recovered a bit from that, but now she has diarrhoea. I will be able to cure her, but she has just calved, so I am afraid they have lost the milk from that animal for the coming year." He explained to me that nowadays an average cow only produces milk for three or four years, so a long period of illness like this means a quarter of the production time. "And will they invest so much effort and money in the animal then? Farmers usually look after their beasts well, but the margins are too narrow for much sentimentality."

Meanwhile we had arrived at a farm with a neat and tidy cowshed and a cow that had had a Caesarian section and whose stitches needed removing. Nowadays Caesarian sections are performed on many ordinary cows. They are impregnated with an embryo from a beef super-cow – a Blonde Aquitaine, because that makes good economic sense – and they valiantly take on the role of surrogate mother; but when the time comes the foreign calf has grown so big it can only be removed by means of a Caesarian.

"Us Mem" looked slightly puny in between the Aquitaine cows; the only piebald Friesian among all those colossal red French beasts. Her flank had been shaved and a broad suture covered her stomach. Next to the cow stood two Blonde Aquitaine calves; one was not her own and neither was the other really – but then again it was.

The last farmer had the splendid, grey-haired countenance of a patriarch. In the cow shed we hunted for the nine cows who were to be vetted for export to Czechia. And then we did some tagging. Four calves were anaesthetised in order to provide them with a yellow ear-tag and remove their horns at the same time. That is done with a sort of large electric apple-corer that drills into the skull.

Horns are taboo in a loose box cowshed, the farmer explained, because you get too much quarreling and thrashing about. Cows, especially bored cows, spend all their time sorting out who is the boss. There is too little room in the loose boxes for them to resolve their conflicts properly. "Loose-box sheds are perfectly cow-friendly, but you do need pretty strong cattle," the farmer said. "The legs especially, need to be sturdy, to contend with all those grids. Weaker sisters have a difficult time of it."

So the arrival of the loose-box cowshed unwittingly heralded a new form of selection between cattle, that of their ability to cope. And a sizeable percentage of cows who had to make the transition from traditional to loose-box cowsheds failed to make the grade. Just like the farmers themselves, in fact.

Meanwhile the calves lay motionless on the straw, their glassy eyes open, their ears young and unsuspecting. The perforating pliers went through them as though they were a thin piece of leather. Afterwards the smell of horn and burning. A church clock rang out across the frozen countryside. It was twelve o'clock.

During those months I saw and heard a lot about nature. The older villagers told me all about milking, about leaning quietly against a cow's flanks, the warmth, the contact with the animal, the aimless thoughts going round in your head while the white jets of milk squirted, the music in the pail. The young people talked about embryo-implants, about synthetic milk and hormones that stimulate milk production and how they no longer need to remain vigilant even if a foal is due: when the pregnancy has run its course they simply placed a tiny receiver between the mare's labia, and when things started to happen the bleeper lying next to the settee at home would go off.

This new and unnatural turn of mind was epitomised by the changed relationship between the farmer and the cow. In the words of a friend: "Before, the cow was always right." A cow never made mistakes. A cow did not really do much at all. It grazed, chewed the cud a bit, had the occasional calf. At 5.30 in the morning and 4.30 in the afternoon a cow would wander over to the gate, for she knew she would be milked around then. That was the extent of her knowledge, and it was enough.

The modern walk-through cowshed brought with it a new phenomenon: the rebellious cow. Or, to put it another way: the cow that would not tow the line. Or, if you prefer, the silly cow.

The more rules a society has, the more deviant characters it produces, and the same goes for cows. The grids and turntables of the modern sheds necessitated the cows walking through in the same order each time, and some were unable to get used to this, even after weeks of training.

The cow that would not tow the line was the same cow who used to scratch itself on the gate, or lick the farmer's trouser leg. The farmer would give the beast a smack on the horns to push it away, half-chastising, half-affectionate. Now I heard farmers referring to them as useless cattle and they had them put down.

In 1995 livestock still came first as far as most Jorwerters were concerned. If a cow fell into a ditch any quarrels between neighbours were temporarily forgotten, and everyone rushed to help. An animal in distress was more important than anything else.

But if only three of a cow's teats produced milk – this can sometimes happen after an infection or an accident – then there still used to be a place for her. Now a cow like that always has to go. The farmers have become entrepreneurs, and a cow is primarily a means of production.

"You used to be able to tell which cow was which and how they were faring, just by sticking your head round the cowshed door," said Gais Meinsma. "Now they all have a number and you can't recognise a single beast any more."

When Cor Wiedijk was outside on the farm, he could tell by the way a cow sighed or mooed if something was wrong; if a cow "called", as he put it. He could even tell if something was up in his neighbour's cowshed. But he no longer knew his own cows by name.

I went to have a look at the annual agricultural show. Rotating within a pyramid of blue and yellow neon lights was the latest wonder of technology: the milk robot. I stood next to a man from Odijk with a large red face, two lads from the agricultural college at Hazerwoude, and a worn-out looking farming couple from Raalte plus their slouching, lanky son, who at 18 already had a bent back.

We all watched the huge revolution that turned slowly in front of us. "The 'Astronaut' gives the cow the freedom to choose when it wants to be milked," the video announced. The voice spoke of a complete system, "well thought-out and animal-friendly". "And last but not least: a quiet cowshed, more time for yourself!"

On the video we saw how the cow pushed open the robot's gate and "logged on" to the computer by means of a chip. "But surely you have to see the udders and backsides of your cows every day?" the farmer from Raalte said. "Otherwise how can you tell if a beast is ill or not?" On the video the animal received her individually adjusted dose of feed while at the same time a laser beam explored the udders.

Next, the valves automatically clamped onto the teats.

"This will totally transform the business of keeping dairy cattle," said the man from Odijk. According to him a machine like this would completely alter the working day, as milking could go on continuously and the emphasis would then switch to control and technique. But the lads from Hazerswoude thought it was all too far removed from nature, and what's more, too expensive. "Just ask the cow. After all, you don't use a machine on your wife either. If you don't like milking you shouldn't become a farmer."

The man with the red face spoke again: "Nowadays there is less and less physical work to do, you have to use your head more and more, and not everyone is able to do that." That you would have to do away with animals whose udders did not conform to the standard model of the machine was a conviction shared by all the bystanders. There was no place for rowdy cows in the world of the "Astronaut". And after the introduction of this system being outside in the summer would also be a thing of the past, unless – and this was often no longer the case – the pastureland was adjacent to the farm.

"There is soon going to be a similar upheaval in the area of feed," said the lads from the agricultural college. "Now we still mow and ensile, but in future the focus of our work will be on animal husbandry. To an ever-increasing extent the provision of feed will be down to the arable farmers. And in future the cow will definitely have to stay inside in summer and in winter, just like pigs do now."

Next to the robot it was chock-a-block with Dinky toys that had got completely out of hand, monstrously large combine-harvesters and grotesque manure-injectors. On display in one corner were computers for detecting when a cow was on heat; there was a new management system for sheep farmers; and the couple from Raalte stood gazing for a long time at a mower with hydro-pneumatic ground-pressure regulation and integrated crushers.

"Only the big and the very big can buy me and survive," that was the robot's message, written in invisible letters on the wall, and all those small farmers, slightly awkward in their best suits, understood this only too well as they walked through the huge congress halls. "You don't have a choice any more," said the lads from Hazerswoude, "you're entirely at their mercy." Their neighbours nodded.

*

One evening Cor Wiedijk showed me the paperwork he had to deal with on a daily basis:

- Keep the milk tank and the cooling system log book up to date;
- Keep the veterinary logbook up to date and keep tally of the daily dose of medicine given to each animal;
- Keep up to date with the national identification system for cows and sheep, which makes it possible, in the long term, to see precisely what a farmer has been doing – Orwell's 1984 has well and truly arrived as far as Dutch cattle are concerned;
- Bring the mineral accounts book up to date: how much of what goes into the cow; what amount of nitrates and phosphates come out again; how much manure has been spread over how many acres and so on;
- the ordinary accounts: it used to be sufficient to note down how much land you had and how many cows and sheep, now you have to fill in whole questionnaires.

"It makes you so damned vulnerable," said Cor. A sizeable bit of pastureland near his farm, some 750 acres in all, had been earmarked as an "ecological development area", or Feathered Friends Fun Park, or area of artificial natural beauty. It was all to be half submerged again, like it was before, for the benefit of the marsh flora and other stuff, and if the plans went ahead at least nine Jorwerter farming concerns would have to move elsewhere.

Farmers used to adapt their natural surroundings to suit their own purposes – with all the disruption this sometimes caused. But in recent years businesses have become more and more detached from the surrounding area. Nature, the countryside, the local economy, none of it matters any longer. Nowadays feed, manure, capital and techniques arrive from all over the world.

The result of this detachment was that the old farming environment appeared on the capital and political markets once more, this time as an independent entity. It was all for sale again to the pressure groups, the property developers, the practically-unemployed farmers and the environmentalists: the countryside, the village, the landscape, what little bit of nature Holland still possessed.

The government wanted to transform more than 3,500 acres of agricultural ground into "strategic green projects" by the year 2020. In the river area summer dykes were to be breached to make room for willow woods and boggy marshland. In the north, the polders would become lakes again and elsewhere pasture would be returned to woodland, heathland and barren sand.

Once again nature followed agriculture – albeit in the opposite direction this time. The reason was all too obvious: work was essential if the countryside was to remain alive and if agriculture could not provide it then leisure activities would have to. But most of the farmers I knew regarded it as a capitulation, total failure, even madness. Excellent land – wrested from the water and the sand by the sweat and toil of their fathers and grandfathers (and indeed, sometimes by their own) – was to be returned to its primeval state, whatever that might be.

"That's not nature," they said, "it's sheer neglect." Some farmers feared for their successors; once a farm found itself in the vicinity of a nature project its survival was under permanent threat. There was concern in many villages too, as pub, church and association cannot live by geese and marsh flora alone. And tourists only blossom for a few months a year.

Nevertheless, the air was buzzing with nature projects. A broad swathe of the old man-made landscape of Gaasterland was to be allowed to revert to an ecologically well-balanced wilderness; in the bare, clay region plans were put forward for an artificial lake complete with beach and sloshing waves, and everyone went on about otters.

I have never heard and read so much about otters as during those months in Jorwert. Just as in the 1950s the statue of "Us Mem" the cow had set the trend, now in the 1990s the otter was the trendsetter.

The otter had become this province's favourite cuddly toy. In the marshy land that lay behind the provincial capital a special otter park was created; hideouts were dug for otters; ponds were cleaned; crossing places created; never a week went by without there being something in the paper about otters. Apparently, if the otters were doing all right then nature and the rest of life would do all right as well.

The farmers began to take advantage of this new penchant for nature too. Some bits of land were designated protected areas: the farmer was financially rewarded for exercising restraint, for not spreading manure, not draining, and mowing only at certain specified times.

But there were those who wanted to go much further. For example, in 1994 the Agricultural Economics Institute put forward a plan by which farmers, besides their other work, would "produce" nature. Flowers growing on the banks of ditches would in future have to be paid for; copses on a farmer's land subsidised; and money would be available to make fallow land attractive to birds. The institute decreed that "nature as a product must become marketable, in the same way as cars, bicycles or holidays."

Certain farmers began to concentrate on so-called "sustainable agriculture". They aimed to produce potatoes, carrots, chicory and apples as well as milk, meat and eggs, in an environmentally friendly way. They renounced fertilisers and pesticides and began to farm organically. They let their pigs root about in the open air again, and propagated old fashioned methods of cow husbandry.

This type of farmer often did pretty well because town-dwellers had gradually become willing to pay over the odds for natural produce. What's more, they usually had little to fear from all the environmental regulations that the government was still drafting: they already complied with them. However, in order to sell their products the organic farmers had to rely on the network of health-food shops in the large towns. And those shops demanded an organic stamp of approval: a highly prized emblem that cost the farmers a great deal of money and effort to obtain.

But they had to, if they wanted to gain entry to the alternative market run by nature's friends. These farmers, then, managed to escape the mainstream bureaucracy of Brussels and the Hague, only to be ensnared by the alternative bureaucrats of Harderwijk and Marum.

By the end of the twentieth century it seemed as though a strange sort of shuttle-movement had been set in motion, from the ultra-technological to the ultra-natural, back and forward from milk robot to flowery verge, from otter to embryo-implant.

Regulating, organising, the Dutch have always been masters at creating their own nature. It was no coincidence that, as early as the end of the sixteenth century, it was the Dutch word *landschap* that permeated the English language as "landscape". In this country, kept dry and habitable by human hand, the idea of a landscape was bound to crop up early on:

a piece of nature whose qualities could be admired or rejected, and that was constantly being created and recreated.

But now something seemed out of balance. Whereas man's relationship with nature during the previous century had been determined by fear and dread, by 1995 only two extremes held sway: pragmatism and pipe dreams.

About 100 years ago, even in a well-ordered country like the Netherlands, the natural landscape was widely regarded as ugly, wild and desolate, waiting for the guiding hand of God and His land agent, man. "The religious society of the nineteenth century regarded flowering meadows as proof of a divine existence," wrote Auke van der Woud. "In contrast, the desolate areas, as countless old folk tales kept repeating, belonged to the realm of darkness, non-land, the lonely place where bubbling bogs, shrouds of mist, fireflies and other phenomena could all too easily adopt the guise of restless dead souls, searching for peace."

However by 1990, nature no longer held any sort of threat; she had withdrawn from the daily environment of most of the Dutch and had become a function, something useful besides town and country, but no more than that. Planners spoke about "illusion landscapes", "façade landscapes" and "adventure landscapes"; and in 1994 when the Ministry of Agriculture and Fisheries held a competition about the landscape in 2010, one of the competitors suggested converting the landscape into a fun-park, complete with "a choice of smells" and "love-making in the hay".

In the words of the Dutch author Koos van Zomeren, nature became something enacted at a distance: "a place that you can go and visit if you have a car".

The appearance of the Dutch countryside underwent great changes during those years, and actually these were often for the better. The landscape became more varied again, there were more trees and birds, livestock became more colourful and diverse, there was more water, it all became less bare and austere, and here and there you even saw cows in the fields with their calves – a scene that had been unthinkable for decades.

Meanwhile Jorwert was still surrounded by flat, green expanses of countryside. On closer inspection that old landscape was just as unnatural. It was the result of centuries of human endeavor and organisation, and there was not much spontaneity about it. But it did have a beauty all its own, that austere, synthetic quality, and we were able to love it the way we love all things we grow accustomed to.

One day I decided to take a look at the new nature. It was an area to the east of Heerenveen, behind the Tjonger, an old river whose current has been going back and forth like a yo-yo for decades, because this watercourse – half-river, half-canal – is used both to supply water during dry periods and to drain it off again during wet ones.

I was taken around by the director of the nature conservation organisation that was developing the area. Above our heads rain clouds like galleons raced over the flat expanse of land, and in front of us the former meanders of the Tjonger wound their way through the landscape: filled in 100 years ago and now painstakingly excavated again. The earthy banks were still sharp and bare, but in a few years time it would look just like the rest of the site in summer: full of grasses, herbs and flowers; like the sort of meadow only to be found at the feet of a medieval Madonna.

"Dragline mechanics are a pretty mixed bunch," the director said, as we walked through the meadows. "There are those who think it's a lot of nonsense; who dig out the bedding of a stream as though it were a rectangular ditch. But there are also those who can accurately excavate an ancient fen; who can tell by the ground exactly where they should stop or continue." Well over a century ago the Tjonger threaded its winding way through this southern Frisian landscape, the nearby heathland had only been reclaimed 60 years before, 20 years ago a land consolidation scheme had swept across the area, and now a laborious attempt was being made to restore it to its original state. Bulldozers were removing the rich, fertile soil and making the site artificially arid again. And in the adjacent woodland, a 100-year-old country estate, the drainage ditches were being filled in to create a natural water table once more: dry in the summer, wet to very wet in the winter.

"Certain exotic tree varieties will perish; gaps will appear in the woodland," the director said, but he was not very bothered about it. "It is going to be a wood again, instead of a collection of timber. There will be variety. Already there are harriers, reed warblers and sometimes even whinchats breeding again in the outlying area – all species that had long ago disappeared."

He expounded enthusiastically on the plants that had seeded

themselves just like that, blown in on the wind. "Normally in an old meadow like this you will find about five different species per square metre. Here there are 20 to 30." So, in springtime, you can walk once more among a thousand bouquets: the yellow of celandine, dandelion and buttercup, then the red of the sorrel, followed by the variegated tints of kingcups, rattles, ragged robins and marsh forget-me-nots.

Here then, nature was being fashioned anew, just as easily as for centuries we had done the opposite. And so the draglines of the Heathland Reclamation Co. and the Soil Co. set to work once more; but this time to undo what they had once constructed with so much effort and expense.

Meanwhile the director taught me the difference between "natural", "as good as natural", "naturally maintained", "half-natural" and "cultivated areas", and I was given to understand that there had not been any natural areas in the Netherlands for a very long time. Even the Waddenzee did not make it any higher up the nature scale than second grade: "as good as natural".

In the wood, with its ponds and scattering of half-rotted tree-trunks, the conversation turned to the question of what nature really is. "Ten years ago here they still swept up all the leaves from the paths in the autumn," the director said. "And the first committee members of our association dug up orchids in order to replant them on their own sites. Cows in the woods: nature conservationists regarded that as a cardinal sin in the 1930s and 1940s. Now we let Highland cattle graze there."

We continued our musings as we walked along. The straight avenues along which we strolled used to be highly fashionable, as were ordered landscapes. Now we idealise the wilderness and are absolutely convinced that nature herself will supply the necessary balance. Tomorrow the emphasis may possibly shift back to the variety of cultivated landscapes in this country, and we will complain about the monotony of the primeval forests, which meanwhile will have taken hold. We continue to project all that we desire and fear in our societies on to the marvel that we in this country call "nature" – even though we have known for a long time that this final mystery is now fashioned purely after our own image.

Jan Koopmans and I were driving through the countryside again. There had been a heavy frost that night and nearly all the farmers we visited were struggling with frozen water pipes. In the old type of cowshed the livestock kept things warm, but the big, loose-box sheds were really cold. One farmer was running back and forth, carting buckets of water with which to douse the cattle, another was setting up a warm-air dispenser and at the third farm the milking machine had packed up and the cows stood bellowing with swollen udders.

We drove by Douwe's former farm, that had blown down one November night a few years before – the vet, who had been one of the first on the scene, said it was a miracle. It was one big pile of rubble, but there sat Douwe, straight as a ramrod, in the middle of it, surrounded by his cows and calves, all mooing. Now there was a sort of midget farm on the site, complete in every detail, only the proportions had been reversed: the house was enormous, but the barn was minute.

We took a lot of coffee breaks that morning. The men's faces as they came into the kitchen were pinched with cold. "In the past 25 years the whole world has been turned upside down," said a farmer. He wore a frayed baseball cap and each word carried weight. "In the old days plain hard work would get you there. Now it is far more important to be able to think things through and do your arithmetic."

"And to have the courage of your convictions," added his wife.

"You have to be enterprising," the farmer said. "But I don't know how this is all going to turn out."

At the end of the morning we arrived at Bonne Hijlkema's. A cow could not rid herself of the afterbirth, and then it was coffee again, as it was too cold to do much outside. Bonne Hijlkema was in a gloomy mood.

"I just do not see the point of it any more," he said. "If I were ten years younger I would have packed it all in long ago."

The radio was on in the kitchen, and beyond the window-pane the grey countryside stretched endlessly. The cattle dealer came in, we drank another cup, and the conversation turned to contentment.

Bonne had devoted a good deal of energy to farming organisations, but he no longer saw any point in it: "It's politics that's raking it in; we never win anything any more. There's no respect for farmers nowadays."

The cattle dealer, whose name was Van der Zweep, began to reminisce. He used to be a farmer himself. "We were content," he said. "At half-past nine we fell into bed, exhausted, me, you, all of us, and at half-past three it was time to start again. We worked ten, twelve hours a day, but our neighbours worked just as hard. That was the way it was and we didn't know any different."

The farmer's wife began to talk about mowing the autumn grass. First you used the scythe, then you shook it out, then you laid it in long strips that you made into haycocks, and then the hay on the cart, with the horse pulling it. Man and beast working together: "If you said 'Hup!' the horse would walk on by himself to the next haycock, and so on, and after that on to the barn, he did it all by himself."

Then everyone began to talk about how warm and cosy the old cowsheds used to be during winter. "I stopped seven years ago," said Van der Zweep. "I had 40 head of cattle. It's all gone and I haven't regretted it for a minute."

The farmer's wife talked about the paperwork.

"There's always something in the post. You can never just get on with your work any more."

The vexed question of "tagging" came up – the yellow ear tags that every cow has to have – that most hated of all laws, directives and registrations, because it encroaches on one of the farmer's most fundamental rights: the right to deal with his cattle as he sees fit.

At first I had seen older farmers wrestling with them. How were they supposed to go in exactly? With the pliers, but where? And later on I saw the cows, scratching, trying to prize them off in the grass, constantly attempting to get rid of the prickly bits of plastic in their ears, their eyes bulging with panic. And I saw what the cows themselves could not see: idiotic, bright yellow bits of plastic with numbers, no use to anyone except the bureaucrats.

The tags were compulsory within the European Community so as to be able to see straight away from which country and which business an animal came. In the case of an infectious disease prompt action could then be taken. The sanction was simple, but extraordinarily effective: no cow could go to market without an ear tag.

Whenever there was a threat of an epidemic the system did indeed provide a valuable service, but as for those ludicrous ear tags, everyone around Bonne Hijlkema's kitchen table agreed: all that unsightly yellow was totally unnecessary.

The registration certificate that pedigree cattle used to have – a card with the name, the place of origin, a sketch of the animal and if necessary a Polaroid photo – that was sufficient surely? What is more, modern cattle-breeders often provided their beasts with a tiny metal tag – and in recent years they had even begun using all sorts of electronic methods, with chips, and neck and ankle collars, simple and discreet.

More than anything else, what drove just about all the farmers up the wall was the stupidity of the forces of bureaucracy behind the measure. The cattle dealer talked about the problem of forgery: "Those bits of yellow plastic are on sale at the cattle market in Leeuwarden." The vet had sometimes witnessed bloodbaths: "The ear tags can get stuck when a cow sticks its head through the railings in a loose-box shed; sometimes half the herd's are torn out." In the paper it said that 10,000 replacement tags were ordered every week.

Sheep and goats were next in line. "Those civil servants know nothing about the livestock trade," Van der Zweep said. "A billy goat, for example, only costs about four guilders. But those couple of bits of yellow plastic cost 40 guilders. The wrapping paper is more expensive than the present!"

"The people who thought this up have never seen a two-year-old bull," Bonne Hijlkema said. Van der Zweep nodded. "I once had a civil servant here in the farmyard who wanted me to ear-tag the last bull as well. I said to the man: 'There he is. Do it yourself if you dare!'"

We continued philosophising, at that kitchen table, about the agricultural industry, and afterwards about the phenomenon of "more", always "more".

"Why are people so dissatisfied?' the farmer's wife wondered. "You can't go on eating when you are full up, can you? But 'more' is never full up."

During that winter I was sometimes reminded of the series of films about the Ten Commandments by the Polish director Krzysztof Kieslowski. Especially his film about the first commandment, "Thou shalt have no other gods before me", in which he tells the story of a man, his small son and their computer. It is freezing cold, the ice on a nearby pond is getting thicker, and each day the man calculates the thickness to within a millimetre on the computer. The son has blind faith in the father and his computer. At a certain point, when the computer gives the signal "safe", the boy braves the ice. The ice breaks and he drowns. The grief of the father.

I saw a photograph of another father in the paper, one who was attempting to skate across the IJsselmeer, a considerable trek of at least 25 kilometres Nobody had checked the ice first. Skating next to him was a little boy of around nine, who was also pulling a sledge with an infant of about four on it. I read that the fire brigade had tried in vain to dissuade the father.

I thought: the man is mad. But he was mad in a special sort of way. He was a typically urban type of madman, the sort of person who takes his offspring for a walk along the pier at IJmuiden during a heavy storm; who goes for a unaccompanied stroll across the mudflats of the Wadden; who crosses the Waal canal when the ice is as brittle as a membrane.

Someone who has forgotten that something called nature still exists, even in this country, and that there are forces that cannot be tamed by pushing a button, presenting a good image and having a polyester lining; that there are elements that cannot be controlled by training and technique; that water, air and human ingenuity all have their own strengths and weaknesses.

During the time I lived in the village a nearby shipyard built a specially adapted seaworthy yacht for an American invalid. The boat was designed to enable the man to sail it single-handedly. You could get around the whole deck in a wheelchair; hoist the sails from a sitting position; there was a lift to get down into the hold and the American could even repair the engine from his wheelchair. "That cost a pretty penny," the lads in the pub muttered.

Understandably, the American saw the boat as the ultimate triumph over his handicap. He wanted to make a solo voyage around the world. None of the shipyards had dared accept the commission, except this one here. The men who built her were rather proud of their workmanship, but they also thought it was a crazy scheme, for they were well aware of the sea's strength. A lift like that could break down, ropes could snap, and the waves would not wait. The lads at the bar knew only too well that nature did as she pleased, and all the technology in the world could not alter that.

However, for a great many townspeople nature no longer seemed to exist. When a flotilla of pleasure craft got into difficulties one lovely spring day, because of an unexpectedly fierce storm, the Dutch shook their fists at the weather forecasters. When, due to heavy rainfall, the water was threatening to break through the river dykes and the forelands were flooded, the government was automatically held responsible. The most that existed outside their own world for these types of people was something called the "environment", something that one was vaguely apprehensive about, a Last Judgement that would be pronounced upon their children, but from which they were protected by governmental "measures". In their eyes everything could be reduced to money, technique and political decisions, and it no longer seemed to occur to them that there were some matters that did not fit into this scheme of things.

The lack of daily contact with weather, wind, soil, plants and animals meant that in modern society nature became mythologised. More accurately: nature was divided into a "good" part that had to be protected and a "bad" part – called "environment" – that we had to control and restrain.

Carl Gustav Jung has described how the western religions gradually lost their devils and evil gods. God was declared "good" and evil was apportioned to mankind. Wicked gods, like those common to Hinduism for example, were unknown in the West.

During these years the same thing happened to our understanding of nature. "Nature" was godly and good – no matter how harsh, cruel and stupid it was in reality. "Environment" was human and susceptible to evil. We accepted freedom and chaos as part of "nature" – albeit with difficulty. And we bombarded the "environment" with all the control techniques we possessed. We recognised that "nature" still had something elusive about it – at least as long as it was restricted to certain reserves. And we used all the rationality of our human understanding to explore the "environment". Farmers took part in this just as much as townspeople, but under the surface there was a difference in attitude.

After all, even the most modern farmers knew better than townspeople that they did not know everything. They did not know what the future would bring, they did not properly know the present, and they accepted the mystery with more respect. They were happy to make use of all the computer techniques God gave them, but they knew that improvements in knowledge would never reduce the magnitude of the unknown.

Because of this, the contrast between the known and the unknown was less marked in the countryside than in towns. Not-knowing was an accepted part of life, sometimes in the guise of magic and superstition, more often in the form of churches, steeples and the Word. But not-knowing was at the heart of it.

Why did farmers do what they did? Why did they "plough on", often in defiance of all the tenets of economic and common sense?

Old Tiennon, the nineteenth-century farmer I quoted earlier, described it as a feeling of indefinable pride and joy:

> When I saw my meadows turning green again; when, enthralled, I observed the growth of my corn and potatoes; when I saw that my pigs were getting fatter, my sheep filling out and my cows bearing healthy calves; when I saw that my heifers were developing handsomely, that my oxen, in spite of their hard work, were bearing up well, that they were clean, well shorn, their tails combed so that I could be proud of them; when, together with the other tenant farmers, I brought cartloads to the castle, that the animals I wanted to sell were sturdy and well-nourished: then I was happy.

What was interesting was that the Jorwerter farmers at the end of the twentieth century still talked in exactly the same way about their ties with the land, the rain and the livestock. They were feelings that could not be explained solely in terms of "surviving" and "money", and almost all the farmers to whom I spoke were themselves surprised by this. They talked about it as if it were a sort of infatuation, a sentiment that conflicted with the businesslike attitude they all too often assumed, but that nevertheless they did not deny.

"Nature is everything," said Bonne Hijlkema. "May-time, the birds. You are at one with nature, you can feel it inside."

"Being with the animals, walking in the fields, the grass, the clouds, it is all so marvellous," Lies Wiedijk said.

In his posthumous memoirs, Sake's father, Tjerk Castelein, wrote about the harmony between a farmer and his cows: "The peace of the cowshed in mid-winter, the vigorous milking of the docile milch cow, they are images that you never forget."

His children called it a vocation. "You work twelve hours a day, the money is not bad, but in the end you still cannot manage," said Sake. His face had retained a youthful quality, but he had a tired physique.

His wife, Yke, was still an attractive woman with friendly eyes.

"You never used to think about it," she said. "We grew up with it, it was a question of getting on with it."

Sake: "When I was 16 we went on an excursion to the Friesland dairy products factory and I saw those people at the conveyor belt. That was enough to convince me: I thought, 'I never want to come here again, it will drive me stark raving mad if I end up here'."

But Tjerk's grandchildren preferred to go into teaching or do social work. It was the same with almost all the farmers I spoke to. We would talk about milk quotas, robots, embryo-implants and hormone preparations, but by the end of the evening the talk would have turned once again to land, livestock and the open air. And the cowsheds were still redolent of the ancient smell of milk, mixed with hay and a whiff of dung, the sweet fragrance that is both timeless and of all times, and that can drive a person mad with nostalgia for something he has never known.

It was a perfect autumn day when we buried the old haulier Tjitse Tijssen. He lay pale and still in the middle of the church in his brown Sunday suit, and his two grandchildren and the son to whom he could never talk, stood beside him.

Broad yellow bars of sunlight fell across the pews. The 50 villagers who were escorting him to his last resting place sat, whispering softly, while the organ played sweet, funereal music. There were no speeches. The only ones who said something were Cor Wiedijk, who had recently become head of the burial association, and the vicar, who did not beat about the bush. At the end of his life Tjitse had been lonely. He sometimes complained that people no longer said hello: "They don't notice me any more." His existence had slowly been extinguished for the village.

While the vicar was speaking, my thoughts turned to the story of Heleen and Annie and the poet, and that romantic spot at the back of the garden, near the churchyard, and to the photographs lying in a drawer at the vicarage, still with holes in them where the eternal traveller Slauerhoff had pinned them to the wall of his cabin, and to what was sometimes written on the back: For Jan, from Heleen, 1926.

Years later Heleen had got them back again from Jan, so that they had eventually found their way to that drawer in Jorwert. By then he was already gravely ill, and he had gone to visit her in Italy specifically to ask her to return with him to Holland for those last few weeks.

She refused. She felt she could not abandon her invalid patient just like that, so he had given her back the two photographs, together with a handful of furious verses.

> Surrounded by enemies,
> Shunned like foul-smelling carrion
> By friends in my hour of need,
> I smile and put on a brave face.

The photograph of Jan on his deathbed was also in the drawer at the vicarage, sent to Heleen by Dutch friends, still in the same rice-paper cover and wrapped in the same tissue paper that she must have unfolded that first time, and perhaps did again later.

> She resides there still,
> I am sure, as
> Hers was a powerful contentment.

I was thinking about all this during the sermon. Tjitse Tijssen had never been one for religion, but towards the end of his life he had asked the vicar if he wouldn't mind doing something. And so we read the epistle to the Corinthians: "And if any man think that he knoweth any thing, he knoweth nothing yet as he ought to know. But if any man love God, the same is known of him" – and then the bells began to toll once more.

The old haulier was carried outside. The churchyard was full of leaves, but the trees still rustled. We passed the grave of the little girl who had died last year, on which the family had placed a tiny Christmas tree. We passed the grave of the butcher and the grave of Durk Siesling's wife that was always covered in flowers; went right around the church until we came to a hole in the ground.

Because it was Cor's first time doing it we had taken a wrong turn coming out of the church, so that the coffin had to be turned around again first. After all, Tjitse had to lie properly, his head facing the right way, just like everyone else in the village has been lying for hundreds of years.

Then, without any prayers being said, he was lowered into the ground. We heard the birds, the children in the playground, the tyres of a car and the two o'clock train. Then it was over.

Chapter Seven

The Winter of 1979

 I DROVE HOME LATE ON A CLEAR NIGHT. THE countryside was in deep slumber, and the only movement in the villages consisted of dozens of cat's eyes that hovered above the road like tiny green lights.

In Jorwert the village street was deserted, hushed and silent in the light of the one and a half street lamps that were still on, and even the trees surrounding the churchyard did not stir. All the houses were in darkness and I could almost hear them breathing in their sleep: Sake, Yke, Folkert, Bonne, Gais Meinsma, Oebele van Zuiden, Eef, the vicar, the elderly solicitor.

What were they dreaming about tonight? I knew what some of them would be dreaming of, and I could make an educated guess about the others. I knew that Oebele van Zuiden always mowed in his sleep, even though he had parted with his horses years ago: "Hup, and back! Hup and back!" Durk Siesling, the old peat-barge skipper, had told me that on moonlit nights he often sailed a boatload of turf, one of his own ships, the *Jonge Durk* (Young Durk) or the *Hoop op Welvaart* (Hope of Prosperity), in full glory, just like they look in old photographs. And the vicar told me that when Tjitse Tijssen was still alive he always travelled the old haulage route in his dreams: Jorwert, Mantgum, Weidum, Leeuwarden, back and forth, back and forth.

The people who were born between 1900 and 1930 have often led lonely lives. They can still tell you about all the sounds that have disappeared from the countryside – that standing in Oostwierum you heard the swishing of windmills all around, and the light tinkling of the reapers sharpening their scythes, and further on, in all the villages surrounding you, the blacksmith's anvil. They can still tell you about it. But they can no longer share the experience with anyone.

Gais Meinsma showed me her old photograph albums. "Look," she said, spreading the photographs out on the table, "there's the village street when I went to school. And there's the amateur dramatics society. And there's the village, with the harbour, and Durk Siesling's ships. And this one was taken in 1939, at the time of the big processions."

The photograph shows a float with a woman in traditional Frisian dress, and a chimney, a stork, a wheel upon which a handful of dressed-up children are sitting. Under the tableau is a line of Frisian poetry by Gysbert Japicx: *The child's world so fragile and fine, within it lies your future and mine.* "That was the vicar, Mr Van Gelder's doing. He wanted to educate us, he was always making us read poetry out loud. 'Death and the garden-er' — we couldn't make head nor tail of it."

A school photograph. "That was my school, 1933 to 1939. There's Anneke Pot, farmer's daughter, moved away. There's Grietje van Hoek, her father sold petroleum, they were very poor; in 1943 the whole family went to work in Germany. Tjebbe de Vries, farmer's son, became an engineer, moved to the city. Henk Oostra, also gone west. Zwaantje de Jong, the baker's daughter, married the postman. Detsje Ikema, labourer's daughter, married a farmer. Her brother Jan moved to France. Anne Dijkstra, carpenter's daughter, married a teacher, now lives in Gelderland. Hendrik van der Veer, blacksmith's son, became a smith himself, till the business was wound up as part of a reorganisation."

A photograph of a beautiful young woman. "Yes, and that's me when I was still at home working on the farm." She would join the Resistance, bear a fatherless child, marry Hendrik Meinsma the painter and decorator, and much, much later, become a student of theology.

There is not a single person in this village above a certain age who has not lived through a constant process of depletion and decline — at least as far as village life is concerned. Of the more than 500 Jorwerters at the beginning of the century there were only 330 left by 1995. Graphs of the village population show only one small recovery, in the 1970s, when 16 new homes were built on the edge of the village.

And that is how almost all small villages fared. In retrospect most of them had their heyday around 1870, with regard to both activity and the number of residents. After that, even when there was some growth in the small villages, the increase lagged way behind the rest of the Netherlands. The natural increase in the population – the difference between births and deaths – was constantly counteracted by the fact that so many people moved away.

That steady decline was interrupted twice. In the 1930s and 1940s any further depletion was blocked by Depression and war; in the 1970s for the first time increasing prosperity gave townspeople a choice that until then had been reserved for the wealthy: the excitement of the city, or the congenial living conditions of the countryside. Hordes of nature-lovers moved to the countryside, and their number more than compensated for the steady stream of country-dwellers making for the towns. The larger villages especially profited from these newcomers. When the economic situation deteriorated in the early 1980s and the housing market collapsed the influx came to a halt. After 1983 the population in half the rural districts of Friesland declined in absolute terms.

But even these figures are too flattering, because – until after the Second World War – a sizeable part of the countryside population lived, not in the villages themselves, but in the outlying area. The older villagers said that Funs and the other hamlets used to "teem with children". The unmarried farmhands and servant girls used to sleep on the farm – sometimes in a cubby hole above the cowshed – and the labourers with families would be in a nearby cottage. This patriarchal system continued for a long time, especially among cattle farmers. Those who grew corn, beet or potatoes could get away with hiring a team of casual labourers when it was time for the harvest, but cattle needed a permanent eye kept on them.

The mid-1950s saw the disappearance of the bunches of labourers' kids who trekked to the Jorwerter village school every morning from the outlying areas. Machines arrived, the ties between farmer and labourer became looser, the labourers bought bicycles, the children had to attend school longer, and gradually it became very tempting to move from the open countryside into the heart of the village. And from there it was but a small step to the town.

That process of depletion did not apply to all villages. When a researcher decided to compare the resident population of the villages of the Frisian

Zuidwesthoek to that of 150 years before, he stumbled upon a remarkable fact: the pecking order of the villages hardly appeared to have changed in all that time. Once villages had achieved a certain status they barely ever seemed to relinquish it. What had changed dramatically were the differences in residential populations. Just as it had between the big and the small farmers, a drawbridge effect had occurred between the various villages: the big had got bigger, the small had carried on shrinking.

Particularly after 1950, the population of the countryside began to be concentrated in larger towns. That was also the aim of government policy: after all, it was there that a broad enough base for schools, shops and businesses existed, and it was also there that almost all the homes were to be built.

The consequences of this policy were spectacular. In 1964 a provincial survey showed that the population of almost all the smaller Frisian villages had declined since 1950 and that a simple rule applied: the smaller the village, the higher the percentage who left.

The extensive grasslands around Jorwert were home to rather more than 100 small villages: in five out of six the number of inhabitants had dropped by 10 to 15 per cent in 14 years, in villages with less than 200 inhabitants by as much as almost 20 per cent.

"If the rural areas as such are to continue to fulfil their function and simultaneously be liberated from the belief that they have been neglected, then the disappearance of the smaller centres should not be regarded as worrying, but rather seen as a favourable symptom," two researchers from the agricultural college in Wageningen wrote in their report of 1957; and in so doing gave a pretty accurate rendition of the views held by the average administrator in those days. While it was true that not all villages with fewer than 500 inhabitants showed signs of decline, there were hardly any policy makers who felt it advisable to risk much further investment in them.

Interest was concentrated on the larger towns. And in the small villages the same disastrous decline occurred as in the neglected inner city areas: there was not enough work; the number of inhabitants dropped – and often it was the pick of the crop who left; the post, public transport and other facilities deteriorated, making the village steadily less attractive to newcomers; shops began to close their doors; now the elderly began

to be apprehensive too; in short, something occurred in those villages
that was akin to ghetto formation, but in miniature and with decorum.
And it happened without a sound. No questions asked.

In the late 1940s Riemer de Groot returned from the Dutch East Indies
where he had been a soldier. He walked into Jorwert, he told me, and
the village felt like a millstone round his neck. He had never felt that
way before. His earliest memories were happy, secure ones: his father
preparing the customers orders; a side of smoked horsemeat hanging
from a beam; ferreting around in the back of the shop among the
cheeses. His parents had sent him to the School with the Bible in
Hijlaard, but apart from this he had never known anything but the
village, and on summer days he had swum in the canal just like all
the other boys, around Durk Siesling's *Hoop op Welvaart*.

But then the war arrived. Riemer had to go into hiding, then to the
Dutch East Indies, and when, after five years, he returned to the village,
he fell, in his own words, into a sort of limbo. "I kept thinking: what
am I doing here? But I didn't know any better. I helped in the shop. I
delivered cheeses to the other shopkeepers on my delivery-bike. I had
my worries, but you had to get on with it." He married his Lieske, and
in 1953 he took over his father's grocery shop-cum-cheese warehouse
and never left it again.

The initial years were prosperous ones. The delivery-bike, with its
sturdy leather handguards, was replaced by a car, and the turnover
steadily increased. "In those days there wasn't much competition,"
Riemer said. "You used to have retail price maintenance, and that meant
that a packet of Douwe Egberts coffee cost just as much in the shop
in town as it did here. So you always had a regular income because
there was always a regular profit margin."

He had nothing to complain about as far as turnover was concerned
either, for households were still large. "There wasn't much money in the
village, but there were a lot of mouths to feed, and the largest part of
the family income in those days went on groceries. Moreover everyone
in the village bought almost everything from one of the local grocers'.
There was one schoolmaster who shopped in town, at de Gruyter's,
because they gave a ten per cent discount, but he was the exception."

In those days, the bakers', butchers' and grocers' shops served as everyday meeting places in Jorwert. A good deal of jawing took place in Riemer's and Lieske's grocery shop too. When Lieske got married she had promised herself that they would never be able to say of her: "She gossips like a baker's delivery girl" – they were the champions in this field. She had her own code of ethics: "You had customers who had run up heavy debts, and who paid them off guilder by guilder, but you never talked about it."

Little was missed in such a close-knit community, and that presented the village retailers with certain problems.

In the first place, village gossip led to the provision of high quality goods: a customer was valuable and if you sold him rubbish you did not just lose the customer, but within half a day you had lost your reputation too.

Second, there was "credit" or "the book". Most customers of a village shop paid once a week. This was a time-honoured tradition – in Jorwert as well – but it was a form of customer relations that cost the small shopkeepers many a sleepless night. "I can still remember who owes me money," said Lieske.

"It set you back 100 guilders if somebody didn't pay a few times running," added Riemer.

There had been cases when Riemer had just managed to get to the door before a customer departed. "I said, 'There's still some owing.' He said, 'How much?' and threw the money down on the table. I thought, 'That's mine!' But it did not always work, and then you were a few hundred guilders short before you knew it. And that was serious, with a weekly turnover of less than 1,000 guilders."

Slowly but surely sales increased. Riemer and Lieske joined the Voluntary Association of Retailers, retail price maintenance was tinkered with, profit margins shrunk, large families became rare, but prosperity increased and people spent more.

"We used to get all sorts of advertising bumph. We sent round a flyer – that was really good for sales. Our range of products kept increasing, and we even had to start using part of the warehouse to stock it all."

The first signs of change began to be visible in the village, but Riemer doubled his turnover.

Outwardly, the village seemed to be doing better all the time. During the first years of their marriage, Gais and Hendrik Meinsma's painting and decorating business provided little more than a minimal existence. They did nicely in the summer, but in the winter it was difficult to find enough inside work.

Hendrik would go odd-jobbing all over the place. He would make a start on the shutters of a farmhouse that he was going to get to work on properly in the summer, or he would paint the farmers' machinery for a special price. Gais found it difficult to get used to the frugal life they lived during the winter. Hendrik grew more and more worried. Gradually however, things picked up, and the other retailers fared the same.

In the early 1950s, Klaas de Jong, the baker, who was fond of the sporting life, was the first Jorwerter to allow himself the luxury of a shower. "It was all very exciting," Gais remembered. "New things in the village. If someone was rash enough to install such a thing, and in a separate room too, you had to go and see. A tap that produced hot water just like that." Gais paid the baker a visit with the specific intention of trying out the shower, and she was not the only one.

Durk Hofstra, a casual labourer, was determined to have one of those things too, but there was no way he could ever afford it. So he took a pail, hammered a hundred holes in the bottom, filled it with lukewarm water, and he had his shower.

There was the same sort of excitement in the air in the villages during the post-war reconstruction years as there had been at the end of the previous century. Gas and water pipes were being laid everywhere. The elderly looked on in surprise as the wooden "privies" were replaced by "mains" lavatories. The "night-soil cart" disappeared – although that particular symbol of backwardness could be found in some of the smaller villages right up to the 1970s; a weekly humiliation for the inhabitants.

De Jong, the baker, was also the first Jorwerter to acquire a television. Once again, everyone was invited to come and admire the novelty. On Wednesday and Saturday afternoons, when a children's programme was shown, there would be 30 pairs of clogs on the doorstep. Whenever there was a football match or other event, the set was placed on the window-sill. Klaas de Jong was soon followed by the solicitor, and after that the whole village.

The car began its advance. In 1919, according to a council inventory, there was one car in the village, belonging to Kingma Boltjes, the solicitor. By 1954 there were three, a year later 25 were parked in the village. Even Hendrik Meinsma got his driving licence – though half the village had been privy to the fact that, in order to spare his nerves, Gais had hidden the examination papers under his pillow, only telling him of the test on the morning itself.

Eventually the Jorwerters began to get a taste of a phenomenon that had until then been the province of the vicar, the solicitor and the school staff: a holiday.

Riemer de Groot was one of the first. From the early 1950s onwards he went sailing for a week each summer. "That cost me a week's turnover, but at the end of the year you didn't notice it." In 1958 the family went to the Veluwe for the first time. After that to Zuid-Limburg, for 20 years in succession. After that they began to go abroad: Israel, Switzerland, the South Tyrol, Spain. The majority of the village followed in the 1960s. "Seeing the world, there's nothing like it," said Riemer.

In the summer of 1978, eight older Jorwerters – Durk Siesling, Oebele van Zuiden, Tijtse Tijssen, Kees Jellema, and their wives – went on the first holiday of their lives: a ten-day cruise on the Rhine. It was a high spot. "You just cannot imagine how beautiful it was," Oebele van Zuiden told me later. "I did nothing but stand and stare; at the mountains, at everything. It was fantastic. And everything was laid on. As much coffee and tea as we wanted." Folkert never went. "Taking a holiday never occurred to me. The work had to go on."

Another change occurred during those years, a change that cannot be traced in any statistics, but that was at least as drastic as the arrival of the car and the television. The outward appearance of almost all the villages underwent a transition.

In Jorwert itself the stinking harbour was filled in, a handful of parking spaces were created, and for a short time there were wild plans to convert part of the vicarage garden into a small square for the whirligig at the annual merke, but Gais was able to stymie this.

In many nearby villages modern times arrived with a vengeance. There was much sawing and felling, overgrown corners disappeared, cobbles were covered with tarmac and ramshackle labourers' cottages were replaced with austere homes of yellow brick. During those years many of the farms lost their characteristic, sober lines: silos were built next to them, outbuildings, loose-box cowsheds, and the shiny black plastic of the silage mounds shone everywhere. New roads were constructed, ancient waterways filled in, narrowed down or rendered unnavigable by the building of low, fixed bridges.

The variety of villages and landscapes gradually began to fade. A sort of standard village emerged, a ready-made design that was "modern", and therefore good, and to which everything else was subordinated.

One of the noticeable things was a decrease in the number of trees. In the early 1950s many villages could have been classified as "leafy". They were full of oaks, beeches and limes, tall and sturdy, often 100 to 150 years old. Twenty years later there were hardly any left. If traffic schemes did not kill them off, then the massive land consolidation projects that swept through the countryside usually did. In most villages they were replaced by the sort of greenery that was all the rage in urban green-spots: shrubs, conifers, the sort of indefinable foliage that was easy to keep trim with a pair of motorised shears.

A place like De Knipe, to the east of Heerenveen – long and narrow and defined by tall trees with a dreamy waterway in the middle – was reduced to little more than a bare thoroughfare. Not only did this type of mutilation seriously damage the appearance of a village, but the village community's image of itself – the village as village – also underwent a subtle change, just as a person's self-image alters if they lose a leg or their face becomes scarred.

One of the first to personally experience this tide of change was the man whose working environment had originally been the main artery of the village: Durk Siesling the local skipper, who sailed back and forth between the village and the outside world with his *Hoop op Welvaart* (fifty tons). From the 1950s onwards all the new dams meant that he could only sail to Sneek by making an enormous detour and getting to Leeuwarden also became increasingly difficult.

Durk had been sailing since his birth in 1916. He had grown up in the oaken smack built by his grandfather. They transported manure, beet, sand, peat and turf in the type of little vessel that tourists now chug around in.

"I was already the breadwinner by the time I was 15," he told me. "My father died young, and my mother was left to cope on her own. As a boy, I sailed all the way to Sneek and beyond, with an extra pram of peat for a customer. Up at midnight, punting, struggling with the pole the whole day long, then home by midnight again, there and back in 24 hours. Slogging away on your own. That's when missing your father really does mean missing."

In 1957 Durk Siesling was one of the last skippers to make the transition to a motorboat. For years he had been a sailor against his will because the family was too poor to be able to afford towing horses or outboard motors. "When I sailed out of the village you could see people thinking: how lovely and peaceful it is on a ship, so quiet beneath the sail. But a life spent carting coal around the village would have been an easier one."

And when the focus of transport switched from waterways to roads in the countryside as well, it did not make the work any less exacting. At fixed bridges, and there were more and more of them, the whole mast had to be taken down. "When we sailed with peat, we left at half past three in the morning, and went on until the late evening. With beet we sailed at night as well, by the light of the moon."

He was used to storms and foul weather. Once he was involved in a collision near Birdaard: another ship tore off his costly outboard motor, which fell, still turning, into the water, and was smashed to smithereens. It had cost him a whole autumn. A lawyer in Rotterdam had insisted on 200 guilders before he did anything. Durk never received a cent in return.

In 1950 Jorwert stopped using "brown fuel", and after 1970 there was not much money to be made from "black fuel" either. "During the holidays the wife and children came with me. Later on the wife came by bus of an evening, to bring me dinner and keep me company for a while. After that there was a time when the boy would pick me up in the car from the ship on Saturdays, for the weekend. But many is the night that you would end up in front of a closed bridge of an evening; you would warm up some food, secure the ship's moorings, scrub the decks, eat, and then down to the cabin and your bunk. You would lie there waiting for morning to come. No, it's not much fun on your own."

In 1974 the *Hoop op Welvaart* transported its last load. "On a day like that you feel a bit wistful. And then, well – it's all over."

*

All of this took place in a period when the word "modern" began to exert a strong attraction on some Jorwerters. They had few qualms about putting out furniture that was not "modern" for the dustman. Older household objects could only stay if they were modern: a wheelbarrow in the garden; a wooden wagon-wheel on the wall; beams in a ceiling where they had never been (where they *were* original they were hidden behind softboard panelling); rustic stoves; a copper pump.

Women like Lamkje had darned socks until they fell to pieces, and it would not surprise me if they still wore undergarments that belonged to the trousseau they had received from their mothers in the 1930s. Although prosperity was continually on the increase, they still seemed to adhere to a strict division between housekeeping money and money for business purposes.

In many households this newly earned money was spent to a great extent on the ideal compromise: the do-it-yourself sector of lawn-mowers, percussion drills, work-benches, grinding machines, welding apparatus, high-pressure paint sprayers, electric screwdrivers, cement mixers, chainsaws and whatever else was required for helping the neighbours, moonlighting, and the on-going embellishment of the family home.

A lot of money was spent on cars as well. Certain villagers were of the opinion that ideally every lad over the age of 18 should have his own car – there were different rules for girls. Less attention was paid to clothes. Most of the older villagers were not very fashion conscious – although they all had their Sunday best, a good suit or pretty dress for special occasions. For that generation to eat out was highly unusual. And at parties one usually limited oneself to cake, coffee, beer and nibbles. The large-scale gourmandising that was common in other parts of the countryside, was very uncommon in Friesland.

For the young people this all began to change in the 1970s. They had more time, they were better educated, they worked in town and in offices, and they usually had more money. They went dancing every weekend, they spent far more on clothes, they even ate out on occasion, and the rest of their spending was more strongly influenced by fashion and trends as well.

It was extremely difficult, if not impossible for the Jorwerter shopkeepers to capitalise on this new situation. Most of the do-it-your-selfers were incapable of taking over the work of the carpenter and the plumber, though painting and whitewashing appeared to pose no problem. Initially Meinsma, the painter and decorator, refused to sell any paint to the do-it-yourselfers. "You're just helping them steal your daily bread," he always said. However, other traditions changed too – including the unwritten obligation to buy within the village – so that Hendrik Meinsma was forced to give in.

What is more, the hourly rate went up, and that meant that the work had to be done more quickly, with big rollers and other new-fangled tools. That was an abomination in the eyes of Hendrik. A very painstaking person, he called the paint- rollers "the curse of the craft". But the earnings were not bad at all.

Riemer de Groot extended his range of products still further, with new washing powders, new brands of coffee and tea, new cakes and biscuits. At first his turnover increased, buoyed up by the wave of prosperity, although it gradually became more and more difficult for him to compete with the assortment offered by the shops in Leeuwarden: five different brands of coffee instead of one; eight brands of soap in place of three; fifteen sorts of cake instead of five; and everyone expected it to be better and fresher too.

And furthermore, a sell-by date was now stamped on the wrapping, after which you had to throw it all away. "Even if the whole village had bought from us, there still wouldn't have been enough people," said Riemer. "With fewer than 400 inhabitants there is simply not a quick enough turnover for a modern shop. In Mantgum they just about managed it. Here in Jorwert we didn't." Refrigeration for milk and fresh food was something they had not felt able to risk investing in.

For Riemer and Lieske, the lifting of retail-price maintenance on brand products was the first step on the slippery slope. "That's when our fixed profit margin disappeared and they were able to start price-cutting and have special offers in town."

After that the car arrived. "If people had not been able to get to town so easily, it would never have happened so quickly."

And then the Miro arrived.

In the early 1970s the Miro was somewhere everyone had to visit: a big building just outside town (into which Riemer and Lieske's shop would have fitted a hundred times) where you could get everything you could possibly imagine. "You knew straightaway when people had been to the Miro. Then they no longer bought much at all."

But Riemer had not given up without a fight, and had used whatever means were at his disposal to admonish his customers. He told me about one of them, a farmer's wife, who suddenly stopped coming. "I saw that she had been to town. She owed us a fair amount, but I never mentioned it. That is until one of her sons let slip: 'Er, mum has gone to the Miro.' Then I phoned her. I said: 'It's been a few weeks since I saw you.' 'Um, yes,' she said, 'this and that.' 'And the lad did mention you'd gone to the Miro.' She went on: 'Er, yes, this and that.' I said: 'Listen here my good woman. It's entirely up to you where you do your shopping. But you are not using my money to do it.' Next day she was back in my shop."

When Riemer and Lieske noticed fewer and fewer sales reps were visiting the shop they realised they could no longer hold the decline at bay. In the 1950s hardly a day went by without at least one dropping by; in the 1970s you hardly ever saw them. Their sort died out too.

Decline is rarely the result of direct confrontation. It is almost always a complex and insidious business, a process that starts from below, while there is still nothing visible on the surface; much in the way that cities during their heyday often contain all the elements of their decline; that trading companies, banks and large organisations often experience one final flowering, more luxuriant than ever, while the signs of approaching downfall are already audible; so too, the fate of the blacksmith, carpenter and the other shopkeepers of this small village.

Initially, as mentioned, the wave of prosperity during the 1960s and 1970s gave the old village economy a fresh impulse. Carpenter Emke Dijkstra worked overtime when the loose boxes were becoming popular, and on new housing projects in Mantgum, Oosterlittens, Weidum and in Jorwert itself, and at one point he had about 15 men working for him.

Gais and Hendrik bought a washing machine and a better radio. The painters and decorators from different villages started to work together. When the Jorwerter church was restored, Hendrik took on the job together with a nephew; and the nephew in his turn put work Hendrik's way in other villages. He did the schools, together with the village painter from Weidum. In summer you could see them both cycling through the countryside of a morning: Hendrik in front, then the five-metre-long ladder, and then the painter from Weidum, tins of paint hanging from his handlebars, the ladder on his shoulder. You could hear their laughter some distance away.

The haulier was kept busy delivering fridges, washing machines, TV sets and irons. Hendrik van der Veer's village forge also did well out of the new domestic appliance branch. Although he had little in stock, most Jorwerters preferred to buy their new fires and fridges from their own blacksmith, partly from habit, partly from loyalty, partly because it comes in very handy to have the chap who can install and repair the thing living just around the corner.

The villagers were in the habit of making their choice at the display rooms of a wholesaler in Leeuwarden – sometimes the smith went with them to advise – and a few days later the chosen article would be delivered by the haulier, to the satisfaction of all parties. The smith had his provision, the haulier his run, and the customer better service than could be found anywhere else.

However, what appeared to be the beginning of a flourishing period was only a time of transition, a temporary reprieve. By the end of the 1970s the whole village was equipped with every imaginable household appliance. And because the smith did not approve of shoddy goods it did not look as though much more would need to be bought in the near future. Moreover, another problem appeared on the horizon: technology itself.

The blacksmith of Jorwert, like many village smiths, was a real all-rounder. He shoed horses, repaired guttering, installed fires, and thought nothing of giving a tractor a complete overhaul. For many years, on some Frisian ice-rinks discarded Renault-4 cars could be seen, ingeniously transformed by him into rink-sweepers. And the Harley-Davidson that he also converted into a rink-sweeper was an unprecedented success. He loved technology for its own sake, but nevertheless technology eventually stole a march on him.

The demise of the village blacksmith, unlike that of Lamkje's butcher's shop and Riemer de Groot's VIVO, had little to do with turnover, imports or mobility, and everything to do with technical advances, increasing complexity and the specialisation resulting from them.

It is probably easier to illustrate the blacksmith's problem by means of an image. First remove the front of an oil heater from 1970 and the casing from a compact central heating installation from 1995. What do we see? Inside the oil heater we come across a few taps, a flue-valve and a simple but efficient float. If anything breaks down – which, incidentally, seldom happens as there is hardly anything to break down – then a few taps and a bit of tinkering with the float usually suffices. But now look at the central heating burner of a quarter of a century later. We stare into a jumble of wires, relays, thermostats, automatic valves, electronic steering-systems, membranes, couplings, pumps and fail-safe mechanisms: an industrial complex in miniature, crammed full of pipes and electricity. And that was where the blacksmith's problem lay.

It all began for Van der Veer with the wholesale invasion of the gas fire. Up until the early 1970s he had fitted practically all the fires in the village. Coal fires were no problem at all, and oil heaters did not require much more than a pair of pliers, a thin roll of piping and a generous helping of practical skill and common sense. He could just get on with it without anyone interfering.

With the increasing popularity of gas fires the provincial gas supplier began to make all sorts of demands regarding technical and safety standards. The blacksmith had to attend refresher courses in order to achieve the status of "recognised gas-fitter", and that really went against the grain.

Shortly after that, practical problems arose in addition to the formal ones. Economical and comfortable central-heating installations became popular; they were installed more and more, even in the smaller village cottages, and began to replace the oil heaters and gas fires. The modern burners were, however, so complicated that they could only be serviced and repaired by fitters who had years of training behind them, and who did nothing else all day but connect and repair central-heating boilers.

Something similar happened with the forge's other line of business, agricultural machinery. When, in the early 1950s, the shoeing of countless horses came to an end the blacksmith lost one of his most important tasks. This gap was filled by machines. By 1970 every village smith could repair most of the machinery on a farm without any problem: tractors, harvesters, milking machines, manure transporters, that sort of thing.

This was no longer the case with the tractors and milking machines that appeared on the market after the 1970s. So much technology and electronics went into their construction that only well-educated young men could get the better of them. An ordinary, old-fashioned smith hardly got a look in any more. In this respect too, the farmers became ever more reliant upon the intangible economic forces of the outside world. Milk robots and other wonders of technology could only be attended to by the manufacturers' own experts.

In Jorwert too the generalist was replaced by the specialist. Fewer and fewer people in the village were involved in the manufacture of real things and with supplying products. More and more people were becoming wealthy by dint of words, paper and intangible matters. And the forge could not keep going by leaky guttering alone.

Most shops in Jorwert were snuffed out like a candle in this way. There was not even time to take leave of the customers. There was simply a clearance sale, and on Monday another shop had closed down. "You knew what was coming when you got a packet of biscuits with mould on them," said the schoolmaster.

When the first village shops closed down it was felt to be the natural way of things. Many of those small businesses had been born of necessity, the last remnants of the Depression years. What's more, for decades all sorts of economic activity had been trickling away from the villages towards the bigger towns; people were used to that. Even the more serious closures happened so quietly and gradually that most of the villagers only realised that every one of their local shopkeepers had disappeared after it had happened.

It had all been unspectacular, just as with the small farmers. Those who went bankrupt were not young people in the prime of life, but older people nearing retirement who, as the elderly solicitor put it, "confronted by the changing times, quietly capitulated".

A number of villagers made a conscious effort to remain loyal to their own shopkeepers and bakers, and struggled within the family to reconcile social loyalties and the demands of the purse strings. "The village provides us with a livelihood, so we must do the same for the village," Dijkstra the carpenter always said to his children; and most of the older Jorwerters agreed. "But that means what they have here must be fresh," muttered the younger ones, voicing their objections. "And to be honest it is much, much cheaper in Leeuwarden!"

"You shouldn't buy things anywhere else," Gais Meinsma told her children. When there were still two bakers she bought bread from both of them alternately. "You could tell by the taste which day it was. That smell of bread baking in the village is something I will never forget."

But there were those who, with the closure of the last shop, felt liberated from a form of social pressure that had become rather too oppressive over the years.

Something disappeared in Jorwert that had been an essential part of rural life for centuries: the local economy, within the bigger one. The boundaries between the two became blurred, more and more holes appeared in the dyke of loyalty and tradition, and suddenly the village economy was washed away and it seemed as though it had never existed.

Riemer de Groot shut his VIVO in 1988. A bit of a sale, and then it was over. The strangest part was that all of a sudden he lost touch with other people. "You still bump into them," he said, "but people have no time for you any more. You have nothing to offer them, after all."

He had left part of his shop intact, just behind the front door, as a sort of tiny museum of his own life. Behind it the sun played on the brown settee, the clock ticked away the time, and the cat lay purring beneath the wall plaque: *Yet thy Father knoweth that thou hast need of these things.*

The haulier stopped work in 1974. The painter in 1978. The carpentry business in 1979. The blacksmith in 1986.

Many small contractors in the surrounding villages got into difficulty once the influx of import that took place in the 1970s came to an end, and the wave of loose box construction had died down. For carpenter Emke Dijkstra the problem was just the opposite: he had too much work, not too little. Emke was a true craftsman. What he liked best was to work with a few helpers, be up on the scaffolding himself, with bricks and mortar, and then complete the administrative work at the weekend. When the other contractors expanded, and the competition got ever tougher, he refused to take part in that race. He gradually cut down on the jobs he undertook and became a one-man business. For a while he did specialised work for a carpenter in Weidum – restoration, spiral staircases, church pews, sash rabbets – and when he reached 60 he packed it in for good.

What happened to the painter was different. Hendrik Meinsma played the accordion in his spare time. He was a lively, sociable person and the driving force behind many village activities. But he was also a worrier. As finding enough work in the village became more and more of a problem, he was urged from all sides to give up his business. Being on somebody's payroll, funds for financial reconstruction, he found it all equally horrendous, and he kept putting off a definite decision. "What I don't want, I don't hear," he often said.

He had just turned 60 and felt he was still far too young for all manner of interim arrangements. And as a self-employed person, to turn oneself over to an employer would, in his eyes, have put the seal on his failure. "Business dropped off more and more, and he felt that this was the cause of his gloominess," Gais said. "But I think that in the meantime he was becoming estranged from society in general."

The amateur dramatics society went on an outing, a festive occasion. That night Hendrik was seized by another panic attack. Gais attempted to calm him down. At 7.30 a.m. he got up. Gais, weary, stayed in bed for a while.

An hour later when she called him for coffee he had already done it, in his workshop of all places, where he had always been so happy.

The small villages especially went into a decline that seemed to reinforce itself and appeared virtually unstoppable. Because inhabitants, businesses and shops disappeared, the government also invested less energy in the region. The friendly neighbourhood police station in Mantgum – from where, in the 1980s, brigadier Riekele Bekkema and his twelve colleagues still cycled around the villages – was absorbed into units of ever-increasing size, until the police themselves barely knew one another. They used to come to Jorwert at least twice a day; they knew every single street and noted any car with a strange licence plate. Fifteen years later they quickly cycled through once a week at most.

The other public services shrunk too. A fair number of sub-post offices were closed down and primary schools in particular got into difficulties. When a new family was seen in Jorwert the first question that was always asked was: "Do they have small children?"

The rural administrators talked during those years about "fighting a losing battle". The population continued to decline – sometimes quicker, sometimes slower, but always declining – which meant that the provision of community services was permanently under threat. And at the same time, the rest of the country was in a fever of large-scale schemes, which meant they were practically blind to the existence of other values. Or, as a mayor once said to me: "Your work as a rural administrator consists for the most part in keeping the last bus, the last shop, the last school going."

The village was hit by an accumulation of developments, and they all affected one another; be it the disappearance of a public transport system; the problems with the schools, shops and post offices; the closing down of the dairy factory with all the peripheral activities; or the increases in scale in agriculture. There was however one constant undertone: the primacy of money and the market above all else.

The school was perhaps the most important focal point of this process. In many cases it was the symbol of the village community, it was a crossroads of activity and encounters, and the school was frequently the last bastion in the fight for the survival of the village.

The population of most villages was ageing in any case – the leavers were generally young – but that process was greatly speeded up when the school had too few pupils and was threatened with closure. When this happened large, young families began to steer clear of the village, the last bit of drive disappeared, and the demise of the primary school was regarded by most as the end of the village as a community. That is why they often fought tooth and nail to save the school. Whenever a village association had the opportunity of handing in a list of requests to the council, they always put new housing at the top of it, "for the school".

Later on, more and more small villages came to realise that "new housing" did not always mean the same as "large families". Properties were often acquired by the well-to-do elderly who wanted some peace and quiet and whose children had left home long ago. And in the street where houses were for rent, they sometimes remained unoccupied for long periods, which resulted in an island of cheapness that chiefly attracted single people, frequent movers and other "low-income" tenants. I even heard that some village associations no longer wanted "new housing". The struggle for facilities had only brought them misery and frustration. There was no longer a pub and no longer a shop, but they still had the community centre that they built themselves, and that was enough as far as they were concerned.

So a downward spiral ensued that, as I pointed out, was vaguely reminiscent of the way ghettos are formed in the cities – though here it all happened in a quieter, calmer and nicer fashion. From the "Atlas of the Underprivileged" – presented by the Dutch Institute for Health and Welfare in 1994 – it transpired that, not only were certain urban areas seriously at risk from poverty and unemployment, but also some parts of the countryside. Whoever leafed through the maps could see at a glance, by the various bands of colour, where the most unemployed, the most elderly, the most disabled and the most people with low incomes lived, and where all those tendencies reinforced one another in negative fashion.

The large cities were clearly visible on all the maps: they lay there like tiny craters of problems, surrounded by a ring of highly prosperous suburbs and commuter districts. But on map after map it was apparent how the rural areas, especially those of the north, had entered the danger zone: incomes had dropped while they had risen elsewhere; within a decade unemployment had changed from a light-mauve colour to dark blue; and migration had changed from green to yellow – which meant that more and more people were leaving. The district in which Jorwert lay had gone, as far as incomes were concerned, from dark green to light yellow within a decade – from the first category to the penultimate.

This impoverishment was however barely noticed because the people on benefit were spread around the countryside, in contrast to the concentrations in the cities. Here, poverty was silent and not given to clamour.

All these changes took place in fairly rapid succession, and with many Jorwerters it was not so much that they engendered concern, more a slight feeling of unease. Towards the end of the 1970s that disquiet exploded into a serious quarrel within the village community, that would

go down in history as the "conflict about Our House". Ostensibly it was
about the exploitation of the new community centre, but in reality it
was about the social basis of the new village economy, by now as thin
as ice that is just two nights old.

It all hinged on the old nursery school. A number of village societies
had been meeting there for years. The building belonged to the Church,
but because the maintenance costs had shot sky-high the church
elders had suggested selling it to the Village Society for the sum of one
guilder. Many Jorwerters saw the advantages in this. The building could
be refurbished, and afterwards function as a community centre, a place
where all the societies could hold their meetings.

Naturally Eef and Jan from the pub took a different view. They feared,
not unreasonably, that two public buildings would be one too many.
After all, everything that the advocates of the community centre wanted
could, according to them, take place in the Baarderadeel Arms, with
its small conference chamber and its enormous room upstairs. "We have
difficulty enough keeping one business going, so let the village at least
concentrate all its meetings, parties and celebrations in the one place.
The village just cannot support more than one pub," was approximately
their reasoning.

The advocates of the community centre emphasised that nothing
would change: the drama club and the other societies promised that
they would continue to meet at the pub in the future, and only those
clubs that already met at "Our House" would stay there, and nothing
more. Even so, Eef and Jan could see a long-term competitor emerging
in the ever emptier village, and they dug in their heels: as far as they
were concerned it was no community centre under any circumstances.

The whole thing escalated, and tore the village community apart, like
a Jorwerter Dreyfus affair. The gulf ran straight through all sections
of society. Eef and Jan, more or less in a panic, mobilised their family,
the more progressive Jorwerters rallied around the community centre.
Skirmishes followed. The drama club, many of whose members were
advocates of the community centre, were suddenly no longer allowed
to perform in the upstairs room at the pub. There was a carry-on
at the fives club, where Jan was voted off the committee in a sorry
fashion. The atmosphere in the pub deteriorated. Old animosities
that never used to bother anyone rose to the surface: old, young,

import, native, everyone was suddenly publicly forced to make a choice.

Eventually Eef and Jan became isolated. The community centre went ahead. Complicated arrangements were made about what could and what could not take place in the community centre, and Eef guarded the rules like a hawk. The women's institute was allowed, coffee and tea were allowed, a funeral supper was a borderline case.

In the end the conflict cost them dear. They had antagonised a lot of customers, and something like that never completely heals in a village.

When I eventually managed to trace Sikke Kooistra, the last shopkeeper of Jorwert (he had since moved) I found someone who looked back with sober acerbity at the 35 years he had spent slogging away there. He was glad to be shot of it, he said.

"When we arrived, Jorwert was a pleasant, lively village. When we left it had all gone. Things were going downhill fast. At the end you had to do all sorts of jobs on the side. And we have our government to thank for that. Anything small had to go."

It had been his fate to become a shopkeeper. He had never enjoyed it. "Always hawking your wares along the same route. Tuesday the mayor, Wednesday the solicitor – and woe betide you if you missed a day, then you lost their custom. But, well, you had a family to support."

In 1953 he started a greengrocer's in Jorwert. "My father bought in the produce, my brothers did the peddling by car, and I did the 'venture-trading', as we called it. I would set us up in an area, my brothers would take over, and I would go on to the next. But after a few years one of my brothers became a nurse and the other a bus driver, and my father started a mink farm. So I was left on my own."

The Kooistras had always been adventurers. Besides the mink farm they had run a chip factory and a dog kennel for a while, they had done a bit of car dealing, refurbished the occasional old boat and even done some property dealing. "In the late 1950s, a large property would cost you about 6,000 guilders, and for the small ones I sometimes paid no more than 1,200. I sold them again for 1,800, well, that was a pretty decent return."

He had also seen the problems looming in the 1970s. "During an average week's trading I would sell one ten kilo bag of sugar, the supermarket would get through 30 or 40 bags." But ostensibly he too seemed to be doing excellently during those years. "Our turnover was really good at that time. We broadened our appeal, and that worked well."

After Christmas, for example, he always did a nice trade in left-over almond pastry rings and almond pastry rolls. "They flew over the counter. I would buy a job lot at 25 cents a piece, and I would sell them again for a guilder. I made more profit on that than on all my Christmas sales combined."

Every year when Sikke Kooistra went to see his accountant he would see that turnover had fallen. But there was always somebody else who shut up shop. "Then your turnover would stay about the same that year. The fall would stop for a while."

His fellow grocers, Riemer and Lieske de Groot, were socially-minded people and they were visibly affected by the disloyalty of "their" Jorwerters. Kooistra never reproached his fellow villagers. He was too much the level-headed dealer for that. "None of you should feel under any obligation to me," he always said. "If it was me, I might go to someone else too." Besides, initially the older Jorwerters in particular had remained loyal to him.

What he did find irksome was the way the newcomers put on airs. "They are the ones who started to run things down. I had no dealings with them at all. And each time they came for coffee they would point out yet again to the other Jorwerters how cheap the Miro was."

Another problem group was the young women from the towns who had married Jorwerter lads. "They wanted things that you just knew would not catch on in a village. They would see something on T.V., so I would order it by the dozen, they would take one and you would be stuck with the rest."

The incidental customers, in particular, aroused his ire. "Come Sunday morning, all at once there was a little fellow of about six standing at the back door. 'Um, mum forgot to buy matches at the Miro.' I pressed the box of matches into his hands, but a few months later that woman still owed me. 'Oh, I completely forgot, but then I don't come here very often.' I had to grip the counter hard to stop myself grabbing her by the shoulders, turning her around and shoving her out the door!"

By 1985, one third of Dutch villages no longer had a grocer's shop. In the Jorwert area you could only do your ordinary daily shopping locally in one out of five villages. A doctor's practice was to be found in only one of three villages. Things were not much better with the schools. The fate of at least half the village schools – including Jorwert's – constantly hung in the balance.

Public transport had generally been improved, except for the small villages – which was curious, because it was precisely there that the inhabitants had to use the bus to get to most amenities. A quarter of the villages in the Netherlands were no longer on a bus route. In 1973 Jorwert too, lost its bus stop, and although one evening a few youthful Jorwerters symbolically hijacked the bus, it never did return.

It was primarily the elderly, women and school children, whose independence of movement was restricted as a result. The children usually cycled to school, but the housewives and the elderly were forced each time to cadge a lift from family, neighbours or friends. The decline of public transport made them more dependent than they already were.

Nevertheless, according to the surveys, three quarters of villagers were apparently "content to extremely content". For the sake of living pleasantly in the country, people were clearly willing to put up with a certain amount of travelling time.

So what was happening in the small villages was not the same as in the deprived areas of the cities. No matter how bad the situation looked on paper, the experience of the villagers was apparently different to that of the inner city inhabitants. The houses did not fall into disrepair, there was no degeneration, and all the surveys indicated that the vast majority of the villagers would not move house if you paid them.

Apparently, the social structure of the villages could support much more than had previously been thought. It transpired that villages, in modern times too, were more than mere economic communities. The inhabitants identified with their village, wanted to fight for it, saw their village as part of an existence that they had chosen, and which had to be defended. Other values did, apparently, exist.

In the mid-1990s, activity in the small villages even began to increase slightly. The differences between large and small villages were slightly reduced. Apparently the changing composition of the rural population did not conform to one simple model: the endless exodus from the small village to the bigger town.

For example, where a village was situated was at least as important: in the far corners of the country, such as the most northerly parts of Friesland and Groningen, small villages continued to struggle, but they fared better if they were nearer the built-up areas in the west of the Netherlands. Everywhere community centres appeared and playing fields were laid out. Mobile shops covered a large part of the country, and in doing so partially compensated for the lack of a village grocer. Village shops that had somehow managed to survive the reorganisations formed co-operatives.

In spite of everything, many village schools seemed to withstand the waves of cutbacks fairly well. There were closures, but ultimately far more schools closed in the cities than in the countryside. The transport problem was solved, at least partially, by small buses that were available on demand, and in some villages they even made plans for the purchase of a collective "village car". In the smallest villages there was sometimes even an increase in the number of inhabitants.

New, too, was the change in government policy. In the 1960s the two per cent norm was paramount: small villages were not allowed to grow by more than two per cent, otherwise planning policy would be thrown into chaos. But the tide began to turn in the mid-1970s. The villages began to rebel against the systematic neglect of everything that was small and fell outside the grandiose schemes.

In some provinces the accent remained on the so-called core villages, but elsewhere the emphasis shifted to clear support for all villages, big and small.

In Jorwert itself there was little sign of the new dynamic – although things were not going too badly. Since the autumn of 1993 even the mobile shop from Mantgum no longer included the village on its run, and in the Leeuwarder Courant only the pub and the mobile greengrocer sent the village their best wishes for the New Year.

But most Jorwerters seemed to have resigned themselves good-spiritedly to the situation. They complained that the village had become quieter and less convivial since the disappearance of the shops, but they had solved the practical problems this presented between themselves. Shopping for the elderly was done by the children, the grocer from Mantgum delivered orders to the door once a week, the commuter-neighbour took her friends with her to town, another neighbour picked them up from the station on the way back, in short, what had seemed a disaster on paper had in practice been solved in excellent fashion by a flexible network of neighbourly help and informal care.

The village community turned out to be tougher than many of those who had penned the reports had ever imagined, and all these problems, large and small, had the effect of strengthening social cohesion rather than weakening it. What was lost lay chiefly in other areas: intimacy, conviviality, seclusion.

In 1979, nature brought the Jorwerters together one last time in a village resembling the cosy one of the old days.

On Tuesday evening, 13 February, it began to freeze, and at the same time a storm blew up from the east. An icy polar wind howled across the flat Frisian countryside. The streets, the roofs and the trees of the village were pelted with black ice, and then the snow came, more and more of it, heavier and heavier. "This is really going to be something," said the men in the Baarderadeel Arms as they sat round the fire, while the snowflakes pressed against the window-panes.

Every now and then somebody would go outside to assess the situation – although it was almost impossible to stay upright in the wind. The young solicitor and the schoolmaster got stuck when they went to see with their own eyes just how high the snowdrifts were in the out-lying area. With might and main the car was freed at half-past two in the morning. Whoever got stuck after that didn't stand a cat in hell's chance.

The following morning the Hilversum radio station announced that "there had been the odd snow shower in the north". In reality the snow was as high as the roof guttering. Nobody could get in or out of the village. The whole of the northern Netherlands was one enormous flurry of snow. That day the snowstorm continued to rage, now and then reaching almost hurricane force, and it got colder all the time.

Things seemed to be calming down the day after. The pub functioned as a crisis-centre. Anyone capable of holding a spade assembled there. Houses and farms that had been snowed in were relieved, paths were dug to front doors, and a special team of "strong-men" attempted to push their way through to the outside world, because the village was running out of bread. Towards evening the wind got up again, and new mountains of snow formed on the paths that had been dug out.

In the village everything was pooled. Riemer and Lieske de Groot's son, who had just had an operation, suddenly developed an unusually high fever, but neither a doctor nor an ambulance could reach the village. In the pub they cooked communal meals. Sikke Kooistra tried with might and main to provide the village with bread. Using Sake Castelein's tractor, an expedition was undertaken to the railway track near Mantgum and the necessary provisions were secured by way of the train. "And who stood at the front of the queue outside the shop, shouting for bread?" Kooistra remembered with grim satisfaction. "The ones I never set eyes on usually. 'Well,' I said , 'you can get lost now, too!'"

During the final years Sikke Kooistra turned his shop into a small self-service establishment. You could get anything there: from groceries to rope, spades and clogs. "We even had books, the Chameleon series, autograph albums, Dinky Toys, handkerchiefs, tea-towels, gas canisters, I lost track of everything I had. In the end it was one big mess."

With the passage of time his shop had grown into a sort of sag wagon for the local retailers. Durk Siesling stopped. Kooistra took over the fuel and the gas canisters. The little textile shop in the village closed down. Kooistra took the smaller wares. Thijssen the café proprietor-cum-trader closed his doors: the clogs and the farming gear went to Kooistra. Lamkje the butcher shut up shop. Kooistra bought a deep-freeze and, in his own words: "subsequently made a tidy little profit with the meat products".

Of all the shopkeepers Sikke Kooistra was the shrewdest, and he fought a long, hard fight against changing times. He kept inventing new things, and in addition he had taken on an extra job: sample-taker at the dairy factory. But he, too, grew lonely. Even the prizes for the village fêtes, that he had supplied all those years, were now being brought in from outside the village by the Jorwerters.

In 1986 he contracted stomach cancer. He stood behind the counter wincing with pain and this did not improve his humour. "I was happy to have a customer, but I was always happier when he or she left again. And always phoning for a gas canister: just as you were having your meal, you'd have to bring one round again. And always comparing the prices to those in town. There came a moment when I thought 'To hell with the lot of you!'"

He stopped not long afterwards. His son tried to keep it going for a while, but just over a year later it was over-and-out for Kooistra's all-inclusive-super-mini-market. The only residents who still worked in the village were the solicitor, the bank manager, the schoolmistresses, Sake Castelein, the greengrocer, the publican and the vicar.

Sikke Kooistra moved away. His son started a dairy business in Drachten.

One of Riemer and Lieske de Groot's sons flew the nest, the other one still lives at home, always reading, always in his room.

Durk Siesling's son went to work as a security guard for the Provincial electricity company. I saw a photograph of him in a coloured leaflet, behind an enormous control panel covered with knobs and monitors. "On average we deal with a thousand communications a day," the copywriter has him saying.

Gais Meinsma got smaller, her face became more leathery, she coiled her hair in a tight plait about her head, but her eyes remained the same. When she reached 65 she embarked on a course of study. "Don't imagine that after these past 17 years I am not enjoying life any more," she wrote to me recently. "Life is too good for that."

Chapter Eight

Intermezzo: the Church Tower and the Wooden Faces

ON SATURDAY MORNING, 25 AUGUST 1951, AT 5.07, the church tower of Jorwert collapsed with a thundering roar. Just like that, of its own accord, after 900 years of snow, sun, wind and rain, simply from pure tower-fatigue. It was an omen, a turning point, or just plain bad maintenance, depending on how you want to look at it.

That morning the solicitor – who had just started in Jorwert – was riding to work on his moped. "As I got near the village I had a strange feeling. Only after a minute or so did I become aware that something was no longer there, that something unimaginable had occurred."

Peet was already at work on the land. "The mist was very thick that morning. When it lifted, all at once we saw it: 'Where the hell has our church tower gone!'" Only the evening before Folkert had been sitting

in the rafters doing some pointing. "I noticed that there were some new cracks appearing in the brickwork." The sexton had mentioned that the weights of the clock no longer hung as they should. "They were just like plumb lines. A sign that the tower was already shifting."

For the villagers the moment of impact itself was like an aeroplane crashing. Gais and Hendrik were still in bed, and Hendrik thought his whole paint shop had tumbled into the canal. The butcher had just gone outside to take a pee when the crash came, and the scaffolding groaned and split into little pieces, and big lumps of stone bored their way into the gravestones in the churchyard. None of the living were hit.

"It was fortunate that our shop windows didn't break," said Lamkje. "They were really expensive!"

According to the newspaper report, by 7.30 a.m., the sexton was once again peacefully occupied with clipping the churchyard hedge.

What you see in the photographs is just a huge pile of stones and bits of timber, as if a bomb has been dropped on it, surrounded by about 30 men, women and children silently watching. The dial of the clock is still sticking crookedly out of the rubble, the hands pointing to the fatal moment, like sometimes happens with earthquakes and other disasters.

That minute at which the tower collapsed, and which everyone remembers, provides us with more than just a newspaper report and a pile of rubble. Thanks to this small disaster we suddenly have innumerable accounts of a single moment in recent village history, one minute of that August month in 1951 frozen in time as it where, that, if played back at slow speed, will tell us everything about village life as it was then.

First there is the time itself. What is noticeable about the accounts is that in 1951 a good many people were already at work by 5 a.m. The local tradespeople were still asleep, or just waking up, but, according to the reports, cowhands came flocking in from all over the fields when they heard the crash.

It is clear that in 1951 Jorwerters organised their days differently to the way they do in 1995. In 1951 the farmers started work at about 4 a.m., and the rest of the village emulated the early working hours of the farmers, albeit with a slight delay. The village was fully active by about 6 a.m.; in the evening people read the *Leeuwarder Courant*, there was a cards club or amateur dramatics, and by approximately 9.30 p.m. most Jorwerters were in bed.

Forty years later the church tower would have fallen into a village that was still entirely asleep. By 1995 the organisation of the Jorwerter working day had been largely adapted to city life. Like most of the other farmers, Sake Castelein started milking as late as 6.30 a.m. Gais Meinsma did not get up until about 7 a.m. "The exodus of the gladiators" took place at about 7.30 a.m.: that was when the commuters started their cars to go to work. In the evening the blue glow of the television could be seen in practically all the living rooms, until about 11 p.m. The newspaper was read less often.

The second conspicuous element in all the accounts of the tower's collapse, is that fortunately nobody was hit because it happened so early and there were few people about, in contrast to how busy it normally was in the street.

In 1951 the men still hung about by the bridge or near the solicitor's crooked railings. The women had their own seat, where they sat crocheting or knitting the whole summer.

There was the *junpraten*, the "evening talk", the next door neighbour who wandered by seemingly aimlessly in order to talk about the weather, the livestock and the world, conversations that sometimes bore more resemblance to ritual formulas, a string of meteorological observations, information about the land, the animals and humanity, sayings and oft-told stories that affirmed a way of life and made it feel secure, precisely because they were so familiar. The bakers, the grocers and the other shopkeepers and tradespeople caused a constant toing and froing. Forty years later the tower could, with slight exaggeration, have collapsed at any time of the day without hitting a living soul.

And finally the third element is the story of the reconstruction of the tower, and the unity of purpose with which, in the wake of the disaster, those few hundred Jorwerters frenetically collected money, organised plays, shows and other fund-raising events, chipped the old stones clean and managed within three years to re-erect the symbol of their village in all its glory.

In this respect village life had altered little in the space of 40 years.

Mutual solidarity and concern for one another were still stronger than in the city. Neighbourly help, as I discovered, was more than a favour – it was an iron law. Everyone kept an eye out for the children. The elderly were driven without fail to hospital or to their GP. It was not unusual for the very old to move in with the family during their last years. Neighbours would help in managing a difficult youth. When one family went on the dole, the whole village was there for them in countless small ways. The dead were still laid out by their fellow-villagers. Gais told me how she was cleaning her windows, the first time she had to do it. "The undertaker's assistant approached. He turned to me and said: 'You'll help her won't you?' Well, it was a question of grabbing a white apron and going round there."

I heard a story about a farmer who was laid up in hospital for a long time with a back injury while his wife and children remained behind in quiet desperation. Their neighbour said nothing, but he kept a discreet eye on things. He looked at the cattle, and at the land, and gave the occasional piece of advice, no more than that. "That cow should go; you should breed from that one; you need a fence here; that piece of land needs more fertiliser." In this way, right at the outset, a social safety net was placed underneath a potential tragedy. And not a word was said about it.

That strong sense of mutual commitment – which you find in villages all over the world – is only logical in a small community where everyone knows everyone else. There is no anonymity, everyone has a name, and because many villages are well off the beaten track people are reliant on each other in good times and bad. Neighbourly help functions here as a sort of insurance policy, a way of spreading the risk, a clever way of exchanging tools, services and labour; in short, as an economy without money.

But that tradition of solidarity in villages is primarily – like it used to be in poor city areas as well – a tried and tested means of collective survival. In many places there used to be pieces of communal land; there was a large-scale exchange of gifts on important occasions; at harvest time and on other dates collective teams were formed; casual labourers usually moved around with others from their village; and people even emigrated collectively from the village to the city. The village was, in short, often a direct extension of the family.

That entire complex of traditional ties was further strengthened by the "we" feeling: "we" as opposed to "they"; "we" the Jorwerters, as opposed to "them" from Weidum and "them" from Mantgum. And if there was one thing that symbolised all this in Jorwert, it was the church tower.

There are great traditions: the traditions of a country; the traditions people are conscious of; the traditions of thinkers and historians. And there are the modest traditions: the traditions that scarcely have a name, the countless routines that are as well worn as a footpath through the grass. Whoever wanted to get a taste of the latter sort could indulge themselves at the Leeuwarden cattle market.

The Friday market had been held since the 1960s in a hall the size of a hangar, and the cafés where most of the deals were done were themselves small halls, several metres in length and breadth. They were bare spaces on the whole, except for the counters with coffee, drink and sandwiches, but by 7.30 a.m. the air was already blue with cigar smoke. The dealers sat at the tables, a dram of Beerenburg with sugar close at hand, the beer straight from the bottle. The cattle hall itself was filled with mooing, with wretched, long-drawn-out bellowing, with horrible suffering.

Farmers no longer came here very often – they did not have the time, and they no longer had any farmhands to keep an eye on things in their absence. Neither was the quality of the livestock anything to be proud of – a good, productive cow would have been sold long before on the farm itself, privately, and the rest usually changed hands for export and the butcher's shop without coming to market.

"If you threw out all the pensioners and those on benefit, it would go really quiet round here," the dealers at my table joked. But even so, there was still a game being played which had a thousand ancient rules, none of which an outsider could ever hope to grasp.

For a start there was the clothing worn by the average dealer. Almost every one of them wore clogs and carried a walking stick or cane. But apart from that they wore every imaginable sort of hat and coat under the sun. Some of them wore a dust coat or an overall underneath, but others were strolling around in their best blue suits, spattered with manure, with a white shirt and tie, and again, beneath that a pair of clogs. Someone else was dressed in a T-shirt and straw hat. A fat man passed by in a dust coat, with a yachting cap on his head. Further up stood a youth in clogs, jeans, an old cap, and a leather jacket with a grey waistcoat underneath. Waving his cane in the air he looked round for some trade, and in the meanwhile he whistled a song. Sometimes there would be a brief murmuring, a small gathering, an incomprehensible slapping of the hands, a few shouts.

Everyone here was acting in their own play, everyone had a different image: the cattle dealers respectable, the sheep-traders small-time hucksters, the horse traders boozy, the knackers quick and efficient.

I found myself at a table with Van der Zweep and his friends, a gathering of older dealers.

"Don't you have any yearlings for me?"

"None."

"But the fields are full of them."

"We'll see."

I gathered that trade was slack. The butchers — major customers here as they need a thousand head of cattle a week — had fixed a price among themselves. Many dealers were faced with the prospect of getting less for their cattle than they had paid.

"They'll cough up eventually, mark my words," said van der Zweep calmly. "They have to get those thousand cows from somewhere, after all."

An old farmer with a ruddy, pockmarked face came by to settle up. Twenty yearlings: 26,000 guilders in a white envelope. Van der Zweep took the envelope and put it in his inside pocket without counting it. "That man would sooner die than do me out of 25 cents," he said, when the farmer had disappeared into the crowd again.

"Have you got any yearlings, Sietse?"

"Yes, but I need them myself."

"Haven't you any spare?"

A secretary from a big export concern arrived at our table. She brought the cheques and the computer transcripts of the latest transactions. She knew everyone, and everyone always came to the Friday market, so it was quicker than the post.

Van der Zweep had the hump: in order to exchange the cheques for cash they used to just walk upstairs to the banks, which had branches on the upper floor of the market. "Now you can't even get 25 cents," he complained. "Cheques, paper, things have only got slower and more complicated." It was against all his principles: when the beasts leave the premises they should be paid for.

When, early on a Friday morning in 1993, a raid on one of the branches of the banks was only just foiled (the robbers had sawed their way down through the roof, but the Securicor van had not yet arrived), the banks had withdrawn this service.

The traders only paid cash among themselves now. And van der Zweep knew of a branch where he could still obtain his thousand-guilder notes. Trust was indispensable in this world. "If a trader fails just once to honour his debt, it will be all over the market the follow-ing week."

The last few cattle were standing in the hall, bony and streaked with shit, the butchers' numbers already inscribed on their flanks in red felt-tip. The whole hall was filled with wailing. At the back the herds were being driven to the cattle lorries. Some of the pigs were leaving on a voyage of death to Italy, to be slaughtered and sent back here as neatly packaged Parma ham.

One cow lay panting, collapsed in an unnatural fashion, foaming at the mouth. Another wandered about on its own, gave a few final high-kicks, slithered its way over the treacherous dung covering the concrete floor. Nobody gave the animal a second glance and later on I saw it sidle up to a group of fellow-sufferers.

"Klaske, could we have another round please?" Klaske made my day. She looked like Doris Day in 1953.

A real village has something timeless about it. The meetings of the Jorwert branch of the women's institute unfailingly take place according to the same abiding routine: a song, a bible reading, somebody reads an extract from a book of Frisian stories, then a cup of tea, a quiz or similar game, another burst of singing, and then off home again.

Social evenings in the village follow a set pattern, with a few acts, a play and a raffle. The plays would not have been out of place in 1955, or 1935: they always feature the same young farmhand, a farmer, a village idiot, a fop from the city and a girl, but everyone enjoys them. The merke celebrations keep to a strict programme: games on Friday afternoon, musical chairs on the fives court on Friday evening, followed by a play and a party, and on Saturday at 8 a.m. the bells are rung to get everyone out of bed for the tilting.

Specific games, specific social events, three times round the church at burials, they were all part of the set rituals that, precisely because they are so invariable, safeguard the unity within the community. You realise just how strict those rules are when someone threatens to contravene them: when Cor Wiedijk accidentally makes a wrong turn around the church; when it pours with rain at the *merke* and the suggestion that the musical chairs be skipped causes a virtual revolt among the elderly; when the young people discover that suggesting that the tilting be held at a different time is equivalent to knocking their heads against a brick wall.

It is therefore hardly surprising, in the wake of 25 August 1951, that Jorwert set about rebuilding the church tower with such vigour. Order had to be hastily restored. The carpenter fashioned a savings box in the form of a miniature tower. Led by Lex Karsemeijer, the Bussum Radio Choral Society, Pro Musica, sang for Jorwert. Folkert collected a bag full of money with his playing. Piet Douma, the village clockmaker-cum-bicycle repairman fished the parts of the timepiece out of the wreckage – he even retrieved some from the surface of the new road that was laced with fragments of tower. A play was performed in the solicitor's garden – the beginning of the Iepenloftspul tradition.

The rebuilding of the Jorwerter church tower was, in short, one great explosion of village solidarity, mixed with a fair dose of chauvinism – after all it did concern the Jorwerters' most important symbol of unity. And all this would probably have still taken place in much the same way in 1995. In spite of urbanisation, individualisation and television, Jorwert had changed little in that respect.

A similar unifying role was played by the Frisian language.

One young man living in Jorwert refused to do his army conscription because – as he explained to the Defence Minister in a letter written in Frisian – there was too great a risk that the Dutch army might one day attack Friesland. And occasionally someone speaking Dutch would be ridiculed, as if the clothes he was wearing were too fancy. But most of the villagers employed their bilingualism with good grace.

The village newspaper continued – albeit after some discussion – to be written in Frisian. "You wouldn't write a Dutch newspaper in English just because there are a few English people living in the Netherlands would you?" Copy written in Dutch was printed in Dutch, as were important announcements.

Nevertheless, the touchstone for every newcomer was a willingness to learn the village's own language. One of the import women told me that she had always felt an outsider until, after about ten years, she learned to speak perfect Frisian. "People spoke Dutch to me, but you could tell they were not at ease with it," she said. "If you learn Frisian it's a sign that you intend to live and work here permanently." But she was still occasionally caught using an archaic word learned on her course that no living person would ever use.

The language, the repetition the and the reliving, brings with it a feeling of oneness that bridges time.

In Jorwert almost all my neighbours ate a hot meal at lunchtime – including those who no longer had anything to do with farming. Many older farmers still rose at about 5 a.m., as if driven mercilessly from their beds by a secret alarm bell. Even though it became possible, once the cooling tanks arrived, to start work at, say, 6.30 a.m. instead of 5 a.m. – since the milk churns no longer had to be at the side of the road by 7 a.m. – it was a few decades before farmers took advantage of this freedom.

In the villages of old, that shared rhythm of life often developed into a system of detailed protocols that kept society ticking over, like the well-oiled mechanism of a clock. Nothing was left to chance. There were rules for everything. For instance, who and when you could visit, who to invite to weddings and funerals, who could visit a new mother and child, what should be eaten and drunk at such times, how to receive new neighbours, who should care for the horses on specific occasions, everything according to a familiar model of longstanding reciprocity. The times to get up and to sow, plant and harvest were all fixed too, and the working methods, all according to a single great unwritten norm.

That mechanical aspect was characteristic of almost all the farming villages of the world.

Polish shepherds had fixed rules, embodied in all sorts of magic formulas and ceremonies – enforced by a *baca* or chief shepherd – for grazing, milking and the processing of the milk, and any contravention was tantamount to evoking misfortune. The same applied to the use of new techniques. Matches could not be used in the milking huts where one was only allowed to strike a fire by the traditional flint stone method otherwise the milk would turn sour.

In Russia, Tolstoy's gentleman farmer Stepan Lewin complains in *Anna Karenina* that his villagers are good at only one thing – ruining all forms of progress: "They sell the tyres from the wheels, and they drink the money: they throw screws into the thresher to render it useless. They have a dread of all those things that, in their eyes, are unnecessary."

In the Netherlands, during that same period, the most progressive farmers were spreading the first fertiliser by night – out of fear of backbiting by the rest. Even the fact that we still eat farm cheese from Zuid-Holland is due to the power of the old village rules. Although by 1900 farmers all over the country were beginning to take their milk to the dairy factory, the farmer's wives south of the IJ insisted on continuing to make their own cheese.

No economic explanation could be found for that difference. However, according to sociological research carried out in the 1950s, the tradition of home-made cheese-making in Zuid-Holland – which meant a great deal of extra work for the farmer's wives – was apparently strongly related to local beliefs about what was "done" and "not done". For women in the vicinity of Woerden, Leiden and Gouda, it was a great honour to be known as a "good cheese-makers". And it was an honour they were not prepared to relinquish.

Villages also had hard and fast rules where money was concerned. When Tolstoy's gentleman farmer visited the city, "the bank notes fluttered from his hand like a flock of tiny birds". He kept thinking that a dinner "represented nine quarter measures of corn in worth" that had been mowed and bound into sheaves, threshed and sorted, graded and measured into sacks.

This applied to the Jorwerters as well. They too retained a certain reluctance to spend money. Many older villagers remained thrifty. Eef from the pub, for example, and she was proud of it too. She loved handsome, good and durable things. "We still have the furniture that we had when we got married 30 years ago," she told me. "Others have replaced their furniture four times over." She thought this was wasteful. "You buy something new if the old one is worn out and can no longer be repaired, and if you want something really special you save up for it, that's what I was taught. I can't throw anything away, no food either, nothing."

Eef, as I have said, was the daughter of a poor farmer who also did some cattle trading, and money was scarce. Or, to put it more accurately, money at home was divided up into two entirely distinct categories. Of course there always had to be cash available for the market and cattle trading, but that was kept strictly separate from the family budget. And if there was any left over it was put away.

Eef: "Money meant business, and you set it aside for a rainy day. Money was not there to spend." After the death of her father, her mother had continued for years with the cattle breeding, and when she eventually stopped she realised that after all the endless slogging she was actually quite wealthy. "Go and buy something nice," her daughters had said, "a few things that you've always wanted, you can do it now," and they had carried her off to the shopping centre in Leeuwarden. But for her too, it was as though the birds fluttered from her hand. All she had done was complain about how expensive everything was and what a waste it all was, and it was only due to the fact that the daughters were aware of her partiality to pretty things that she now sat, very contentedly, in the midst of her new possessions.

A farmer prefers exchange in kind: the products should be passed from hand to hand, not the money. Money is not there to be circulated, but as insurance against bad times, disasters, illness, and failed harvests. That is why even rich farmers are seldom generous. Many older farmers who stopped farming had great difficulty in accepting that they were suddenly rolling in it. The novel money situation brought unheard of problems with it.

In Jorwert they told me about an old farmer nearby who divested himself of his business. According to the calculations of the men in the pub the transaction must have made him a multimillionaire, if only on account of the sizeable milk quota and the large chunk of land that he had sold. So everyone waited with baited breath to see what he would do.

Nothing happened. He just went on living in his immense farmhouse. He had never owned a car, and he did not buy one now. He continued to do everything by bike.

People he knew convinced him that he really ought to take the wife on a holiday. A holiday, just doing nothing and spending money, that was something they had never done. They spent a week in Appelscha and were thrilled to bits about it. A meal in town with the children was a sensation that they talked about for days. "Those old farmers have no idea how to spend money," they said in the pub. "They should leave that to us!"

Lamkje told me hundreds of stories about her husband's illness, her children's studies, about the end of the business and her own illness. Only later did I realise that she had been talking about money the whole time: college expenses, hospital expenses, the funeral. "I have as many as five boxes of pills, that's five times one guilder!" She converted every important event, all the struggles, all the pain, all the joy into money, because there was hardly any room for anything else.

And then there were the portraits, the eternal portraits that hung in every living room: the wooden faces, practically expressionless, wary of showing any feelings; the couples fused together and sexless; the hands heavy in the lap like tools or implements; the clothing black.

They had usually married in accordance with the traditional conditions: the man had to be hardworking and sober, the woman should ideally bring some land or money with her, and if she had a strong pair of hands as well and was canny with the purse strings, she was seen as an extremely attractive party. And if she was also known as "pretty and obedient", why then she was ranked as ideal.

Their portraits belonged with such sayings as: "The best piece of household furniture is a good woman," and "The farmer near the cattle, the wife near the kettle." Throughout those years their tasks were always strictly divided by that same system of immutable rules. And the productive work outside the house always took priority over the more domestic work – cooking, sewing clothes – inside the house. "As long as it stays in the cowshed!" the farmer's wives used to cry whenever a cow died or if there was another form of financial setback. They meant: as long as a problem does not affect life in the farmhouse itself we should not complain.

We know little of the emotions that lay behind the wooden faces, as they were usually people who spoke solely through their labour, their harvest and their cattle. Moreover, in the eyes of many townspeople they were crude and uncivilised. They overlooked the fact that the sensible marriages of convenience of many farming couples could indeed contain within them genuine feelings of respect, affection and comradeship.

The classic farming marriage was no better or worse than the sort of marriage that had developed in the cities since the nineteenth century, it was simply different. It was less romantic, but it was also less fragile. It did not proceed, as it often did in the city, from a strict separation of home and business, between the private domain and the rest of the world.

The marriage of those portrayed was part of a much broader way of life encompassing family, farm, cattle, harvest and village, and the feelings that the spouses had for one another were inextricably bound up with all of that. Their affection was based on one another's work and skills, on the shared joy and pride in the harvest, the cattle, the horses and the farm, on getting through the hard times together, on the same hopes and expectations. And love and tenderness were expressed through events interwoven with that life. "You are so delicious, my sweet buxom darling," a French farmer-lover once wrote on a postcard, "and you smell so fresh the only thing I can compare you to is a big field of cabbages."

In one of his books Robert Redfield summed up what were regarded by a rural culture as the distinctive characteristics of "a good life" and "a good person": "An intense attachment to native soil; a reverent disposition towards habitat and ancestral ways; a restraint on individual self-seeking in favour of family and community; a certain suspiciousness, mixed with appreciation of town life; a sober and earthy ethic."

These characteristics were visible in all the rural cultures he had studied, whether in South America or Surrey. He explained that this system of values was grounded in a constant interaction with nature. "Peasants find in life purpose and zest, because accumulated experience has read into nature and suffering and joy and death significance that the peasant finds restated for him in his everyday work and play. There is a teaching, as much implicit as explicit, as to why it is that children come into the world and grow up to marry, labour, suffer and die. There is an assurance that labour is not futile; that nature, or God, has some part in it."

It was this universal system of unspoken commandments that lay like a second dimension beneath the surface of rural life. It was an order that was often encapsulated in religion and the rules of the Church – but that was based in reality on the norms of rural tradition. An order within which time was not a continuous line of progression, but a cycle, like nature itself. It was an order within which life was not an end in itself, as it was in the city, but an interlude, with ideals in the past and commitments in the future.

And above all it was an order that was unimpeachable – and the plot of any country saga, from The Odyssey to the regional novels of Reinder Brolsma, always turns on this one theme: the restitution of this Godly Order. Amid the chaos of nature it was the only means by which people could keep fate at bay. Only in this way could they allay disaster, illness, failed harvests and other calamities – apart from death eternal, the ultimate fate of every mortal. And even that could be triumphed over, because a person could live on in immortality, thanks to sons and daughters.

Nowadays the old gulf between city and countryside has largely disappeared, and each way of life tends to complement the other, rather than be opposites.

With the passing of the years the village has not only lost a certain serenity and sense of tradition, but also much of its isolation, its oppressiveness, its repression, its cruelty, poverty and privation. And if anyone is conscious of this it is the villagers themselves. Nobody wants to return to milking in the cold November rain, or to toiling in the hot hay meadows, or to the fear of flooding, illness and plagues. Nobody wants to go back, and any farmer worth his salt nowadays surrounds himself with the latest technology.

Even so it is noticeable how city and countryside persistently differ from one another in some respects. Why do people in the cities tend always to be searching for novelty, while people in the countryside still prefer to steep themselves in their well-tried ways? Why does the city plump for speed and the countryside for slowness?

During my months in Jorwert I found myself one afternoon at Thom de Groot's. Thom was one of the last farmers who had refused on grounds of principle to provide his cows and sheep with the infamous bright yellow plastic ear-tags. His "Conscientious Objectors to Ear-tagging Action Group" had originally boasted more than 2,000 supporters, but this had eventually shrunk to not more than 250. Faced with this system of registration almost all Dutch farmers had capitulated.

We were sitting at the kitchen table in the family's centuries-old farmhouse in the middle of the wide-open Frisian countryside beyond Gouw. Thom was furious. He had just returned from a hearing at the agricultural board in the Hague. "It was just like a tribunal," he fumed. "The gentlemen had allotted us exactly half an hour; after that they were off out for dinner. A colleague heard them laughing behind the door, probably at us stupid yokels."

While the gentlemen dined, Thom had driven home to his cowsheds bursting at the seams with young cattle, his muckheap, his rapidly diminishing stock of hay, his chickens, cats, sheep and lambs that roamed all over the farmyard, his 15-hour working day, his sleepless nights, his principles and his farm, as full as Noah's ark.

Few people knew better than Thom what it was like to be on the receiving end of the authority wielded by the agricultural dictatorship. Slowly but surely his business was being strangled. In the meantime the calves – unsaleable for the past two years because they did not have ear-tags – had grown up. His business, suitable for roughly 25 cows, had expanded to double that amount. Officially he was only allowed to send cattle without ear-tags straight to the slaughterhouse, but the cost of the special transportation plus inspection was almost as much as the amount the cow would fetch. Moreover he had dairy cattle not beef cattle.

Everything that made a farm business viable was gradually being stifled at Thom de Groot's: space in the cowshed, land, manure, milk quota, feed, labour, capital, even his organic farming license was under threat. "I recently had to buy 2,000 guilders worth of extra hay," he told me, "otherwise we won't make it through till Spring."

One of his cows had to go for emergency slaughter, but it was not allowed to leave the premises. He calculated the losses for me, 15–20,000 guilders, apart from all the futile work involved. "You're battling against an authority you can't get to grips with," he said.

He knew that the end was imminent. The previous spring, as a result of all the unrest, a few young bulls had been able to break out and cover a few of the yearlings – still practically calves themselves. One of the victims of this "rape" had just calved – much too early. The tiny calf, hardly bigger than a dog, lay on some straw in the middle of the aisle of the cowshed. "It isn't long for this world," Thom mused. The chickens scratched around it, the calf jerked its legs spasmodically, and made little barking noises. "I don't know what's wrong with me," he said. "You suddenly feel so full of hate. And that's a feeling I've never had before."

"The conservatism of peasants is not about the preservation of power, but about the preservation of values," wrote John Berger, after years spent sharing the ups and downs of life with his neighbours in the French Alps. When Thom de Groot talked about his conscientious objections, he referred to "something from within". "We employ certain norms in our life and work. An animal too, should be respected for what it is. But now we are being driven into a corner, and there is nowhere to go any more."

Each trade has its own norms and its own aesthetics, whether it be carpentry, law or cattle-breeding.

Old village carpenters hardly ever worked from drawings or blueprints. All their technical knowledge was based on memory, and was restricted to the repetition of a few basic models and a number of variations upon them. In that situation rituals, routines and traditions are at least as effective at transferring knowledge as ordinary teaching – not in our dynamic city society, but in the old static country world where the future was seen as an uninterrupted continuation of the present, and the present as a true-to-life rendering of the past. The traditions were always passed on in the same simple and reliable way: through stories – often in the form of short, pithy, rhythmic proverbs and sayings – and by means of clear, practical examples.

The same went for the farming profession. Moreover tradition was an excellent method of passing on the intuitive knowledge, so indispensable when working with beasts and nature. After all a young farmer not only had to learn how to milk quickly, to repair his tools efficiently, to hammer a pole in deep, plus a thousand other skills, he also had to learn to trust his intuition, he had to learn to "see" that a cow was sick, "feel" that the weather was turning, "know" that the corn must be gathered in. And the wealth of experience saved up from generation to generation was indispensable to this process, in spite of all the nonsense and superstition that had crept in over the years.

*

Let us return once more to the everyday tradition of Van der Zweep and his fellow tradesmen, to their habitual methods of payment and their noticeable preference for payment in cash. That tradition seems at first glance to be merely irksome: it forced every trader to carry enormous wads of notes around, with all the inherent dangers of theft and robbery.

But that ritual of payment did, nevertheless, have an exceptionally practical background. It was of course useful as far as the taxman was concerned. At the same time it was an extremely effective way of symbolically transferring responsibility from the farmer to those buying from him. Because livestock is exactly that – "live stock" – anything can happen to it at any time, during transportation as well. As soon as the money was handed over the farmer was relieved of this type of risk. The cash payment also gave the trader an alibi to visit the farmer again, to angle for another deal, and by the same token the farmer kept in touch with the traders as a matter of course.

But above all it was a form of silent protest. "All cheques mean is even more control over the tradesmen, still more control over the farmer," said Van der Zweep, and most of the dealers in that market café in Leeuwarden thought the same. In their eyes cash payment was the action of an independent operator who viewed the powerful city institutions and the hectic nature of the times with disdain.

It was the same silent resistance that caused Sikke Kooistra to repeatedly refuse to stock Ginger Ale. "We don't drink that stuff in Jorwert," he would say, each time the teacher enquired whether he had it.

It was this same feeling of self esteem that drove Lamkje to keep her empty butcher's shop as neat and tidy as it used to be: the counter spotless, the red scales on top, the big slicer and the mincer behind. They had remained there, in defiance of the passage of time, red and stately in the white tiled interior, as a tribute to the deceased butcher.

And it was that same proud obstinacy that made the Jorwerter church tower indispensable for the village, and its absence inconceivable.

A peasant retains his traditions, wrote John Berger, "not only because it appears to assure the best chance of the work's success, but also because, in repeating the same routine, in doing the same thing in the same way as his father or his neighbour's father, the peasant assumes a continuity for himself and thus consciously experiences his own survival." When a farmer resisted the introduction of a new technique or working method it was not that he did not see the possible advantages — his conservatism was not stupid or lazy — but because the risks were too great for him: if the technique failed it would mean not only losing his investment, but also being cut off from the routine of survival, that steadfast stream of tradition in a changeable world.

According to John Berger the conservatism of peasants had nothing in common with the conservatism of the ruling class or the respectable middle class. It was not about retaining or obtaining certain privileges. The conservatism of peasants, Berger wrote, "is a conservatism not of power but of meaning".

It was an attempt to retain the experience of life of previous generations of peasants during a time of constant and irreversible changes.

In their eyes they were guarding an ancient store of riches.

Chapter Nine

The Goodness of Akke van Zuiden

 THE SECOND WORLD WAR SWEPT PAST THE VILLAGE like all great events, as something that was happening in the distance and from which only an occasional stray splinter would land in the village.

Hendrik Meinsma, Klaas De Jong and a few other men had to go to Germany to work. The associations were suspended, the skating club closed, the church tower was silent, the bells were winched down and taken away.

There were some who were on the right side and there was some who were on the wrong side, but when the vicar had to go into hiding between the roof boarding of the church, he did not have to worry about taking an evening constitutional around the village. Nobody would betray him.

Dutch people from outside Friesland came to try and get potatoes; hungry children from Amsterdam came; people who had to go underground arrived; now and then a German car appeared, and suddenly everyone in the village had forgotten where Kees Greijdanus lived.

One Sunday morning the vicar appeared in the pulpit again. Shortly after that – one glorious Sunday in the middle of April – he said in his sermon: "Liberation is at hand". That afternoon a few girls cycled out of the village to the main road. They saw tanks, and soldiers who were distributing chocolate and cigarettes. On the way back they picked large bunches of flowers, spring arrived so early that year, and when they got home they described what they had seen.

That Sunday evening it was as warm as summer. Everyone had gathered at the fives court, games were played, and there was dancing. There was no music, but everyone sang, "Rosa, Rosa, flowers on your hat" and the whole village danced as they sang to the accompaniment of a mouth organ, under the trees and under the starry sky. Many years later, on a cold afternoon, sitting by the fire with a cup of tea, while the rain pattered against the windows, Gais told me what had taken place:

"On our farm we knew quite a lot about what was going on in Germany, even before the war began. All manner of tradesmen were constantly visiting us, and they always had stories to tell. And one day there was a man, he came after supper, and he had just come from Germany. And he talked and talked. About all the things Hitler was doing, that he was having the roads made twice as wide, and that all the factories were on a war footing, and everything else that was brewing there. And I was so engrossed that I was almost late for school. They talked and talked, my father and that man, and it made such an impression on me that I never forgot it – and I was nine."

As soon as war broke out they gave shelter to a Jewish family, the Rozenbergs from Leeuwarden. A man, a woman, an elderly German lady, a blond daughter and a dark-haired daughter. They came to Jorwert as early as 10 May 1940, because they were afraid that the Germans would bomb their house. They were to remain with the Greijdanuses for two months, and Gais formed a close friendship with one of the daughters, Erna.

After the Occupation, father Greijdanus soon landed in prison, and by way of Scheveningen and Amersfoort he ended up in Vught. His motto was: "You're asking for it if you confess." Eventually he was released again.

"When he returned it was November," said Gais. "He had a very strange smell about him." Greijdanus was never to talk about that experience.

Not long afterwards Gais was removed from school. She was needed at home too much. Her mother was expecting another baby, and Gais had to clean the milk churns and help with the milking of an evening, and do the washing on Monday, the bleaching on Tuesday, the bedrooms on Thursday, and all the rest of it on Friday and Saturday.

In the meantime Erna Rozenberg and her family had drifted from one address to another, and they eventually disappeared in Buchenwald. "Because of their fear, because of the way in which they were threatened, I started to hate the Germans," said Gais.

Two young men arrived to hide out with the Greijdanuses. They slept in the storehouse attic. "We didn't have much to eat the winter of 1944–45. Trees were cut down all over the village, as there was no fuel any more, nor was there any power. You went to bed early with just a piece of wick floating in a saucer of oil. It was actually quite cozy, as no one here went really hungry; there was always enough milk and potatoes."

It was generally known who was sheltering people, but nobody was betrayed. "There was one paid up member of the National Socialist Party in the village, a farmer, but he was a really soft touch." That last winter, nobody went out after 8 p.m., and it was the claustrophobic atmosphere in the village that she gradually began to find oppressive. "It wasn't betrayal that was the problem, but rather the atmosphere of hatred and malice."

She found herself in the Resistance. "I was 16. I delivered weapons that were small enough to fit into a cycle bag, covered with cloaks and overalls. The way it was organised was extremely naïve. A young country girl didn't arouse suspicion. I just cycled around, I didn't know the others either, I carried out my own crusade.

"During the final year, especially, large amounts were involved. When you heard on the radio that such and such a 'delivery' had been made, and you had been involved, it was enormously exciting, but at that time I was primarily driven by a feeling of 'We will get through this, but if we are going to, then something has to be done.'"

Gais was one of the girls who had cycled to the main road on that legendary Sunday in April 1945, and had seen the Canadian soldiers handing out chocolate. She had picked flowers too, she had laughed that evening during the games, danced to the mouth organ under the starry sky – "all the pretty girls are so sweet" – and only she knew that she was pregnant.

"He was married, he was going through a difficult time. You lived in such close proximity to one another, and then that sort of thing happened. We lived from day to day. I had a lot of faith in that relationship. I thought: 'It's going to be all right.' But it was not all right."

She carried her secret around with her for months. "I only told my parents in July, and in August I left the village for a while. I could not give birth at home – that was not an option in those days. Eventually it took place in a hospital. I still remember phoning home, it was 5.30: 'The baby has arrived, it is a boy, his name is Cornelis, and I am fine.'

"My parents were upset at first, but they accepted it completely. Besides which, my youngest sister was one and a half – little Cor fitted into the troop nicely. My father said: 'He will be just fine,' and I was really grateful to him for saying that."

A similar feeling of trust prevailed in the village. "I was never bothered by people gossiping or talking about me. Everyone just carried on as normal, people accepted things as they were. I took Cor out with me, he went with me to parties, on the merry-go-round, everything. And later on he was always known as Hendrik and Gais's Cor, never just Gais's Cor."

She met Hendrik in 1946, a small, brown-haired, nimble man, who alternated between the two sides of his character: anxiety and cheerfulness. He was usually cheerful. He had been away during the war, and there was a difference of eight years between them as well.

"We had to perform in a review, and he had a good voice and could play the accordion well. We practised in the cow shed. The wonderful thing about Hendrik was that he was fine about everything. 'If we ever get married,' we always said, 'we will start off with the three of us.'"

After the birth the real father had in fact suggested that he divorce his wife and marry Gais, but she did not want that any more. "At Christmas he wanted to talk again, but I said: 'It's my child. I'm caring for it, and it is fine by my father.'"

Gais told me all this on the last afternoon of autumn. That evening there was a hard frost. The sky above the open countryside was dark purple, with here and there a few last yellow sweeps of light. The moon was thin and sharp above the horizon, a typical Saint Nicholas moon befitting a long, cold December month. All of a sudden it was sheltered and snug inside the village, people called out to one another cheerfully in the street that there was a nip in the air, that everything should be given the once-over, that it could easily drop to minus-seven at the weekend, that it was time to get the skates out. The arrival of frost was the talk of the village, scarves were donned, warm clothing was taken out of the wardrobe, and Jack Frost was slowly received into the village.

The following morning the landscape was petrified. The sheep stood silently in the cold sun, 50 grey-white statues in the meadow, as though frozen to the grass. The ditches were covered with a wafer-thin layer of ice. A heron stood, also motionless, where the water had not yet frozen over. The spell was broken only by the geese: they flew in from the distance, and all at once the sky was filled with their honking. There were at least 50 of them, three big flights woven together; cackling incessantly among themselves, they sheered over. In the village the cockerels crowed in the freezing air.

In the pub that evening all the conversation turned to skating and more skating. Was there enough water in the ice rink? Did we know that the ice rink sloped, and that consequently some parts needed a good metre of water in order to have at least 20 centimetres in other parts? Or that, worse still, the ice rink actually leaked?

The skating club committee had held endless discussions on these matters, but they had yet to come up with a solution.

Meanwhile, at the bar, they were talking about a boy from a nearby village, "one of D——'s lads," who at approximately 13 years of age, had been youth champion of Friesland once already. His achievements were weighed up with tender loving care, rather as though he were a young bullock. Nobody had properly observed him, let alone talked to him, but all the skating aficionados had him sized up.

"He is fine on the straight," said one of the men. "Only the bends, they are a problem."

"That's because he's left-footed," someone else felt. "Being left-footed is always extra troublesome, it means you have to train really hard."

"Yes, you have to overcome that."

"But mark my words, that young fellow has a lot of potential."

Meanwhile a few dozen metres further up the street, the Women's Institute was holding a meeting at the community centre. For the most part it was the older women who got together (for Lamkje it was one of the most important outings) and later on the following report would appear in the village paper:

After the introduction, the singing, and the report, we were ready
for our first cup of tea. When the break had ended everyone got
out their old autograph albums. Thereupon our oldest member

suggested that everyone read out a few verses. One woman read aloud a verse written by an old school mistress and others read one written by a vicar's daughter and one by an evacuee from Jorwert. The first pages were usually covered in rhymes written by parents. Here is one of them:

> May roses surround you,
> Flowers, soft and pretty,
> They spread their scent
> Throughout life's round
> And banish every worry.
> No rose without a thorn
> Is a saying old and true,
> May life bring many roses
> And but few thorns for you.
>
> 28.03.1912

After this we chat a bit more while having a cup of tea. Then we continue reading aloud from our albums and sing another verse. This evening gave us a real taste of our schooldays. Autograph albums were passed around mostly at school. We had spent another pleasant evening together, and all of us returned home content.

Next morning, the roofs of the village were white with powdery snow. The houses were huddled closely about the church, the branches of the trees bare and black, reminiscent of a Breugel winter landscape.

But that evening there was another club: the dancing club, or the cards club, or the drama club, or the singing club, or the billiards club. Or the *Iepenloftspul*, or the senior citizens association, or Amnesty International were holding a meeting. Or there was a reading organised by the Society for Public Advancement, about antique toys, or homeopathic medicine, or a trip to South America. Or the fives club, "Take Courage" was holding its annual meeting: "Treasurer's Report: everything approved and two new members nominated."

A total of just over 300 people, but Jorwert was well able to keep itself occupied during such a winter.

As long as the frost persisted, the ice rink was full of mothers and children during the day. The scraping of skates on the ditches and waterways could be heard everywhere. A solitary hare ran across the open countryside. Occasionally he would stand up straight on his back legs, look around, then start running again, across the fields, over the frozen ditches, zigzagging over the canal, stand up straight again briefly, ears pricked, then full speed in the direction of the village. The washing was hanging out to dry at a farm: red, brown, blue, white, against the white-green landscape. Behind the farmyard the muckheap lay steaming.

The clock in the church tower struck three times. A calico cat with hesitant paws stepped onto the canal. Oebele van Zuiden returned with the other ice-stewards: using a type of pickaxe they had made holes everywhere to measure the thickness of the ice. Together with hundreds like them in all the other villages, they formed the mysterious society of old men that people called the "ice-ways headquarters", and that every once in a while blossomed into the spectacular Elfsteden skating marathon.

"I have not seen such good ice so early on in 40 years," said Oebele with satisfaction. A couple of ducks waggled along in the middle of the village street. I went with him, and we turned left towards the new housing development. "If it keeps freezing for a bit longer it will be thicker than ten centimetres everywhere, then we will no longer need to do any measuring." Oebele was a thick-set man with a friendly ruddy face. He had started as a labourer and ended as a farmer, and was now happily retired in a terraced house with a tiny garden back and front. We stumbled inside and straightaway there was a grandchild on the line: "Grandpa, I won a prize!"

Oebele and his wife Akke started to unfold their lives to me. They told me how they had come to live near the village in 1944. He had been a labourer, together with three others, at Groot Battens, Meindert Algera's farm, where, in 1912, the first milking machine in Friesland had stood chugging. "A farmer was still a farmer then," said Oebele. "We were given our coffee in the cow shed."

He had stayed there, with a few interruptions, until 1952. Then all at once it had been over and out between him and Algera. "It was like this," Oebele said. "For 49 years I always started at four in the morning.

And I was always the first. Then one morning I overslept, and I got to the cow shed at ten minutes past four. And the farmer was standing in the doorway and he said: 'Damnation! Are we going to get started at all today?' I replied: 'I have been here for such a long time, I don't deserve this. I'm taking my labour elsewhere.' How that farmer regretted his words."

Akke: "He came home, still a bit pale around the gills."

Oebele: "We never mentioned it again. The farmer and I settled our accounts on 12 May, we smoked a cigar together, then parted in complete harmony."

After that he had worked at Tjerkenest for three years, for his neighbour, farmer Fopma.

"Fopma had a simple business, he did not go in for breeding or anything. I bought a bull for him – first of all he would have nothing to do with it – but the following year we had a number of splendid calves. 'Take them to the veterinary inspectorate,' I said. He said: 'I don't wanted to go to the inspectorate because it's not the cattle that get inspected, but the farmers.' Then his wife said: 'Do as Oebele says, he knows what he's talking about.' So I went to Mantgum after all. I stood in front of the gentlemen, and I saw that my calves were put into a good category. Fopma gained an A-prize and a B-prize at one and the same inspection. Well, I could not cycle fast enough to get home and tell him. But Fopma didn't want to go, and he didn't want the medals either. 'Those are for you,' he said."

The Fopmas did not have any children or other successors: "One morning in March 1955, the farmer came into the cow shed. 'We are thinking of stopping,' he said. 'The wife and I discussed it yesterday.' I said: 'I don't know what to do, since there's no chance of me getting the farm.' Then he said: 'If someone else can get it, why shouldn't you? But on one condition: that you take it over just as it is.' After that there were discussions with the land agent and with the owner, a lady from Wassenaar, and I was checked out. Fourteen days later the land agent dropped by. I took a deep breath and I thought: 'Here goes.' He shook my hand and said: 'The owner is very happy too, Van Zuiden.' Well, I ran home crying tears of joy. Suddenly I was a farmer! And with 30 cows as well! Someone like me, the sort that never had more than about six cows in the cow shed! And the first person to congratulate me was my old farmer, Algera. And he also said: 'If you ever have a problem, or need help, you know where to find me.' That was decent of him and after that we always remained on good terms. Now we bring him his food, with meals on wheels."

Although everyone in Jorwert was equal in the eyes of God, under the surface lay a society with well-defined social positions. What Oebele and Akke Van Zuiden did was still fairly unusual in the 1950s: they rode roughshod over the village hierarchy.

Jorwert too, had its regents, its managers, its old and new rich, and its old aristocracy. The Kundersmas, the Casteleins, and the Algeras were prominent family clans wielding a great deal of influence. These old farming families were looked upon rather as the village aristocracy, the bearers of the characteristic village mentality, and that effect was further enhanced by the fact that the cowhands and milkmaids who worked for these cattle farmers traditionally lived in – and the farm labourers lived very nearby – the farm. They usually left the daily happenings in the village itself to those who lived there – the tradesmen, the shopkeepers, and the labourers – but as in many villages, the surrounding area was the domain of a few farming families who were all related by marriage. And when it came down to it they called the shots.

The exclusion of the village inhabitants by the farmers expressed itself in all sorts of ways. There were villages with dancing clubs that only admitted the sons and daughters of farmers. Then again there were certain skating competitions in which only labourers could participate. Initially the Jowerter Society for Public Advancement had been balloted – and in practice this had meant that labourers were not welcome. The village hierarchy expressed itself in the same way as it did in all other societies worldwide: excluding some groups from certain forms of knowledge, owning specific tools, eating specific foodstuffs, and inhabiting certain types of housing,

In his youth Oebele had hired himself out as a farmhand in Abcoude, because he could earn one and a half times as much there as here. "That farmer had 80 apple and pear trees. But don't imagine that us laborers ever received so much as an apple. The farmer's wife was the only one who occasionally put something our way. One evening he said to us:

'I have just seen something I have never seen before: a farmer's wife walking arm in arm with a labourer's wife!' – Abcoude!"

When Oebele and Akke became farmers, all at once they gained entry into a different class, as though they had suddenly been promoted from sergeant to captain.

Oebele: "Before 1955 you were just Oebele and Akke, nothing more. After 1955 all at once it was Van Zuiden."

Akke: "I went into the draper's shop, and the woman said 'Akke – oh no, I have to call you Mrs Van Zuiden now.'"

Oebele: "And you were invited for coffee by the other farmers, something that never happened otherwise. We would pay our neighbours a visit and have to make a tour of the farm to see how everything was doing, and we would be told all the ins and outs of the farm, even about the labourers, which ones you should and which ones you shouldn't employ. But there was one farmer who said: 'What on earth is a farm labourer doing here, playing at being a farmer!'"

Akke: "When you went to a performance organised by the Society for the Public Advancement all the farmer's wives, with their *oorijzers*, would be sat in front with all that gold and silver on heads and bosoms, and it was all: 'Oh, come and sit here Mrs Van Zuiden, or here.' But I said: 'I am sitting where I always sit, next to Aaltsje.'"

Oebele: "The workers from the flour factory came with food. They never got anything from the farmers. They had to eat their bread in the cold shed, and they had nothing to drink all day. We always let them in, I never forgot that I'd been in the same boat. After that they always slipped us the best straw."

Oebele's predecessor, Fopma, was not fond of modern fads, but it was all grist to Oebele's mill. "Old Sije Hogerhuis worked for us. But we had borrowed a good deal of money and it all had to be paid back, but we managed it. We started breeding bulls with other farmers. Erik was the first bull, he went to Poland for 65,000 guilders. Carlos was the second, he went to France for 9,000. That was a nice little earner."

Eventually Oebele's success was his revenge. "A few years later that same farmer who had said that about a labourer playing at being a farmer, was standing at the door with a cow – could she be serviced by our bull? That is something I could never go along with. We hadn't forgotten what he had said. And eventually I got on to the board of the governors of the dairy factory, something none of the other farmers had managed."

Oebele and Akke stopped farming in 1978 when the milk churns were discontinued. "We would have had to buy a milk tank, and have a dairy parlour built and a completely new driveway would have had to be constructed for the milk tanker. I was 62. We sat round the table together with the boys and girls. It would have meant an investment of more than 200,000 guilders, and in order to make it pay, more land was needed as well. My eldest son would have liked to succeed me, but he said: 'So much extra debt makes it a less interesting proposition.' He already had a good job. The children had all left. Come milking time, we were on our own. I said: 'I've been working since I was 13 – it's time we made a plan.' After that we looked forward to it."

The auction-day was on 26 April 1978, and in the end it had been less difficult than they had thought.

Oebele: "My daughter and our grandchildren wept. They thought it was awful. But apart from that it was a good auction day, except when it was all over and the cows were being loaded into the lorry. Then I did think: 'There go my beautiful cows!'"

Akke: "When we came here, to the new housing development, we were suddenly on top of one another and we thought: 'What on earth are we going to do here?' All our belongings were new."

Oebele: "We were used to having space. On the farm you would watch the sunrise and it was so beautiful and then we would say to one another: 'Can you imagine that there are people still lying in bed?' But since we came to live here we aren't such early-risers either."

The tin containing the medals was produced from the cupboard. CARLOS FIRST PRIZE FRISIAN AGRIC. ASSOC. BAARDERADEEL DIVISION 1964. TIETSJES PAUL, THIRD PRIZE 1961. And at the bottom of the tin lay that simple gold-coloured medal with which it had all started. On it were two cows and a farm, and a message that nobody would understand in years to come: 1954, FR. AGR. ASSOC. DIV. BAEDERADIEL, 1ST PR. B. CLASS 5 OF F. L. G. FOPMA.

On one of those dark November afternoons, Gais took me with her to the school attic, where it smelled of mothballs and where hung the clothes from 40 years of plays in the solicitor's garden. There were racks, metres long, with hundreds of suits, skirts, jackets, coats, black capes, knight's armour, monk's habits, and party dresses. There were boxes full of shoes, shelves filled entirely with gloves, whole racks of accessories, everything by which the old village faces could be transformed into personages unknown. And Gais supplied the narrative.

"These were the dancers' costumes in *A Half-baked Gentleman*. This apron with quills was made for the servant girls in the piece in which the man of the house could not keep his hands of any of the women. We made this especially for *Don Quixote*. We were given these capes by the burial association in Baard, they belonged to the pall-bearers, they're bound to come in handy again sometime. This jacket belonged to Ollie the Bear."

While I walked around that school attic I considered a phenomenon that my friends in town always mentioned whenever they talked about villages. I shall refer to it as the oppressiveness of villages.

I realised that it was not without reason that plays, masquerades and dressing up were so popular at village celebrations: it was the ideal way to get away from it all, even though you were with the same people, to swap roles and patterns of behaviour, for the farmhand to become a farmer and the milkmaid Cinderella. It was the ideal way of cutting through the oppressiveness for a moment.

It was beyond dispute that a village could sometimes feel very oppressive to someone from the city. The curtains that were parted when someone passed by, a silence you could cut with a knife when you entered the pub, the little gestures and remarks. It was the other side of the picture: the inevitable counterpart of all that solidarity, caring and neighbourliness, was a large amount of social control. That oppressiveness could vary greatly from place to place, but a big triangular eye always hung above each village: we, the village, see everything.

We see how the vicar enjoys a meal in the garden, and what he eats and with whom. We see how our ailing shoemaker's wife is doing, as she lies wasting away behind the window – just as she herself, for that matter, performs the function of all-seeing eye for as long as possible. We see the visitors. We see who goes to which shop, and we count the clogs on the doorstep. We see who gets up late, or who has a boyfriend or girlfriend staying over. We bang on the door: "Ids, why haven't you gone tilting?" We know everyone's place. And because we live in such close proximity we hear everything.

When city-dwellers complained about what in their eyes was a village's oppressive atmosphere, they unconsciously touched upon the most essential difference between the city and the countryside. What they called oppressive was in fact an essentially different relationship between individuality and collectivity.

The houses and doors were generally left open during the day in Jorwert, and you could simply walk into people's homes. Nevertheless, this was where the eye came up against a boundary line. By means of few subtle signals – the type of welcome, the chair that was pulled up – the visitor was immediately made aware of whether or not he was welcome, and for how long. The "boundary line by the door" had simply been shifted to the kitchen and the living room.

Privacy turned out to exist in villages too, it was just that the codes and relationships were different to those of the city. People knew remarkably little about one another's financial affairs – they often remained hidden even from the children. In conversation the Jorwerters were generally more open-hearted than the average city-dweller, and I regularly heard more than was good for me. But at the same time I was certain that countless village secrets remained hidden behind the doors and windows.

In a city relationships are more businesslike and straightforward than in a village, because a city is largely based on individuality. It was the individual city-dweller who was addressed, who caused conflicts and made peace, who preened himself to avoid being swallowed up by mass anonymity, and who dressed according to the latest fashion, to avoid being seen as a backward idiot. In small, orderly societies none of this is really necessary, because people know each other anyway.

In 1995, people still lived closely together in this province. Illness and death were less distant and anonymous than in the city, and life itself was closer. Practically all fatal accidents were described in detail in the Leeuwarder Courant: a young man in a car with his younger brother hits a tree at high speed; a schoolboy is run over by the local train to Sneek; someone is stabbed at a disco . . . and each time, in the days that followed, waves of death notices filled the pages, and we got to know the dead better and better: parents, in-laws, uncles, aunts, grandparents, friends, parents of friends, neighbours, the school class, the fellow students, colleagues, the ex-colleagues, the neighbour's children, the friend from the pub. It was not unusual for there to be a couple of dozen death notices for one person, tiny black-edged monuments of solidarity.

Small villages continued to exist in the twentieth century because the traditional structure – based on farmers, on small shops and on walking distances – simply could not adapt to modern times that speedily. This was a blessing in disguise.

Unnoticed, a new division had developed within our highly developed society: that between the quick and the slow. The slow were not pathetic or deprived, but they were "awkward". They were the ones who, for example, were too slow for present-day social contacts and networks – so that they could not get or keep a job. They were the people who had difficulty with the modern type of relationship – so that their friendships were stranded. They were sometimes the families who, in the midst of a consumer society, lacked the discipline to cut their coats according to their cloth, and who consequently drifted into criminality, or who got into almost insurmountable debt. They were also the boys and girls who were unable to manage in an educational system that was complicated and often lacking in discipline – so that they left each school they attended without any qualifications.

The slow and awkward had always existed and would always continue to do so. The work they used to come by was of a low standard – but it was work. There was a minimum of care – but it was the sort of care that they understood. They had relationships that, in the eyes of the city dweller, offered little variety – the eternal and exclusive family contacts for example – but that family was at least there.

For years the countryside was an oasis for the awkward. The villages offered them support and structure. But more than that: the villages valued them for what they were because a lot could be learned from the slow and awkward – although they were not the usual sorts of things.

In short, in the countryside collectivity was stronger, and individuality weaker. In Jorwert I regularly heard older people speak about themselves in the third person. Many farmers spoke of "the wife" while their spouse was seated next to them, women addressed their husbands as "the farmer" or by his surname, children were addressed in the third person – "he has to sit down like a good boy!"– and at Lamkje's it was "would Geert like a sandwich?".

The first-person pronoun, "I", was unpopular in the countryside. This is well illustrated by the documentary It has been a Beautiful Day, in which the director, Jos de Putter, recorded his father's final year as a farmer in Zeeland. At one moment de Putter senior is sitting at the breakfast table, it is early in the morning, he chews his bread, listens to the farming news, it is one of his last days as a farmer, and his son asks him: "Father, how do you feel about it personally?" The father says nothing for a minute, then another minute, and another, the camera keeps rolling, and then he says: "How do you mean, personally?"

The Jorwerters had one annual explosion of collective feeling that put all the others in the shade: the annual fair or merke. The merke was – and is – a festivity given by and for the village community, and very few outsiders are admitted. It is not advertised, there are no large posters pasted up all over the surrounding district, you either know about it or don't know about it – and that knowledge simultaneously defines the boundary between insiders and outsiders.

On those days the Frisian flag flies from the tower, the swallows fly screeching around the church, the streets are decorated, near the fives court there is a merry-go-round, a cake stall and a shooting-range, and the field outside is a carpet of daisies.

In front of the church, children play with a huge kangaroo-ball. In front of the vicarage there is a race in progress that ends with an ingenious construction whereby the winner jumps on to a plank and launches a rocket. At Castelein's farm the children are doing something with beams and buckets. And at the neighbour's they are all walking on extra long slats of wood, a sort of cross-country skiing, but with six a slat.

The music for the matinee emanates from the pub. It is 12.30 p.m. Sake Castelein's pretty daughters are already seated at a table wearing fantastic silver-paper masks. The group is called Cheers, the female singer Jacky, and she is determined to knock us into shape. Her arms, legs and upper torso move as though she is mopping the floor, and on her face the word "work" is writ large. She rams the festivities down our throats like a gym mistress. Only when she's got us waving our arms in the air like madmen to the tune of the song "My Bonny Comes over the Ocean" and "Helaloe, Helaho, Hehe" does she permit herself a wan smile.

There is a lot of dancing in groups: in congas, in rings, everybody crouching down, yes, you too, – "Oh, the hokey-cokey-cokey – knees bent, eyes down, ra-ra-ra!" – and then up again. Ups-a-daisy! The twist: the singer is mopping the floor again, the whole place is shaking, and the young people of the village start to perform a frog-like dance. Glasses break, and a wig falls to the ground, high jinks with water pistols. The two strongest youths of the village have put one of the women in a tub, and are swinging her around as though she were a feather. Meanwhile Folkert is dancing with the Casteleins' enthusiastic blond daughter, Wiepkje, as though it were the most normal thing in the world, which of course it is.

Then it's time for the conga: "In, out, in, out – that's right – that's the way to do it!" We weave our way out of the door, and right around the graveyard, jigging and singing, past the graves of every Tom Dick and Harry, and then there is a spread laid out for everyone in the vicarage garden.

In the early evening it is time for the traditional musical chairs. It is raining, the grass on the playing-field is soaking wet and Lamkje sits in her electric wheelchair, shivering with cold under an umbrella. But it must go on, the musical chairs, it is a ritual to which the elderly villagers are especially attached. The men walk in circles in time to the music and the women stand stock still, grouped together on the field, and function as living chairs. One of the women gets a small ball pressed into her hand, and whoever is holding on to her when the music stops is out. In this way the group gets smaller and smaller, and at the end the winner receives a piece of cake. Next it is the women's turn.

Another game: passing buckets of water around very quickly. After that, something with wheelbarrows. A tombola, with handkerchiefs, oven-gloves, a bed-spread, a home-made cake, a basket of fruit, a cycle-pump, a small folder containing yellow serviettes, a pair of curling tongs, a bottle of wine, a radio, a cheese and a small basket of dried flowers as prizes. Lamkje wins a string of garlic.

A fire has been lit at the corner of two streets. All the village children are encouraged to write down on a piece of paper what it is that they are most frightened of, and then cast it into the flames. The children sit on the kerb writing gravely. They write down: "big spiders", "swords", "ghosts", "thunder and lightning", "racism", "the beheaded", "UFOs", "snakes", "vampires", "child-molesters", "murderers", "secondary school" and "having to die".

There is a performance in the upstairs room at the pub: a pantomime with a car, everyone sings along with the song "In wood and open field", Gosse Guchel spirits away a farmer's watch – to the genuine fury of the farmer's wife; Ymke van de Heide is dressed up as Dolly Parton; and a boy and a girl put on a Richard and Judy show, with a toilet brush as microphone and real pigeons glued to the stage. In the room the men sit on the left, the women on the right, and only the centre table is mixed.

And then it's dancing again, this time with the Jafros: two middle-aged men, a middle-aged woman, a 20-year-old girl punk and an immense synthesizer; they play polkas and the veleta. The older generation whirl around on the wooden floor as if they met one another for the first time only yesterday.

This is what a Jorwerter village fair is always like, be it 1995, 1990, 1980 or 2010 – even though, as we know, people and times change.

The Jorwerters' strongly developed community spirit had traditionally made certain things problematic. Conducting trade, getting invoices paid, as well as marriage and courtship, were often complicated affairs in a village. A marriage was not just about love and affection, it was also a leave-taking from the family, a transition from a large collective whole to a newly begun small collective whole, and it was something in which everyone took part. Often the choosing, building and furnishing of the house were joint activities. They would all join forces to help get the new business off the ground. And again, they all got together to help the parents when it was the time for the harvest or the spring-cleaning.

In the city a network of relationships was an address book from which you could choose to go to so-and-so for this, so-and-so for that. This wealth of choice was largely missing in the villages. If Folkert or one of the other elderly villagers danced with one of the young girls at the Jorwerter *merke*, nobody raised their eyebrows, because they all formed part of the same whole. In the city, farmers like Fedde and Minne would presumably not have given one another a second glance, but the remote spot where fate had deposited them both, made everything different. Your neighbours were a given, there was only one pub, and you had to make do with Folkert, Sake, Gais, Cor, Bonne, Riemer and all the others, whether you wanted to or not.

That made versatility a necessity – and often village life was indeed less divided up into little boxes than life in the city. Marieke Treep, one of the Jorwerter import women, talked in this context of the lessons she had learned from the village: "My friends in Amsterdam are unaware of so many things, because they always remain within those closed circles of friends."

"In the village you're always getting dragged to something or other, even if it is only a play," said Wiepkje Castelein. "How often in the city do you rehearse with 70- and 80-year-olds evening after evening? Very rarely if you ask me."

In a city you could walk away from ordinary life, conceal yourself among the masses, in the anonymity, or within exclusive circles of friends. This was impossible in a village.

Sometimes a village would divide up into smaller "villages of the mind". The entire Netherlands, for example, was dominated for decades by the division between Catholics and Protestants. Because few Catholics lived in the vicinity of Jorwert, in these parts it was primarily a question of the "religious Protestants" versus the "secularly-minded", or the "stricts" versus the "civils".

The gulf ran very deep. The children of "stricts" did not usually play with the children of "civils". "Stricts" and "civils" had their own schools, basketball clubs, grocer's, baker's, even their own local politicians and newspapers – the *Friesch Dagblad* and the *Leeuwarder Courant* respectively.

Even in the 1960s some villages still had two village fêtes, an "Orange celebration" for the "stricts" and a *merke*-type fair for the "civils". Children scolded one another: "Your father belongs to the wrong fête." And as late as the 1970s an important local fusion between two agricultural organisations fell through because the "stricts" insisted there should be prayers at the start of the meeting. The "civils" responded: "We're not at a damned church service!"

This rigidity of clan and belief had one advantage: it brought clarity and orderliness to a socially complex situation. It is no accident that that

division between "civils" and "stricts" was at its most virulent during
the first half of this century, when workers, small farmers and the petit
bourgeoisie had, each in their own way, embarked upon an emancipation
process. People began to earn a little more, children started to attend
school for longer, the contacts with the city became closer, and workers
and "modest folk" acquired political aspirations. In the short, everything
in the villages was in a state of flux, and the old order was thoroughly
shaken up.

In that situation not only did the "stricts" and "civils" groupings
provide a vehicle for emancipation, they also signified an attempt to
reorganise the village world — albeit with somewhat different principles,
and with different guiding lights and extremely oppressive boundaries.

I noticed few of these religious disputes in Jorwert itself, and
according to the older inhabitants this sort of thing had never played a
very big role. Jorwert was traditionally a Protestant village with a secular
school, and only true-blue "stricts" — like the family of De Groot the
grocer — had gone to Hijlaard for a Christian education. Apart from that,
Riemer De Groot had played with the other children in the normal way.

But I heard later that when he started attending Christian primary
school in Leeuwarden, he usually cycled to town on his own. And there
were those in the village who did not buy from his shop because he was
a "strict", and did not really belong.

Oebele van Zuiden had sometimes had his difficulties as a non-
believer: "If the churchwardens were parcelling out land and you weren't
a member of the church — oh no, you got nothing, there was no point
in even thinking about it."

There was another aspect that could enhance the sense of oppressiveness
in a village: a city has need of variance, the countryside has need of
regularity.

Not without reason did people in villages keep things quiet and
harmonious: once a serious quarrel had broken out it tore through
family, neighbours and friends with the speed of a fire-cracker, and the
end was often an inextricable tangle of explosions and fire.

The row about the pub and the community centre smouldered on
for years in Jorwert, like a sort of heathland fire. Eef and Jan Dijkstra,
the pub's owners, belonged to one family group, the advocates of the

community centre to another group, but, in addition, they all sat together on other committees: the skating club, the drama club, the village Society for Public Good.

So that the conflict was fought out on more and more fronts that had originally had nothing to do with it. Advocates of the community centre who were no longer welcome in the pub started their own card club. Fifteen years after the affair, there was still squabbling between the pub-owners and the committee organising the Iepenloftspul. The pub complained about the noise, the committee about the quality of coffee that the pub served to visitors. The full cups were carefully counted.

The conflict between Cor Wiedijk, Bonne Hijlkema and the other inhabitants of Funs (it started, I was given to understand, with a difference of opinion about the maintenance of the approach road) seemed impossible to disentangle. Those involved were known to me as none other than pleasant, open-minded people, but once we got on to this thorny problem they became taciturn, or said things like: "They won't even look me in the eye. Well, at least I know which way the land lies." "I haven't done anything wrong." "It doesn't bother us." "We are quite happy living here on our own." "It's a pity, but it's for the best."

So it was well worth a village's while trying to prevent this sort of conflict. That is why almost all small communities recognised a number of unspoken principles that gave stability to the whole, and which were quite strictly adhered to.

For example, in small communities almost everywhere in the world the principle of reciprocity existed – albeit often in the long term and in a complicated and roundabout way. As well as this there was often the principle that the young were subordinate to the elderly. Then there was the principle of the sense of family, of neighbourliness. Above all there was that most classic of village principles: the precedence of the community over the individual.

It was this last principle that caused people in many traditional communities to disapprove of individual behaviour. If someone paid more attention to his or her appearance, or behaved in a slightly different way, people were quick to ridicule them. "In Jorwert you always had a quick glance in the mirror to see how you looked, before you opened the door to go out," Wiepkje Castelein said. "You were always afraid that they knew things."

Just as change and regeneration are necessary in the city, so stability and predictability have enabled many rural communities to survive down the centuries. In a city children are ridiculed because they do not keep up with fashion, in a village precisely because they do keep up with the new.

It is sometimes assumed that rural repression was all to do with survival: for small, isolated societies it was vitally important to keep everyone on board. Too much individual freedom brought with it too much unpredictable behaviour, and consequently formed too great a threat to social cohesion. Nature itself was, after all, unpredictable enough.

I must say that social pressure in Jorwert was, in every respect, less than might have been expected. It was clearly evident that these regions had been strongly linked to the city for centuries, and the system of the thousand commandments had lost most of its sting generations ago.

Furthermore Jorwert boasted – undoubtedly influenced by relative prosperity and a series of enlightened vicars and schoolmasters – a traditionally open-minded and relatively liberal climate. Just as grimness and conservatism can intensify over the centuries until they form a black vortex that hurls cheerful souls from its path and sucks in the religiously orthodox, so the opposite had occurred in Jorwert: for openness breeds openness and tolerance more tolerance.

But countless other villages still remained, populated by hundreds of mothers-in-law with thin, darting lips, strictly governed by the triangular eye. And as well as that there was the continued prevalence of "the rural type of latent mistrust" as the doctor from Brabant called it 80 years ago. Even in Jorwert, people usually proffered unasked explanations for any action that was out of the ordinary, for anything that could appear not quite normal. You explained why you were walking round behind your neighbour's meadow. "It's more out of the wind there." You explained why you got the doctor out of bed for a sick child. "Then she went such a funny shade of blue." You explained how you could afford to drive around in a spanking new car. "My boss leases a number of new cars each year."

So, in most villages there existed a small, informal security service, and it was in part due to this easygoing system of consideration and responsibility that you could often leave your bike unlocked. But the downside was that all country dwellers were far more prone than city dwellers to ask themselves: "What will people think about this?"

This question is posed wherever people live and work together, but people in a village ask it more often, and because the margins are so much narrower, with more apprehension.

Will things remain the same in Jorwert?

During the 1970s, Jorwerter street life was still dominated by a whole series of old men and women. By Sije Hogerhuis for example, the Van Zuidens' cowhand, and provincial draughts champion; by old Kees; by Jan Siesling, who took his meals, day in, day out, at Dirk, his brother's; by old Ale and old Mientje (a bow-legged German woman); by old Hans, a man with an enormous head, ears from a Roald Dahl illustration, and a habit of hawking-up of a morning that could be heard by the whole street: "Hawaagh! Hawaagh! Jesus Christ! Hawaaagha!" – "Old Hans is warming up again," they would say in the village.

Sometimes they would walk five or six abreast, and later on they would stand on the bridge chatting. Meanwhile old Kees would baby-sit his granddaughter: he had tied some twine around the child's middle to keep it away from the water. Five old men, a piece of twine and a child. But with the exception of the child they have all disappeared from the street.

When I lived in the village Sije Hogerhuis was still alive. He was 99. He lived in a small house near the school and he paid the same rent that he had paid 30 years before: six guilders a week.

Every morning at 9.30, Akke van Zuiden set off to visit their old labourer. She helped him out of bed, lit the stove, tidied things up a bit, did some shopping, at noon she brought him a meal, at 4 p.m. she popped in again briefly, she did his washing, and at 7 p.m. she helped him into bed again. She had done this for 16 years.

At holiday time one of the neighbours filled in occasionally, and Akke also stocked up Sije's fridge with eight day's worth of food in the freezer and two day's worth in the fridge, all divided up into individual portions, plastic tubs with carrots, meatballs and pancakes for after's, to keep him going while she was away.

"After all, we have known him for 40 years," Akke said. "He used to come here every Sunday, for a cigar and a couple of drams. He lived with his mother who he in turn had cared for endlessly."

Sije had recently acquired new neighbours. Import. They did not even bother to visit him. As for help, he could forget it. Neither were the other neighbours very keen to help any more. "Yes, it's different nowadays isn't it?" said Akke. "But it's the only way I know."

"And it's the way it should be," Oebele felt. But Akke admitted that it occasionally got too much for her, especially when he had problems at night.

The strong village ties gradually loosened.

In 1993, research carried out by two social geographers from Amsterdam in the districts of Litternserediel and Boarnsterhim (which includes Jorwert too) showed that a wide gap was developing between the younger and older women of the village. While few older women worked outside the home, the younger ones clearly maintained a different, more modern lifestyle. "Their participation in the labour market is relatively high," wrote the researchers in their characteristic jargon, "they are of a relatively high professional standard, seldom work in the traditionally female professions, and for the most part have substantial part-time jobs a long way from home."

However all this also had a downside. According to the researchers these young country women made increasingly high demands upon their immediate environment, but were less interested in the social side of things. They predicted in their report that "as a result, the Frisian rural centres will loose their social flexibility."

Oebele van Zuiden felt that the village community had been changed by the import. "That's my experience. They're different, the townies, say hello less often. They live here in the village, but work outside, and the village itself no longer interests them."

Ids Meinsma, Gais's youngest son, blamed it on the lack of economic ties. "Nine out of ten people are no longer dependant on the village for their daily bread. The pub wouldn't make a penny if it all had to come from here. Twenty years ago that wouldn't have been a problem."

Marieke Treep saw the role of women changing: "A good housewife was someone who used to be highly respected here. They had an important function within the village and that included, for instance, neighbourly assistance. But as more women go out to work, all that is disappearing. I no longer drag myself over on my last legs to visit so-and-so either."

Sikke Kooistra, the former grocer, blamed the car: "Before the car, everything had to take place in the village. The whole village looked forward to the fair. This or that is coming next year, a year before it was due to happen they were already talking about it. Now the youth even go dancing in Groningen."

His wife: "It's the times you know, the times."

He: "You can't stop it."

One of the signs that something was changing in the smaller villages, was the increasing number of reports in the paper about neglect of livestock. If a farming business, through whatever circumstances, gets into such difficulty that the RSCPA and the authorities have to be called in, this says something about the social support within a village – or rather the lack of it.

A journalist friend of mine on the *Leeuwarder Courant* told me that when he had had to print yet another story like this, he had phoned up an acquaintance in the village concerned: "What the hell is the matter with all of you in the village? How can neighbours let one another down so badly?" According to him things like that did not happen in a healthy village.

In Jorwert a slight disintegration of the community could be seen in the lessening of interest in the *merke*. The merry-go-round used to be the sensation of the day. Just after the war it was still transported here by cargo ship, and the youth of the village would walk for kilometres through the meadows to meet the merry-go-round boat. In the 1960s, from the first moment the lorry arrived in the village it was impossible to keep Ids Meinsma and his friends away. But by the 1990s the children on their mountain bikes gave it at most a quick glance, and on the *merke* committee a suggestion had already been mooted to replace it with "something more active", a trampoline, or something similar. "It used to be one huge easygoing mass of people all together," Oebele told me. "We danced the polka, the veleta, all the old dances. Nowadays, we do still go, at lunchtime, then we all get together in the upstairs room at the pub, but there's not much going on for us senior citizens anymore."

"All the ladies went to the hairdressers in order to look their best," said Lamkje. "And you ran up a dress, and how they danced!"

Folkert: "And at the top of the Ferris wheel you could kiss and cuddle."

Ids: "The *merke* is still popular, but it is nowhere near the festivity it used to be. Not only has it to do with the city, but also the Jorwerters themselves are more individually minded too. It is 'quite' nice, 'quite' enjoyable, and it's 'quite' fun to take part, but it mustn't clash with your holiday plans. In the 1960s and even the 1970s that would have been unthinkable. It's only happened in the last ten years."

Very gradually the *merke* changed from being a home-made festivity to a more commercial occasion. According to most of the senior citizens, the "Variety Evening" was now but a pale shadow of its former self. "There's no point us going any more," concluded the elderly, after one of the farmers from Funs had leapt around the stage waving a bra. The volunteers who had worked themselves to the bone for the *merke* wanted out too, but there was no one from the younger generation that wanted to take over. The number of participants in the communal meal dropped dramatically. The three village viceroys – Gais, the bank-manager and the solicitor – no longer put in an appearance.

There was another type of article in the papers that caught my attention during the winter months. *The Leeuwarder Courant* regularly made mention of 80- and 90-year-old drivers, who had been plucked from the roads of the province because of dangerous driving. Sometimes they no longer even had a driving license, but they kept on driving anyway. Quiet roads, stubborn country natures, one could think of all sorts of possible motives for this phenomenon. There was one other reason: necessity.

Oebele van Zuiden explained to me: "I'm almost 80. I still drive, but once I can no longer drive, we will have to move somewhere else. The only way to still see people is in the old people's home. There, everything is within easy reach, you get your food and help is at hand if necessary. What's more, if the wife survives me, she will be on her own. She can't get around. What's she supposed to do then?"

Akke: "In days gone by we would have done things differently."

Even the Van Zuidens no longer dared put their trust in the village.

*

Just as village solidarity, on closer inspection, turned out to be a very complicated mechanism, so too was its disintegration; a process that could not be explained merely in terms of "city", "import", "car", "individualism".

First of all there was the role played by the government. While the papers were full of stories of "self-care" and "self-reliance", it was noticeable how little in practice the government capitalised on the possibilities still offered by the sense of community in the village.

Most of the big changes in Jorwert – the filling in of the harbour, the new housing – were almost all thought up by the inhabitants themselves. In later years this sort of initiative was hardly ever followed up. The path to the fives court, for example, was one big pool of mud, but when Willem Osinga offered to spend a few Saturday afternoons, with the help of a handful of men, putting it right (there were some tiles left over somewhere) and all the council needed to provide was a load of sand, his offer fell on deaf ears. The council later did it themselves. Cost: 30,000 guilders. "We could have done a lot of other things in the village with that sort of money," grumbled Osinga.

A second, not insignificant, factor in the disintegration of village solidarity was the role of television.

In the nineteenth century, as part of the formation of a new national State, a valiant effort had been made by the French government, operating from Paris, to civilise the countryside. To achieve this aim a *gendarmerie* was built in every village, as well as a boys' and a girls' school, where language, arithmetic and history were taught under a strict regime. This attempt to turn the rural population into respectable citizens was tremendously influential.

Something similar happened at the close of the twentieth century, but now to the rural population throughout the whole world. This time it was not the *gendarmes* and the schools that were the bearers of the new "culture", but electronics. And this invasion was no longer regulated by governmental rules, but by those of the market.

Television came to Jorwert gradually, along with countless other changes. The triumphal progress of the new medium was particularly visible in the falling number of visitors to the lectures run by the Society for Public Advancement (SPA). In a sense there was a sort of capillary action between the TV and the village SPA. The room at the pub could easily accommodate a hundred people, as indeed it did in the old days. But by about 1995 often no more than 25 Jorwerters turned up, 50 at most.

Willem Dijkstra, the contractor's son, who together with Ids had grown up in the village, put it like this: "Everything of importance used to take place within the village. Now everything takes place outside the village."

Marieke Treep: "It's no longer a tightly-knit culture. Everyone watches television the whole day. In the pub, topics of conversation used to be strictly limited to the territory of the village, and now they talk about foreigners and all sorts of other things. The village seems to be becoming less insular."

In the 1980s the journalist-anthropologist, Richard Critchfield saw how the television set had invaded all the villages he was studying. He watched the new medium gain ground in Brazil, Morocco, Poland, Sudan, Vietnam, Bangladesh, India, Nepal, Egypt, Java, everywhere his researches took him. The speed was bewildering. In the most remote Ghanaian villages it was almost impossible by the early 1990s to find someone who had not, on occasion, seen a football match on television, or the Gulf War. Even in the most far-flung hamlets of Mongolia the technicians and development workers had brought satellite dishes larger than the tents the villagers lived in, even before they had brought water. And the world of MTV and CNN swamped their universe, their universe of camels and naked poverty.

In those same years Critchfield, the expert on villages, signalled a significant change in the villagers he had observed over a long period of time, something in their mentality: "They felt the future would no longer simply repeat the past, as it always had done," he wrote, "but could be radically improved."

At the same time he saw how the universal television culture took over everything in the villages within a very short space of time. He cites Greece as an example: within two decades the ties of village and island were replaced by a mixture of individuality, and a universe that was mainly directed towards Athens. He quotes two older black American women from the USA: "There was a time when, if a boy got a girl pregnant, he had to marry her. That was the way we were brought up. Now you look at television and say: 'Hey, that's okay. This is okay.' And you find yourself changing your life, your standards, your values."

"TV's great power is the way it replaces words with pictures," wrote Critchfield. "Seeing is believing and needs no translation."

The exact influence of the arrival of television on the Jorwerter community is impossible to gauge – the city had always been close by, and anyway people change. But there can be absolutely no doubt that the bombardment of new game shows and "soaps" left deep traces. The traditions, the rigidity, and village oppressiveness were all affected too.

In 1986, Gais was the first woman to appear at a meeting of the burial association. This had always been a male province, the sort of meeting that starts at 8 p.m. and ends at 8.45 p.m. with a dram of Beerenburger. But now the women had lots of questions. Why did a man always have to be laid out by two men, why not by the women who had nursed him all the way through? Once, when a man had died in the middle of the night, the undertaker's assistant could not even find a second man to lay him out, why did it have to be like that? Why did the undertakers assistant always order the flowers? Why did everything have to be the way it was, why that way?

Whereas in the 1970s the youth of Jorwert only fraternised with the youth of Jorwert – anything else was unthinkable – in the 1990s the children fraternised with the youth of Mantgum and Weidem and Leeuwarden as well.

The villagers, including the elderly, got used to other fashions, ways of life and cultures. Whereas the one stranger that behaved in a "city" fashion used to be stared at everywhere he went, nowadays, evening after evening, whole hordes of equally strange people paraded by.

It was not just television that broadened their outlook; their activities too, became less one-sided. Farmers and farmers' wives were compelled to look for other activities besides their business, and this brought them into contact with new people and new worlds. Yke Castelein had, for example, become well known in the world of quilts, those artistic pieces of patchwork. She had been to art school in Utrecht, and her patterns had even been reproduced in a Japanese magazine.

Artists came to live in the district, and non-Frisian Dutchmen who had fallen in love with a farmhouse just outside the village. And people like Willem Osinga, who had close professional contacts in Texas and flew to Milan and back on business, but who could nonetheless be found holding forth to Willem Wonder the following evening in the Baaderadeel Arms.

And Gais, who as a child had even been afraid to go to school – "such big doors, such enormous classrooms, we had never seen anything like that at our place outside the village" – Gais started doing voluntary work, she became a home-help supervisor, did her training and followed courses, got her driving license, obtained a permanent job, and gradually became a working woman. "Of course it was nice to finally have enough to buy that little bit extra. But it also gave me a good feeling to be able to take care of others, especially as they took such good care of me when all that happened with Cor."

But Hendrik sometimes found it difficult to accept in the pub, when they referred to his Gais as always being out somewhere.

It was on a cold winter evening that Ids Meinsma appeared on television. He had apparently entered himself for the national lottery show. Main prize: 100,000 guilders. Everyone was talking about it, about Ids, and especially about that 100,000. It was a quiet evening.

Snow was expected. The door of the Baarderadeel Arms banged open and shut, and snippets of conversation spilled out onto the street. The farms loomed dark in the landscape. Just a few yellow lamps shone here and there in the cowsheds. In the dying light five children skated on the ice-rink. Their nylon skating-suits reflected blue and pink against the snow. Their voices rang out over the frozen countryside, and the scraping of the skates was magnified tenfold by the ice mass, as though it were the membrane of a giant inner ear.

Folkert came into the pub. He had been carrying the telephone number of one of Eef and Jan's children around in his pocket for a while, a lad who now lived in faraway England. He had thought it odd that you could simply dial England, as if you were phoning Leeuwarden. Now he informed us, casually but proudly, that he had done it. "I've just called England" – and for a while it was all they could talk about.

Then Willem Wonder, grumbling and cursing, took his place at the bar. His car radio, complete with carriage, had been lifted from his car;

they must have been professionals. It had happened in town, while his wife was attending the animal first-aid course. "I didn't want her to go in the first place. Now if it had been a computer course."

"Yes, the city," said Eef. "It's always the city."

After that the whole pub was glued to the television. All the Meinsmas were present at the hall where the show was taking place – members of the family had arrived from as far away as Germany.

While the whole of Jorwert watched with bated breath, Ids and his girlfriend moved quickly back and forth across the screen, in an armoured jeep they knocked over a 20-metre-high tower of tins, strung numbers together, scrambled and ran like Knights of the Holy Grail for the number 1, manœuvered with plastic letter cubes, made guesses about expensive cars and ignition keys, puzzled over an elusive password, climbed, fastened rings to magic wands and pursued obscure goals.

Chapter Ten

The Town, the Castle and the Village

 EVER SINCE THE UNFORTUNATE WATTIE VAN Hania was bumped off in his bedroom at Groot Hesens in 1569, public authority seems to have fought an uphill battle in Jorwert. The Jorwerters prefer to manage their own affairs. I do not know what it was like at the time of the *grietmen* and all those other eminent gentlemen, but by the end of the twentieth century one seldom saw a representative of officialdom in the village.

The head of the council's department of public works sometimes used to cycle through Jorwert of a Sunday afternoon, on the look out for illegal structures. Once there was also an attempt to check on the closing times of the Baarderadeel Arms — on entering the policemen found the solicitor, Folkert, and an old farmer, and they were duly evicted from the premises. And on one occasion there was a large police raid at Hendrik Meinsma's, when he forgot to renew the firearms license of the skating club's starting pistol. "Here comes the Baader-Meinsma group!" they shouted from the pub when he returned from the police station. The rest of the time they took care of themselves.

When the village children repeatedly damaged their letterbox on New Year's Eve, Harry Kaspers and Wytse Blanke simply rounded them up and gave them an hour-long talking-to. According to the report in the village paper it had emerged that:

     – that sort of thing happens when you have drunk too much

     – we sometimes get bored in Jorwert

     – eight people were involved in the letterbox incident

     – what happened was ridiculous

     – it must never happen again

*

Up until the 1980s the village fell under the jurisdiction of the police station in Mantgum, then under Grouw, later still the Jorwerters had fallen under the jurisdiction of Bolsward, and by then most people were not sure any more. They still had occasion to phone for the police when someone noticed a suspicious car, but the two constables who had driven out from Leeuwarden had lost their way.

One of the policemen whose beat used to include Jorwert was Riekele Bekkema. I had asked him if I could accompany him on patrol sometime, and so it transpired that one night the two of us were the sole representatives of central authority in the flat triangle which began near Leeuwarden and ended somewhere around Stavoren – some 800 square kilometres of farms, country roads and villages. Only in Sneek and the vicinity of Joure were there two other patrol cars; apart from that we were on our own.

It was a quiet evening. We had driven hard to Warns, 40 kilometres off our route, for what turned out to be a false alarm; we had listened to an account of an argument about a football in a garden; and there had been a report about a neighbour deliberately driving over another neighbour's bicycle. The engine purred, the two-way radio crackled occasionally, the torches were within easy reach, and we drove around for a bit.

Meanwhile Riekele Bekkema reminisced about Mantgum and Jorwert. "In those days you were really involved," he said. "If something was wrong they phoned and you went, whether you were on duty or not. Now you work from eight to six, you do as you are told, and then you go home. That is how the powers that be prefer it."

The area of his beat now covered more than 50 villages and two small towns. During the summer, because there were not enough waterway police, the "land force" also had to deal with most of the problems caused by water tourists. None of the villages had their own policeman any more, it was all centralised and streamlined from the central control room in Leeuwarden. Even the police station in Sneek was no longer manned at night.

"I used to know all the lads who damaged bus shelters," said Bekkema. "You had years when the village school suddenly contained a class of troublemakers, lads who kept crossing your path. Even when they were older and had left primary school. For a few years you'd keep getting trouble in their village, then it would suddenly stop. And then you'd get it in another village. But nowadays everything has been regionalised and streamlined. I don't know who the lads are any more."

Later that evening, while Riekele Bekkema wrestled with the necessary paperwork at the empty police station, I read through the weekend's duty reports:

A cycle had been stolen in Workum — *Have idea who the culprit is, will investigate.*

A certain Klaas K. had been to the station to file a complaint about being beaten up by a certain Rommert F. I read: *Rommert informed witness K. that he did not like his face and was therefore going to beat him up.*

In the Juliana Park, a man had been apprehended for feeling up two underage girls and uttering obscenities, *suspect's behaviour entirely according to type.*

There had been a fire at a farm in Pingjum.

A packet of cigarettes costing fl. 4.60 had been pinched from the Poimar supermarket in Bolswaard. When apprehended the female suspect had *reacted with waterworks.*

After that we had driven once more through the far-flung, depleted police district. "I don't want to sound complaining," Bekkema grumbled. "But if I am in Weidum, and there is a stabbing incident in Stavoren, that is 54 kilometres and three quarters of an hour away."

He explained that they were completely on their own at night no matter what happened: injuries, theft and minor arguments, but also fatal accidents, suicides and gang fights. "My colleagues in Joure will sometimes take a peek when there is that sort of serious report, but they are usually many kilometres away. On the other side is the sea, and you can't expect much help from that quarter."

In the middle of the night, at 1 a.m., while the villagers were sleeping, all those still awake had gathered in the police canteen in Sneek. The crews of the three police cars, that covered half the province at night, were having their traditional meal break: sausages, croquettes and salad from the nearby snack bar. The men from Sneek and Joure acting tough, Bekkema and his female colleague rather more restrained. The talk was about jobs on the side, sex and promotion. I gathered from my companions that one of the most disastrous things that happen on night duty was if someone hanged themselves or there was a fatal accident. "First you have to attend to the actual situation, then you have to notify the family, and the rest of the night is taken up with doing the paperwork."

"But if a drunk driver comes careering along the road that can be a real pain in the backside too," mumbled Bekkema. "Blood tests, confiscating the driving license, unearthing an assistant prosecutor from somewhere in the province in the middle of the night, and then you have to find somewhere to put the detainee, in spite of the fact that everything is shut."

The cell monitors indicated that all was quiet; on television there was a debate between a left-wing politician and a liberal politician; apart from that the building was hollow and empty.

Later on we drove crisscross through the district once more: Weidum, Mantgum, Jorwert, Oosterend, Spannum. "Just what on earth are you supposed to look out for, with just the one car in an area like this?" In Scharnegoutum we smelled burning near a farm. We looked round the farmyard, shone our torches in the barn and the cowshed, the guard dog began to bark, but the rest of the house remained quiet as the grave. We found nothing. In the back of the police car there were detailed ordinance survey maps showing every imaginable dyke and country road – since the reorganisations the regions had become so large that even for an experienced policeman there were whole areas that were *terra incognita*.

2 a.m. We drove through the south-west corner. The moon was high in the sky and a thick mist rose from the ditches and lakes. "Mist," said Riekele. "At night around here it can get so that you can't see your hand in front of your face. The only thing you can do then is pray you don't get called to an incident."

The strong arm of the law in town seemed to have left the villagers to fend for themselves. Only in the early hours of the morning would the first signs of life appear on the road again: the milkman, the post, the newspaper delivery vans.

Farmers are tied to their land, and throughout the centuries that simple fact has made them extra vulnerable. In the eyes of townspeople farmers were seen as foolish or naïve – but how could they help the fact that they could scarcely get away to gather information for themselves? They were viewed as being submissive – but you try and organise resistance when you are forced by the nature of your work to live in small units, spread throughout the land. They were viewed as an easy target – but how can you hide your livestock and your acres from robber barons, tax inspectors and EEC bureaucrats?

Practically all over the world, as Robert Redfield wrote, the farmer was more or less held to ransom by sections of society that were both recognisable and alien to him. He preserved his traditions by making compromises, by paying his taxes, by treating priests and political leaders with respect, by following the policy of his professional interest groups through thick and thin, by chasing after organic farming franchises, by recognising that there were people outside his field of vision who knew more about things than the people in his village. But there were always those other dimensions of existence: the life of byway and blasted heath, life in the terrifying city, life at the imposing castle.

There exists an extraordinarily interesting piece of research on the influence of city life on rural cultures. Between 1918 and 1920, the Polish-American sociologist duo William Thomas and Florian Znaniecki analysed hundreds of letters sent by Polish farmers who had emigrated to America. They found that certain phenomena typical of the city gradually crept into the correspondence between the leavers and those who had stayed at home, and that these undermined the traditional norms of the countryside.

In the first place they observed a slowly burgeoning individualism. They described, for example, the case of two sons who, despite their emigration to America, were still dominated by their father at home. One of the brothers was the "good" son. He was submissive, gave in to the father's whims and in doing so he maintained the old tenets of family solidarity, in the city as well. The other brother "was a bad lot". In his case the father's tyrannical behaviour led to rebellion: he broke away, he individualised.

The second fundamental change that Thomas and Znaniecki noticed in the letters of the emigrants, was an increasing hedonism – the idea that it is not bad to spend money on something you enjoy. Linked to this they noticed a marked striving for success, an ambition that could sometimes degenerate into servility or pushiness.

A third factor that according to them undermined the norms of the countryside was the steady conversion of all norms and values from "qualitative" to "quantitative". It was not the nature of an object but its price that became more and more important. It was not the value of a specific action that counted, not the joy in the activity itself, but how useful it was and what it would yield.

Now the Dutch countryside, as previously stated, was a special case. The differences between farmer and city-dweller in the coastal provinces were certainly less marked than elsewhere in Europe. Of course there were walls and gateways and embankments that divided the city in a judicial sense from the surrounding countryside, but in a social sense it was more a case of a gradual transition: from big cities, by way of towns and medium-sized villages, to the tiniest hamlets. Both worlds coexisted, as it were, without wanting to know too much about each other.

Most Jorwerters were indeed ambivalent in their feelings towards the city. On one hand the city was nearby, on the other hand far off. As late as 1970, a survey of the neighbouring villages (Jorwert itself fell just outside the area surveyed) found that half the residents seldom or never paid visits outside their own village. Only ten per cent occasionally visited the city – and in villages like Huins and Lollum it was only three per cent. But at the same time, according to the census carried out a year later, more than half the working population of Jorwert was already working outside the village and the vast majority earned their living in the city.

I found that most Jorwerters exhibited the same old ambivalence in the 1990s. On the one hand they were in practically daily contact with the city, but on the other hand anti-city emotions proliferated.

There were those who had a real dislike of city dwellers. "People in the city only drink mineral water," said Cor Wiedijk. "But if there is a war they will need us." Others regarded the city primarily as a miserable place. Wiepkje Castelein, who had moved to Leeuwarden, hated being surrounded by all that brick and stone. "In the city you hardly notice it when everything is iced over. In the village people talk about nothing else."

Wiebe, my neighbour, told me that the roar of the motorway had driven him mad. "When I decided to move to Friesland I simply looked on the map to see which village in the vicinity of Leeuwarden was farthest from the motorway."

The city had become too chaotic and hectic for Marieke. Or rather, it made her too chaotic and hectic. She felt sheltered here. "If you have to go to the city during the winter months, you always travel out of the village into the darkness."

"You can turn a knob and get music everywhere," said Lia, the wife of the teacher, "but where can you turn a knob and get silence?" She thought the city stank, and while she was still living there she tried to eat outside town as much as possible, at least then she could sit among the cow parsley. "I was scared in the city, here I'm not."

"If I had to live in one of those flats, I'd jump out of the window," said Folkert.

In the late 1960s a new map of the Netherlands came into being – and it was not distance that was mapped, but time. And on this map Jorwert was scarcely further away from Amsterdam than Leeuwarden or Heerenveen. That made taking the step towards village life a real possibility for some city dwellers.

Marieke was one of them. She had felt a need for peace and quiet, and a rather more compassionate community, and had come to Jorwert from Amsterdam in the late 1970s. In those first few weeks, when each morning she took her little boy to the bus for the infants school in Weidum, all the mothers stood in a circle talking. When Marieke said hello they did not reply. After a few weeks some of them began to return her greeting. And eventually the circle opened when she approached – but that was three quarters of a year later.

Most of the newcomers initially found themselves on the new housing "estate" that had been built between 1970–71 on the old land belonging to the church. It encompassed one street in its entirety – the Pastorijfinne – with blocks of houses with through lounges, plus a handful of detached properties. The whole thing was more or less tacked on to the old village.

The first time I walked through the area was the day that bulky household rubbish was collected. Plastic rubbish bags lay here and there, broken garden chairs, mattresses, old carpets, cupboards, a broken plaster garden ornament, and outside one house were two old television sets.

It was 12.30 p.m., everyone was eating and the cats had the street to themselves. Jan Dijkstra was sawing firewood, and you could hear it throughout the village. The man from the council was raking something.

A woman was cleaning the windows with a chamois leather. A handful of sheep wormed their way, bleating, through the village street.

A few days earlier the bell had chimed for a child, and one of the new houses now had a wooden stork in the garden, a garland of flowers hung on the door and in the living room a festoon of congratulations cards was visible.

The neighbours opposite had purchased a new, wrought-iron letter-box, grey, with a red post-horn embossed on it. Brown posts had been placed around the yard, together with an iron bollard painted white; they had also been put around the parking space, like a small landlocked harbour. Many of the houses had large nameplates made from clay or roughly hewn tree trunks, with the names burnt into them. *Peter and Rieckie*, it said, on one of the house fronts.

People in the village were no stranger to the import phenomenon. Labouring families had always trekked from place to place, and Jorwert was actually extremely popular because the pay was better and you could find work more easily.

But the wave of import that had arrived in the village during the 1970s had a different character. They were people like Armande, who found a second home in the village after her divorce, like the teacher, who was smitten with the dusky snow-filled skies and the far-flung landscape, like Marieke, who took a two-year rental on a house here, married the carpenter's son and never left again.

Their motives were no longer based on economic necessity. It had more to do with the fact that Jorwert was such a pleasant and attractive place to live, that the children were far less fraught than in the city, that a garden was such fun, and that commuting was not that bad really. It had been one of many choices they could have made, and most of the newcomers did not originally come because Jorwert had anything special to offer them, or because they were dependent on the village.

That also gave something noncommittal to this import: the Jorwerters regularly saw the new housing change hands – a frequency of removals they had only encountered with the poorest casual labourers in the old days. That gave the new housing the stigma of transience. If someone from outside renovated and moved into an older house it aroused great interest. But a newly arrived couple in one of the new houses, well, that merely occasioned a general shrugging of the shoulders.

So there were basically two villages: the small, detached Jorwert of the new housing estate, and next to it the larger Jorwert, ancient and settled.

That did not alter the fact that the first wave of import to arrive after the new housing had been completed seemed to the village like an invasion. All at once there was an increase of about 50 extra souls around the Jorwerter church tower, out of a sum total of 300 souls at most.

"We kept bumping into people we didn't recognise," Ids Meinsma recalled. "Yet another one that we didn't know, and another, bound to have come from the new estate too. The numbers alone were a shock."

Gais had found the import to be an enrichment of village life, precisely because the motivation and preferences of the newcomers were so different to what she was used to. In the old days you only saw women in the pub on Sunday afternoon, now the import women came and had a beer on Friday evening too.

That freedom made a huge impression on Gais. "I'll never forget a newcomer saying: 'You people here have no idea how wonderful this pub is. That you actually have a place where you can meet up with one another at the end of the day!' It was the import who opened our eyes to how special the atmosphere in the village was. During that period I went to the pub more frequently. You had really good conversations, people no longer went just to booze and shout."

Marieke had rented a house in Jorwert as an experiment. She planned to see how it went. Her initial impression of the village was how small it was. When she braved the pub for the first time everyone stopped talking. "So I took a deep breath, and I plunged on, towards the bar. Afterwards people said that they had really liked the way I did that, but they didn't show it at the time." The village reminded her of a series of closed ranks, and she got the strong impression that she would have to fight for her own space.

Willem had grown up in the village in the 1960s. He belonged to Ids' generation. They had never been bored. "That hanging around that you see nowadays in the school playground, there was none of that. We were always doing something, playing fives or football, building dens." When he was about 15 they started playing billiards in the pub, and now and again they also played street games in larger groups, with the girls as well. Later on they went out, to the informal bashes in Beers, or the community centre in Weidum, or to the disco in Grouw, always with the same group, always the same old larking about. Once in a while they went off to Leeuwarden at night to eat a doner kebab, but they did that in secret because Leeuwarden was dangerous. According to them city girls were all tarted up, and you could smell them coming a mile off. "And there was no talking to them either."

Marieke had moved to Jorwert with all sorts of ideas about small-scale coexistence. The reality was extremely lonely. "You were intruding upon the village culture, and you felt it. They said you were a mother who had deliberately not married, and all sorts of other things, and nobody asked about how matters really stood. That was due to a sort of modesty, but it did mean that rumours continued to run riot."

There were a few people in the village who took her under their wing a bit. "In the beginning nobody would dance with me on the dance evenings, but Ids always asked me."

And apart from that it had been a question of persevering. Marieke had very deliberately become a member of the merke committee, had helped organise all sorts of children's activities. And then she had met Willem.

Marieke did not really fit into any pigeonhole. I noticed this when I attempted to apply the classifications of C. D. Saal, a sociologist from Groningen, to the Jorwerter import. In 1972, Saal had been one of the first to attempt to map the city import in the countryside, and he had distinguished between three types of newcomers.

He called the first type "the recluses: those wanting to enjoy peace and quiet in seclusion" – the successful business types, those who had taken early retirement, artists and others who had bought up old farmhouses and had withdrawn to the country. They went unnoticed or hardly noticed by the village, and by the rest of the world as well, and that was exactly how they wanted it.

He called the second sort the "pragmatic dualists" – people who wanted to live in the country, but who made certain urban demands at the same time. With regard, for example, to shops, schools, swimming baths and the like. These pragmatic dualists, Saal noted, often got quite involved with the village, campaigned for schools and against motorways, and were significantly enough often the fiercest opponents of plans for further development in the village. These import types were known as Sudeten-Frisians, and if they formed a coalition with the indigenous Deep-Frisians they could make the life of an administrator well-nigh impossible.

According to Saal, the third category was formed by the "want-to-have-it-both-ways group" – the people who remained narrowly linked with the city in all sorts of ways, and who only lived in a village because it was pleasanter and cheaper. Their entire social network had remained in the city. And the fourth sort – closely related to them – he called the "captive commuters" – those who had been forced out into the villages by the housing shortage. You could also call them the Reluctant Villagers.

In Jorwert those categories were rather jumbled up. I knew a few recluses, quite a lot of pragmatic dualists – although most of them did not have the airs that Saal implied; while on the new housing development the "want-to-have-it-both-ways-group" and the "captive commuters" came and went.

"If a stranger from the same district settles in the village, and he is pleasant and obliging, then he is soon permitted to do everything a fellow villager also does: freely enter the houses, call the children to order, and he is even allowed to administer light punishment," wrote P. A. Barentsen at the beginning of the century about his village in Brabant. "'Familiar strangers' are a different matter, local worthies who frequent the village, like the vicar, the mayor and the solicitor. People are never familiar with them, but they are subject to extremely critical observation from a distance."

The actual name of the teacher I have mentioned a few times already in this story was Douwe de Bildt. He worked in a nearby village school, and was the instigator of countless plays, social evenings and other important events in Jorwert. He was square-built, with a splendid curly beard and laughter came easily to him. His wife, Lia Duinker, was a bit smaller, and dispensed gardening tips from a little office in their old Jorwerter house. They lived with their two children in the flat countryside beyond the village, between a few trees on the canal.

Douwe arrived at the village in 1971, on Tjitse Tijssen's lorry. He was 20 and at a secondary school. Through a school friend he had helped a Jorwerter farmer during the holidays, and one day he approached the vicar. Was it possible to rent a room? That is how it started.

The following morning at 6.30 a.m. Hendrik Meinsma, who was doing some painting there, woke him by banging on the door: "Are you still lounging in bed you great lummox?" That evening they hit the Beerenburg together and it was the start of a beautiful friendship. At first the rest of the villagers were unsure quite what to make of the young newcomer, but Hendrik and Gais became like a mother and father to Douwe. More especially, they were the key to his subsequent life in the village.

At exactly this time the old oppressive side of village life began to disintegrate, and Jorwert, in its own way, experienced the student, hippie, sexual, women's, and new-age revolution – all mixed up together. While the import was arriving, the youth of the village were beginning to make their presence felt, together with those who were less traditionally minded. They were the Jorwerters who had already managed to prise themselves partially free of the old-fashioned village or who – like Folkert – had always been outsiders.

These two groups came together down the pub. It was full every evening. The painter was there, and the carpenter; at midnight the solicitor would come in to partake of a night-cap, and Durk Siesling did his Tarzan imitations. "You Jane?" he called out to Ms Boonstra as she was passing. "If so, I'm going to drag you to the Raarder coppice!"

At first Douwe spent all his free time there. "It was a sort of *Coronation Street*. You heard the most fantastic stories." Nobody stayed home to watch television. "We all knew that Folkert was a terrible liar. We all knew what had really happened. But oh, what a marvellous storyteller he was!"

Douwe became the owner of a little house near the bridge. Hendrik painted it in exactly the same colours as the pub, "otherwise Douwe will have withdrawal symptoms". Jan Dijkstra laid a wooden floor. Someone else installed the electricity and fitted a lavatory in a bedstead. "The only thing I had to do was provide a crate of beer now and then," Douwe told me. In this way he was carried into the village by his friends from the pub, and he was never to leave again.

Later on Lia moved in with Douwe. She too had deliberately chosen to live in the country. "Children and lots of space, that's what I wanted'. During the winter months she gave sewing lessons at the pub, all the women took their sewing machines with them under their arms, and the pieces of cloth were cut up on the billiard table.

The voluntary fire brigade, consisting of a red handcart, a hose and a few firemen's uniforms, grew into a veritable entertainments committee. Each year Douwe, Hendrik and the other firemen spent a day sailing in Durk Siesling's ship, with a crate of Beerenburg on board. When Sikke Kooistra's chip shop caught fire, Hendrik Meinsma was standing on a ladder painting in another part of the village. "Is it burning well?" he called down. "Okay, then in that case there's no need for me to come." The last fire was in Sake Castelein's smouldering muckheap, which had ignited. They made such a mess of it that the Mantgum fire brigade took over for good.

They were years in which anything could happen. A play week was organised for the Jorwerter children, with dens and pancakes all week long. The matinee at the merke was one big fancy dress party. A gay man came to live in Pastorijfinne street; then a mother who had chosen to remain unmarried; and a divorced man; and a divorced woman; "natural" untamed gardens appeared and some people hung black, wide-mesh curtains at their windows. A group of dissident Salvation Army members, consisting of one family and a lodger, all dressed neatly in home-made uniforms arrived a bit further along the street.

On 24 December 1971, the first alternative Christmas service was held in the church at Jorwert. Its motto was "For the dying child". I found an old newspaper cutting with the programme. There was to be an anti-war protest march through the streets of the village, the film Z was to be shown in the church, the pop group Earth People were to perform, there was to be an alternative Christmas dinner and chocolate lovers could even buy "alternative chocolate".

In 1978, Wiepke Castelein still had a knitting club with five of her friends, a different stitch each week, each week another ten centimetres. She played cowboys, built dens; the boys played football and propelled themselves along the ditches in upturned car roofs. Three years later she made the following entries in a secret notebook :

17 July 1981. *Jellum disco*. ("I think that's where I drank my first beer.")

26 September 1981. *With Sietse and Dan to pop group Fuck in Weidum*. ("My parents had no idea what that meant.")

10 October 1981. *Disco in Jorwert*. ("With my boyfriend, but we hardly spoke to one another, we were too shy.")

30 October 1981. *Disco in Weidum*. ("Cycled home late afterwards")

23 January 1982. *Fuck in Weidum*. ("I think I had been grounded for the previous few months.")

30 January 1982. *'t Holt in Deinum*. ("That was very unusual, I had to do a lot of persuading.")

27 February 1982. *'t Holt in Deinum, BZN performing*. ("At that time I had a friend who had older brothers.")

27 March 1982. *Disco in Jorwert*. ("I was gradually developing my talent for partying. After the *merke* there was no stopping me. I went further and further afield too.")

25 July 1982. *Treemter in Grouw*. ("The folks were angry because I'd been told not to go – it was much to far.")

The following pages of the notebook show us that the groups, the disco's and the parties became ever more frequent, until they were taking place every weekend, while young Wiepkje's sphere of operations grew ever wider: Brainbox in Wommels; Doe Maar in Irnsum; Golden Earring in Grouw. "In the end you knew them all. You just had to go, you couldn't miss it."

Wiepkje had met her boyfriend Pier through the band Fuck. "He came from Weidum. The boys had their own crowd, mostly from the same village, and they had their own place at the bar. They talked about women and football and the world; it was all about nothing really, they would jump from one subject to the other in such a way that no outsider could ever get the drift."

The lads drank heavily – for a time it was even regarded as a sport to tear along the country lanes and give the police the slip in spite of your drunken state; that only stopped after quite a few lads had killed themselves. But when they found themselves next to a girl at the bar, they could hardly get a word out.

Only: Pier had a band, and he played all over Friesland. "They knew perhaps four numbers in those days, but that didn't prevent them from playing the whole evening long in the Baarderadeel Arms. The same four numbers over and over again. We thought it was great."

Leeuwarden remained dangerous and risky for a long time. "Even at secondary school we formed a village class within the city class. The city kids were much bolder than we were. We didn't like spending time there."

By about 1600 the national poet Brederode was already warning the "gentlemen" and the "burgers" to "avoid village fairs: they are seldom very elevating". He described the different phases of such a fair. "There is such feasting, supping, singing, thronging and dancing, dice-playing and gambling. People call for wine, that is the way it always is. Each peasant ends up blind drunk."

Four hundred years later little had changed. At the Whitsun market in Oudeschoot they started imbibing at about 7 a.m., the shouting began at about midday, the fighting at about 1 p.m., and by about 2 p.m. the lads would be slouched senselessly against the houses or lying collapsed in the kerb, others would be zigzagging all over the road, pushing and pulling, sometimes punching and hitting, unaware of their own strength. After that the miraculous homecoming could begin.

Something came to the fore at these types of fairs and markets that had little to do with the old rural way of life, and that also had nothing to do with fashionable city trends.

While city dwellers from The Hague to Istanbul more or less conformed to the trends dictated by the world of television, many young people in the countryside dealt with it in a contrary manner: some elements were picked out, but many of the current trends were ignored. Just as in the cities, they had split up into societies and sects, according to taste, musical preference and brand loyalty. Only here they did not call themselves "discos", "antis" and "studs", but "housers", "braves", "bikers", "relaxos", "critical alternatives", "computer freaks" and "farmers".

They adopted a Rambo-style posture from TV series, but remained largely unmoved by the "well-known" brand names – Nike, Levi's, Oilily – that so affected the youth of the city. Rapping and graffiti also seemed largely to pass by the youth of the countryside. From the flood of TV entertainment and information they did unerringly pick out a number of elements from Texan rural culture: there were dozens if not hundreds of village bands playing country music, big American cars were hugely popular and at every market you always saw a few people walking around in Texan cowboy hats.

For the most part this sort of nonconformism had to do with the simple fact that practically all the fashions and trends came from the city, and once again were meant for city dwellers. You could not get far in high heels on the land, neither was an Italian suit of much use to you on the tractor, and a stylish café life was not there for the asking in the polder either.

Those who lived in the countryside were used to regarding advertising, TV shows, newspapers, leaflets and everything else that emanated from the city with a certain detachment. Nevertheless the platitude "That is just not meant for our sort of people" was heard less and less in the 1990s. A new catchphrase was becoming popular, a rebellious cry: "We will have no part of that." This tiny sentence said a lot. Not joining in with the city had for years been a question of not being able to, whether from financial reasons or from practical ones. Now it was more often a question of refusing to.

For decades the countryside had been regarded almost entirely negatively, not least by the inhabitants of the country themselves: it embraced everything that was non-city. And rural culture was simply a culture that was not (yet) able to be urban, due to lack of money, communication problems or general backwardness.

However, as the cities got into more and more difficulty, people in the countryside became more conscious of their own values. Normaal, a pop group from the rural east of Holland, gained enormous popularity with their songs about "shacking up", "puking", "slogging", "down days", "boozing", "fooling around with chicks and slapping their bottoms" and "causing a rumpus". Roughly translated it all came down to the same thing as Brederode's "supping" and "thronging". During Normaal's concerts – and also, for example, those of Rowwen Heze (a group from North Limburg) – a rural youth culture that no one had ever mentioned was disseminated: the booze, bonk, slog culture of youngsters who could not and did not want to follow city fashions, who gave their all during the week, who were not eloquent but were extremely strong, and who, once a week, on Saturday evening, went totally out of their minds.

They gave the cussed, self-willed culture of the young farmers a name once more, and with it a separate existence, a separate identity, free from the imposed world of city and TV.

What was noticeable about the breaking free of village youngsters like Wiepkje and Pier was that they were simultaneously returning to their roots.

The lads, for example, mostly went around in "crowds", groups that stayed together for years. It was not unusual for these "crowds" to be formed early on at the village school; they cycled in long columns to secondary school in town; they went to parties together and only when the first of them got married did the troupe begin to disband.

The language in which the "crowds" conversed was almost always Frisian, and preferably a particular Frisian dialect, like "Bildts" or "Stellingwerfs". Frisian was also the language in which all the songs and the ballads were sung. Pier's band inspired others. After Fuck came Disturbance, and they were the founders of the so-called "Bildt-rock". In that district almost every village eventually had its own band, and around the sheds and classrooms where rehearsals took place a completely separate mini-youth culture developed, with its own language and its own atmosphere, village-like, but still worldly.

So that in place of the traditional ties a new awareness began to develop, a new attachment to the village and everything connected with it. In Jorwert, for example, a campaign was organised to protest against the removal of the bus stops and the closure of the school; there was group concern about threats to the appearance of the village; people tried their utmost to restore the old drawbridge; the Iepenloftspul in the solicitor's garden got more resplendent each year; it was always crowded at the merke, despite the decline in interest; and the young people organised their own annual pop festival near the village, called MUKPOP. People had to stand their ground against the city, and this forged ties.

This increasing village pride was a common phenomenon in the countryside — indeed sometimes the term "village nationalism" would have been more applicable. Everywhere in the vicinity of Jorwert there was a noticeable attempt to provide villages with something unique, something special that would differentiate that village from other places.

In Beers, for example, they wanted to erect a 15-metre-high steel construction that would be an "open-air reflection" on the former Unia

estate. In Tjerkwerd the ancient Walta castle was reconstructed in miniature for a village fair. Near Drachten people attempted to excavate the
foundations of an old monastery. In Jorwert the vicar had a special church
seal made – it looked as though it had existed for hundreds of years.
Grouw and Terhorne battled over the question of which of the villages
had inspired *De Kameleon*, the popular series of boys' books. In Grouw they
wanted to erect a statue; in Terhorne a theme park. Elsewhere people
made plans to rebuild missing castle gates and to dig out ancient village
waterways. In yet other villages derelict churches were restored – one
village of fewer than 400 inhabitants coughed up 70,000 guilders without
complaint. And everywhere villages were renamed and given the old
Frisian names, Grouw became Grou, Tehorne became Terherne, Jorwert
became Jorwert, road signs were replaced, official stationary reprinted.

All those feelings were strengthened and stirred up by rituals, by
village festivals, fairs, processions, clothing, use of language, booklets
of old postcards, parades, the skating club, the village idiot; in short, by
all matters and happenings in which recognition and repetition formed
the most important elements. And the banner under which all of
this took place was the Frisian language, which resonated more often
than ever, during church services, in official documents, and in other
important matters.

The activities of the village societies played an important role in this
process. In the council archives I found a list of eleven Jorwerter village
societies dating from 1923. All except two were still flourishing in 1995
and there had even been several additions.

Jorwert was not alone in this. In spite of the car and the television,
village societies were still doing relatively well compared with 50
years before. However, their purpose was different. While the classic
nineteenth-century societies – like the Jorwerter Society for Public
Welfare – were dedicated to stimulating the general education of the
members and breaking through the isolation of the villages, most
societies in the twentieth century were primarily concerned with their
own little village: the social and travel societies flourished especially,
and the skating, draughts, and fives clubs, and the pensioners get-
togethers and the amateur dramatics societies.

*

The new village pride was reminiscent of the rise of community consciousness in the big cities, of local action in the 1970s, of the "us-together-against-the-rest" of the old districts in the 1980s. By the 1930s, the Jordaan district of Amsterdam had already been romanticised in a series of films as a village within the city where everyone knew each other and neighbours went through fire and water to help one another. But the films — with titles like *Bleke Bet* and *De Jantjes* — had little to do with the real Jordaan. Amsterdam had already been through decades of modernisation. It was already a busy and anonymous city. But that is possibly just why those films were so terrifically popular: they conjured up an illusion that everyone dreamed of, they painted a picture of a district that had disappeared years before, but for which grandparents and grandchildren were still nostalgic.

A similar sort of thing was going on with the new village pride.

It was clearly different to the village bonding of the past. That had been a system of traditions, part of a static community that was now in decline everywhere. The village pride was relatively modern. For example, it was apparent from surveys held among villagers that people with a progressive lifestyle in general also identified strongly with their village. It was a phenomenon that, just like the "Jordaan-feeling" of the 1930s, was boosted by all the changes.

It was furthermore an expression of the "regionalism" and "communalism" that was again stirring throughout Europe; the new solidarity in the countryside between people who at first glance had little in common and that expressed itself in, among other things, all sorts of language questions, in the rise of local and regional parties and in an aversion to central authority in general.

Something else was noticeable too: almost all the newcomers to whom I spoke regarded Jorwert in the first place as the village of those who already lived there. The village belonged to the others and they were joining it. There was a sort of unspoken agreement: nobody was forced to adapt, but it was incumbent upon people to accept the village for what it was.

That did not mean, though, that overnight Jorwert had become the open society that the townspeople were used to. Unmarried couples were initially not admitted to the married couples dancing club. The *merke* remained – in spite of the literal meaning of "market" – an insular event, where a stranger was regarded with some mistrust. Cor Wiedijk experienced some resistance when they wanted to appoint him under-taker's assistant as – although he had lived in Jorwert for 16 years – "he did not come from here".

It was indeed the case that in some villages the "arrogant Dutch" from outside the province lived up to their name. Some of them seemed to have gained their opinion of the countryside principally from certain television advertisements, and refused to accept that a cow shits, that a farm sometimes stinks of manure and that a village blacksmith, on occasion, has to turn on his welding machine. Others had scarcely moved before they began to impose urban living standards on their new environment, and armed with the Public Nuisance Act they got quite a long way.

In nearby Poppenwier for example the ancient village pub was squeezed out of existence by the new neighbours, who demanded rural peace and quiet and were prepared to go to the Council of State to achieve it. In Britsum, a lawyer had blocked the traditional path the mourners always took with the coffin because, according to him, it was by rights his. In Birdaard, an import family wanted to get rid of the blacksmith's-cum-bicycle repair shop, "because of the noise of the grinding and welding", although the smith had plied his trade in the village for 60 years, and had been licensed for 40 years.

These sorts of excesses did not occur in Jorwert, but people did some-times have difficulty with the slight sense of alienation that the import brought with them. The older villagers had only ever known people with concrete professions. But now all at once they were sat in the pub evening after evening with people about whose working lives they knew nothing.

They all knew that Keimpe was a bus driver, as everybody regularly saw him driving around. But what Gijs van Woudenberg did in Amsterdam with all those computers, and why Willem Osinga had to go to Milan, and what Frans Langemeijer's work as manager with the child protection agency precisely entailed, they had no idea.

Many import villagers in fact led two lives – a Jorwerter life, and one in the outside world. And for the Jorwerters it meant that the second dimension of existence was once more manifest: the dimension of the city, the dimension of the terrifying castle, and the dimension of the safe village within which no one knew – or wanted to know – anything.

That worked well enough, just like in a complicated marriage, as long as these worlds did not encroach too much on each other. But there was a limit: the children. The Jorwerter school had been a real village school for decades: the children were prepared for secondary school, agricultural school or a specific vocational course, but the tuition was not particularly suitable for the city and the castle, so there was a problem.

The policy of the school was determined by a parents association that stemmed from the old village. That commission had dealt fairly harshly with the then head teacher – and not without good reason. But just as with the conflict around Our House, the quarrel between the school head and the committee quickly spread to all sorts of groups who had nothing to do with it.

When Douwe – who taught in a nearby village – tried to apply for a position in Jorwert, he was informed: "We know you can't do anything about it, but because the head is in favour of you, we are against you." And when they were called to account for this by the parents, the questions remained unanswered. "That is confidential," they replied. Or "We will discuss that among ourselves."

The differences of opinion came to a head in 1985. Under the new Primary Education Act every primary school had to have an advisory body. This did not present a problem in most villages: the parents association was more or less automatically transformed into this new advisory body.

However, in Jorwert they decided to play it formally. Everyone gathered at the school, a vote was taken, you could cut the silence with a knife, and when the result arrived it emerged that the former parents association had been completely swept away. The members slunk off; it was not a very edifying spectacle, and it would be years before the wounds of that evening healed again.

In one way the conflict around the village school was a crucial moment in Jorwerter history, like battles and presidential elections can be in the life of large nations.

In the first place, the conflict was a collision between the new and the old village elites, between those who wished to be consulted on important matters in the modern manner, and those who wanted to deal with things through the traditional networks.

In the second place, the conflict was an almost unavoidable phase in the process of change the village was going through. A confusing period like this almost always expresses itself in one or more village disputes: what are we to do with all those newcomers? Why have all the shops suddenly disappeared? Why don't we see one another any more? What do our children hope to find in the city?

Usually after such a conflict a new balance is achieved, sometimes the village adapts completely to the newcomers, and sometimes it opts for a new isolation.

In the third place, the conflict made painfully clear how far the make-up of the village had changed since the early 1970s. Circa 1985, Jorwert was still outwardly more or less the same village as it had been in 1971, but if you looked at the figures you saw that gradually more and more houses had been occupied by newcomers. Many older families had disappeared: the youngsters to the city, the elderly to old people's homes.

Once when I asked him, Ids Meinsma took the trouble to work out exactly who had moved away since he had left school. He made a mental journey through the streets of the village and counted: that house, that house, they have left, they have left, they are new, and them and them; the score quickly mounted up. The result surprised us both. According to his private statistics at least half the village, and perhaps as many as three quarters, had settled there within the past 20 years.

In the same way that a new body is formed unnoticed after a few years because the cells of the body replace themselves every so often, here a new village had silently come into being.

Meanwhile the comings and goings continued. In each issue of the village paper the feature "May we introduce . . ." included one or two newcomers: a mechanic at the Frico dairy factory; a civil servant on the council; a nurse from Leeuwarden; a couple from Groningen, of whom the husband had something to do with computer courses and the wife coached trainee secretaries; a manager of software courses from Hilversum; a female student; a project manager from Sneek; a carpenter from Wirdum; a bank clerk from the Bildt; an old lady from

Gerkesklooster; a Leeuwarder operations manager with the hauliers Van Gendt and Loos.

"Life in Jorwert really suits us," they wrote. "Peace and quiet and a lovely view." "My hobbies are reading, knitting, embroidery and cross-word puzzles." " Maaike enjoys fiddling about with cut flowers, likes handicrafts and reading." "It is as if time has stood still here."

To some extent the government paved the way for their arrival by its policy.

The overfull conurbations in the west of the Netherlands began to eject people. While the population increased, the statistics for the cities showed a slow but steady decline in inhabitants. More and more of the Dutch preferred a half-urban, half-rural environment. National research on where people wanted to live indicated a similar inclination to flee the cities. The majority of those who lived in the cities would, if it were possible, prefer to live somewhere smaller. Only a quarter preferred the city. Outside the western conurbations it was exactly the opposite. Almost three quarters of those interviewed in the smaller places were quite satisfied and did not want to leave. Only one in twelve would have preferred to move to one of the cities in the west.

The consequences of all this began to make themselves felt. The IJsselmeer coast between Lemmer and Harlingen became a popular alternative to the Gooi suburbs, and in addition, many Germans – who had enough sand and forests at home – were attracted by the characteristic Frisian landscape of wide-open skies and bare, flat countryside. In the early 1970s Douwe bought his house for 1,000 guilders at the solicitor's. Twenty-five years on, it was worth at least 100 times more.

Bungalow projects sprang up all over the place – more and more frequently in the form of imitation farms, complete with thatched roofs and plastic dormer windows. In at least five locations in Friesland there were plans to create prestigious country estates, with gardens, woods and water features, and of course, splendid houses for the wealthy purchasers. For now that agriculture was fading away, other functions for the countryside had to be found, and other types of employment. Many administrators and project developers would have preferred to see the countryside become a typical residential province, an attractive and peaceful alternative to the conurbations of the west, the Florida of the Low Countries, only colder and wetter.

*

It was scarcely possible to measure that new stream of immigrants and the changes that they brought about within the villages. There was, however, one way of gauging it: the language.

Despite all the interest in the Frisian language, Dutch was in the ascendant in many villages, and it was most audible in the school playgrounds.

The teachers whom I spoke to had noticed a definite change in the mid-1980s – at least in the import villages. Before then, new children had learned Frisian as quickly as possible, of their own accord, in order to be able to join in the play; after that time the Frisian children began to learn Dutch. Soundings taken by the Frisian Academy indicated that by 1980 a third of Frisian youth no longer spoke Frisian with their friends. By 1993 that figure had become more than half. Many Jorwerter children no longer knew what a word like *dongje* (muck-spreading) meant.

The age make-up changed as well. In many villages the young people continued to leave because courses and career opportunities lay elsewhere. By contrast, the elderly leisure-seekers streamed in. Many ex-Frisians who had taken early retirement tried to realise their dreams by purchasing an old house in a village. It was not uncommon for those who were selling to ask a price that was tens of thousands of guilders higher than the real value, in the hope of ensnaring an idiotic Amsterdammer with a sudden desire to live in Friesland. It often worked.

In villages with a more extensive layer of import, a second elite often formed, consisting of early retirers, managers, scientists, senior civil servants and similar wealthy residents. The Dutch-speakers founded their own societies, choirs and chess clubs, they drank like one of the lads at the village fair, and in addition they had their own garden parties where everyday country folk were anything but welcome.

And then there were the so-called second homes. The odd arty type who bought an old labourer's cottage never used to bother anyone, but it was a different matter when that quiet enjoyment began, in some districts, to take on massive proportions. According to a survey in the *Leeuwarder Courant*, in the winter of 1995 40 of the 400 houses in Woudsend were empty; in Wymbritseradeel 450 of the almost 6,000 houses were of a recreational nature; in Gaasterland, 350 of the almost 4,000 houses were registered as second homes; and in the village of Langweer there were 15 to 20 empty homes in the winter.

Those searching for a second home rarely spent any of their income in the village itself, so the local economy derived little benefit from them. They did not support the school, they did not usually take part in the societies and the church, and for three-quarters of the time their houses stood dark and empty in the village street. Besides which they forced up house prices considerably, so that it was often almost impossible for the village's own young people to acquire a reasonable property.

So, something that was a delight for the city types became an affliction for the villages.

When I drove with Riekele Bekkema through the flatness of the dark Frisian countryside, the city was simultaneously far away and near.

The city was nearby in Sneek, when within one hour, in the early evening, there were suddenly three reports of running amok, madness and nervous exhaustion; and Bekkema had had to interfere in order to pacify these unemployed, divorced or otherwise broken people. It wasn't that something like this never happened in a village, but not three times in an hour.

The city was nearby when we met up with a "domestic" in Oosterwierum. In the only house where a light was still burning sat a young distressed import woman who had had her mother to stay from Apeldoorn. They had had an argument about the children – "That's exactly why I moved here, I thought I'd be able to deal with it now!" – and subsequently the mother, still fuming, had walked away into the night. There were no longer any buses, she was nowhere to be found; perhaps she was wandering around lost in the countryside. We searched for her in vain.

The city was nearby, due to the increasing prosperity. There used to be one break-in a month at most on Bekkema's patch, now it was happening a few times a week. The perpetrators used to be mostly professional burglars, now they were often young men seeking to alleviate a temporary shortage of funds for the disco or drugs. "The professional thieves used to leave a place neat and tidy," said Riekele Bekkema, rather nostalgically. "Now they turn everything upside down."

The city was nearby, on account of the fact that the cattle dealers could no longer drive around safely with ready cash, because of the increase in vandalism due to a decline in social control and authority, and a number of other things. Bekkema: "A rule is no longer a rule. The matter now has to be a bit more serious before we get involved."

The city was also nearby as a result of the bureaucrats and pen-pushers who had decided that safety in the countryside could be guaranteed equally well by extending the district covered by Rieke Bekkema and his colleagues from 150 square kilometres to 1,800 square kilometres, and who were of the opinion that this could be compensated by an extra two-way radio and a handful of ordinance survey maps in the boot.

But elsewhere the city remained far away. There was crime – but, viewed through city eyes, it was all rather innocent. There was stealing, violence, drunkenness and rape – but then there always had been. There was disruption and disturbance of the existing way of things – but nevertheless the villages remained villages.

Once, in Jorwert, all the parked cars were broken into during a performance of a play, and for the past ten years fewer front doors had remained open, but apart from this the increasing feeling of insecurity had largely passed the village by.

In contrast to some of the other villages, Frisian was still spoken on a day-to-day basis – although the village youth, under the influence of a few trendsetting import children, were using more and more Dutch words.

The problems second houses brought with them were unknown in the village, because for years the rural district council had pursued a far-sighted policy. In the villages proper second houses were completely taboo and, in the outlying districts, recreational homes were only very occasionally permitted under stringent conditions. The canteen at the skating rink was sometimes rented by a Dutch family during the summer, but that was all.

Many of the village youngsters, who in the 1970s had enthusiastically taken part in the merke, the Iepenloftspul, the recreational weeks and other festivities, had eventually left for the city. First of all they had broken free of traditional family life, and afterwards they had broken free of the traditional territory as well.

"Ten years ago we used to have sing-song evenings in the pub, with Folkert and his accordion," said Wiepkje. "Age didn't matter at all. That's all finished now. Nowadays the 16- and 17-year-olds haven't even got their own bands any more."

After a number of boom years, the import received a setback. Most of them got on well with everyone, but the period of intimate seclusion was at an end. For them it was largely the big rituals – the *merke*, the *Iepenloftspul* – that still kept the village together.

Douwe and Lia had withdrawn somewhat from village life. Douwe still played the leading role in the solicitor's garden in the summer of 1995, for the umpteenth time. On this occasion as Anatevka, but entirely in Frisian, performed in a mock-up of a complete Russian village, with choirs and dancers and live music, and real cows in the byre – without ear-tags. Apart from this they relished the solitude each day, the skies, swimming in the canal, the freedom the children had, the non-city life.

One day they too had received a visit from the project developer. In this region there was really only one, a certain Johan de Jong: a portly man who scattered plans around like pigeon feed and who intimidated half the province with his blue pinstripe suits and enormous cars. He was a fast operator who was usually quick to leave the district again, but not before he had left a few deep scars.

De Jong was a determined operator. He enjoyed wild speculation, he had dealt in real estate and bungalows in all sorts of villages, he had plans for whole villa parks in the Bildt, and suddenly there he was on the canal, at Douwe and Lia's.

"This is where the farm restaurant will be situated," he had said, "and those trees will have to go." After that, armed with a camera, he had heaved himself into a small boat, rowed, puffing, to the other side and taken a few photographs.

"Yes, a bistro," he said when he returned. And then he had outlined his dream: the land from here to Mantgum would become a built-up area, the canal would be drained, and eventually a large commuter village would emerge with a direct link to the Snekermeer.

"Yes, that's the way it will be," the portly man said decisively, and in his blue pinstripes he strode back and forth over Douwe and Lia's property, as though he had already acquired it.

Now I wish to give praise to pious men,
Our fathers, to their descendants,
To whom the Almighty granted much glory,
And who were great in times gone by.
Wealthy men, relying on their strength,
Living peacefully in their region.
They were all honoured by their contemporaries,
And were famous in their time:
Some of them gained such a reputation,
That people continued to talk admiringly about them.
But there were also others, who people no longer remembered;
As soon as they passed on, it was finished.
It is as though they never existed,
Nor their children.

Jesus Sirach 44: 1–2, 6–9

Chapter Eleven

An Island in Time

 I ONCE SPENT A WINTER UNDER THE SPELL OF two weighty tomes. I read them in bed or during meals, I read them whenever I possibly could; my hair stood on end, and the fright they gave me taught me Frisian. They were the tales of an old skipper's son. The stories went something like this:

A young girl asked her boyfriend to pluck her a wedding bouquet from the Enchanted Hollow. The boy went to the bog, and while there was turned into a snake by a wizard.

The girl went looking for him and found him with the wizard. He made her do maid's work and one day wanted to sleep with her. The girl said yes, but tempted the wizard away from the bog and onto the heath, where his spells had no power. She started to tickle the wizard, so that he laughed so hard that he opened his mouth wide. The bewitched snake saw his chance, and shot into the wizard's stomach.

The girl tied the wizard to a tree and starved him of food and water. The snake suffered too, but would not leave the stomach until the girl crouched down next to the wizard, lifted up her skirts, and peed on the heather. As soon as the snake heard that trickle he crawled out of the wizard's behind and changed back into a young man again.

Together they threw the wizard into the bog and lived on without hindrance.

End of story, and there were hundreds of similar stories in those two books. They were the last original Frisian folk tales collected some 60 years ago by the narrator, Steven de Bruin. As a boy, De Bruin had sat up night after night behind the cupboard doors of the bedstead in the ship's cabin, secretly listening as family or friends began their story-telling. Because he had a memory like a tape recorder he was able to remember hundreds of these stories almost word for word: about the Coach of Darkness belonging to a dead Frisian king, that thundered across the skies at night while the monarch hurled his fiery axe at the earth; about ancient hills on the heath, full of magic pots of gold; about skippers who received a secret commission to set sail at night, the ship full of the souls of the recently dead, whispering, invisible.

I got to know these strange stories of Steven de Bruin's thanks to the Frisian poet and scientist Ype Poortinga. In the early 1970s he realised that Frisian old people's homes were a gold mine of stories and sagas that had been handed down over the years, but that he would have to act quickly as, along with these old people, the stories were dying out too. So, when he was about 60, Poortinga embarked upon his life's work: he took driving lessons, learned how to operate a tape recorder, and within no time he was travelling from village to village in his tiny Daf, on the trail of storytellers and stories.

The results were breathtaking. Elderly housewives, with a few years primary school at most, produced ancient legends about gifts for the dead that their grandmothers had once told them. Old farmhands used terms that had disappeared centuries before. Wodan and other Germanic gods turned out to have lived on in other shapes and forms, as had the Greek ferryman Pharon, who ferried the dead across the river Styx. And through an illiterate skipper an unusual variant of the Orpheus and Euridyce legend was discovered that had been handed down over many generations.

The stories were unexpurgated, sometimes they were plain dirty or crazy, and they entirely lacked the smooth, polished quality of stories by classic storytellers like Andersen or the brothers Grimm. But precisely because of their simple roughness they were as magical as the shards and fragments at a newly discovered archeological site. Since that winter it seemed to me that our communal memory extended for hundreds or even thousands of years in depth, deeper than our written knowledge, deeper than our consciousness, deeper than we ever thought.

That he knew the cowshed and the barn, the garden and the pasture?
That he was in the corn byre and with the men in the hay meadow?
That he knew the smell of the wood in the pile-driver drilling on
   the dyke,
Of the boat steering past the nets and of the tannery at the back of
   the fisherman's house?

That he knew the houses with the stone floors
And the low smoke-blackened attics?

Every community has need of a collective memory. Having such a memory binds, explains, and adds new dimensions to daily life. And the greater the threat to a community, the greater the corresponding need for such a communal memory will be. The only question is whether it is still the collective memory of the community that is being preserved, or whether they are impressions formed by others. The smaller or more marginal the community is, the greater that risk becomes.

In the case of Jorwert that collective memory resided first and foremost with the church. The building had supposedly been built sometime at the beginning of the twelfth century, thanks to the missionary zeal of a nearby monastery, and it still had the same rough-hewn walls of boulders and sandstone. Generations ago the many-coloured frescoes of Marias and saints had been plastered over and replaced with reformation and sobriety. Now all that was visible were white walls, brown benches and a pulpit with an hourglass. But the roof beams were still the rough, half tree-trunks of old. This was the oldest building in the village.

People here had treated other historic sites with less respect. As late as 1952 the oldest property in Jorwert, the eighteenth-century mayoral dwelling or *grietenijhuis* – "a simple building constructed of yellow stone, with a gable roof between two incorporated neck gables" – was demolished to make way for a sturdy new building. No one had shed a tear.

The terp had been largely levelled off years before, for the sake of the rich terp earth, as had most of the other terps and ancient fortified farms – or "stinzen" – with which the Frisian countryside used to be covered. On a map made by the cartographer Schotanus in 1718, there are about 120 extra-high terps – or *hege wieren* – that could also function as fortified farms. On the maps made by the cartographer Eekhoff between 1849 and 1850 they were almost all still visible. By 1995 there were only five left.

The village's past was only really to be found in the churchyard, the place where the Jorwerters had buried their dead for at least a thousand years. In the council archives I found an inventory dating from 1973, and all the major families of the village were buried there: the Kingmas, the Kundersmas, the Hoogenbrugs, the Sieslings, the Greijdanuses, the Hallemas. Some names had been registered in the village for more than two centuries. The members of Gais's family, the Greijdanuses, had lived in the village since 1781. The register entries for Durk's family, the Siesling's, were unbroken since 1813. But it was very much a question of names only.

Bouke Sijkes Kundersma, 1894–1918: *Rest in peace dear departed one / Brought here all too soon / In thy short life thou / Hast always tried to do thy duty.*

Eelkje Oene Hoogenbrug, 1846–71: *Look upon this grave oh wanderer / In quiet solitude / The wife that God once gave me / Has here been laid to rest / She died resigned to her lot / Looking towards her God.*

So we knew that much about Bouke Sijkes and Eelkje Oene, but it did not really amount to a great deal more.

Just how far does the concept of "living memory" extend? Are old people really the "living books" the French historian Michelet once wrote that they were; books that unfortunately close each day? Are they the annals, though not always aware of it, the providers of a thousand answers, who can enlighten those who are able to consult them?

In the vicinity of Jorwert there were a few villages that were still clearly recognisable, 400 years after the Reformation, as Catholic enclaves in a protestant district – purely because, after the reforms, a clandestine priest had dallied there and continued his work.

In a few seventeenth-century trial documents dug up by Jolt Oostra I read an account of a fantastic neighbourly dispute at the Jorwerter solicitor's. "Loitering" – hanging around outside on the doorstep – was apparently already a favourite pastime by 1698. The Jorwerters had continued to do this, same time, same place, for nearly three centuries, right up until the 1950s.

Tilting had been played here for at least two centuries. After all, everything needed to play was there for the taking in the farmyard: a stick, an old cartwheel and a ball – probably a round piece of chalk in former days. It used to be a popular pastime all over the Frisian grasslands on Sunday afternoons during summer. Now it had become a rare attraction that could only be seen in Jorwert and perhaps one or two other villages.

For that was the flip side: at the close of the twentieth century traditions were disappearing as rapidly as plant species in a Dutch meadow – unless they were consciously preserved. Separate mourning attire – normal until the 1950s – had fallen into disuse. The "formal announcement" of someone's death was discontinued during this same period. Up until the 1960s, women with eighteenth-century ornamental *oorijzers* sat at the front of the church in Jorwert, their heads hidden under lace bonnets. After that time those sorts of attributes were only to be found in museums and antique shops.

Until the Second World War the "Scottish jig" and the "ice-polka" were regularly danced at the Jorwerter *merke*. Gais told me how she and her friends, as young girls, had often had fits of the giggles when the oldies suddenly began to "jig" around. But after the war – there had been no *merke* celebrations for a few years – that became a thing of the past. The traditional folk dances were only seen at performance demonstrations by specially trained groups.

I can still recall a winter afternoon with a young friend. We played in the hay, the cowshed was warm and cosy, the cattle fidgeted, buckets rattled; sitting at a wooden table with the whole family we solemnly drank a beaker of warm milk, and in the evening, going home on the bus, the passengers sang. That was sometime during the late 1950s. Thirty years later the sheds were open and gaping, and the redolent smell of muck heap and hay had disappeared. The atmosphere of that Sunday seemed as old and ageless as the world, and yet it has still somehow or other been lost.

Another memory: the route taken year after year by the haulier Tjitse Tijssen. In the summer of 1827, Doeke Wijgers Hellema noted in his diary, not without some surprise, that they were in the midst of laying a high road between Zwolle and Leeuwarden. On 5 November, when the work was nearing completion, he went to have a look. The old road "was always boggy", he wrote. "When they began to talk about laying this new road, the Frisians consigned the idea to the realm of fantasy and believed it to be unfeasible, yes, well nigh impossible, because of the difficulty of transporting material – and yet, behold! There is now a high road!"

That same high road, albeit in slightly altered form, was still in use 100 years later. I remember cycling along it as a boy, bumping over the cobbles, the wind in the high trees that bent over in an endlessly long row.

In the early 1960s a spanking new motorway arrived, circumventing the villages, the newest of the new. Barely 30 years later there were great mounds of sand all over the green countryside for yet another new road, a four-lane motorway this time.

The country roads with which our Wirdumer farmer grew up, were 400–500 years old. The high road that he watched being laid lasted for almost one and a half centuries. The motorway was written off within the span of a single generation.

During the last few weeks that I spent in Jorwert, I often asked myself how history would remember all these changes. What would they say in later years about the four remarkable decades in which all the farmhands and milkmaids had suddenly disappeared from the farmyards; in which, after thousands of years, the co-operation between man and beast was severed by the arrival of the tractor; in which the interests of agriculture were superseded by other interests; in which the dynamism of the village had melted away within ten years?

How would this strange period be described? Would tales be told in later years about the silence and the hardship, about the warmth of the old cowsheds, about the bell and the shuffling in the village shops, about the goodness of Akke van Zuiden?

The way in which most Jorwerters regarded their own history could at best be compared to an upturned pyramid: whatever had recently occurred was extensively discussed and considered, but interest quickly faded after about 20 years. Everyone knew about the collapse of the church tower, stories were always being told about the war, and Folkert was able to give me a detailed account of the big fire on 15 August 1930, when no fewer than four farmhouses burned down due to overheated hay and a storm. "It was a quarter past twelve. We were having a meal. All of a sudden there's someone standing at the window: 'Van der Hem's place is on fire!'"

But most of the stories and memories in Jorwert apparently stopped after that. They were not much more than stones that skimmed high over the waves of one or two generations, then disappeared, forgotten forever.

Durk Siesling (he had become quieter and lonelier since the sudden death of his Aaltsje) once told me that round about 1885 his grandfather had ferried endless loads of sand for the building of "the railway". That was 110 years ago. I heard from the elderly solicitor that his grandfather had skated the Elfstedentocht in 1890. Nothing was organised in those days, they just had a piece of paper with the signatures of the innkeepers on it. That was 105 years ago.

And in a nearby village they could still point out the exact spot where, in 1887, the promising son of the local vicar fell through the ice and drowned. That was 108 years ago.

While time quietly flowed on, the collective memory of the village was apparently remarkably short, and selective besides.

For 20 years the charismatic vicar Hille Ris Lambers had set the tone in the village, with his books on Chinese philosophy and the recitals given by his pretty daughters Heleen and Annie.

> At the bottom of the garden a shallow pool began
> Where we found one another of an evening under branches.

Sometimes I would see the Jorwert of old appearing between the lines of Slauerhoff's poetry, but the ties were not so strong the other way round. After 80 years the poet, the vicar, and his daughters had been forgotten by the village – except by Gais, the present vicar, and a handful of intellectuals.

I had asked Folkert about it: the only thing the elderly man remembered about the Hille Ris Lambers family was the "fart gas" – marsh gas that he obtained from the same "shallow pool" Slauerhoff had described, and that was transformed into a small car park in the 1960s. "At the time of the Great War that vicar, Lambers, found a way of obtaining gas, of all things, from the smelly canal," Folkert recalled. "And they used that confounded 'fart gas' for cooking as well."

One evening I paid a visit to Philippus Breuker, former teacher and subsequently Professor of Frisian Language and Literature in Amsterdam, but still interested in everything going on around him. Breuker lived in the nearby village of Bozum. He had delved at length into the history of the community and in actual fact was still delving.

"As far as concrete events are concerned, collective memory does not extend farther than about 100 years," was his impression. He told me how he had discovered a family that had resided in his village without a break since the fifteenth century, from father to son, for five consecutive centuries until the present day. But the family themselves had no idea of their line of descent, let alone how far back it went.

"I came across all manner of things — accidents, quarrels, thievery, all sorts of stuff — weighty matters that had often taken place less than 100 years ago. But when I questioned the grandchildren and the great-grandchildren of the protagonists about them, they could no longer tell me anything. There was once a local vicar who threw the entire province into confusion by predicting the end of the world — 8 May 1774 to be exact — and 60 years later they were still writing about it in Friesland. Some years ago I spoke to a great-great-grandson of his, who was as old as the hills, born in 1875. But he had no idea that he was descended from such an illustrious forefather, he had never heard anything about him."

There were, of course, exceptions. The Jorwerter solicitor was able to recall how his great-great-grandfather had been conscripted in 1830, had paid a replacement 100 guilders to go in his place, and how, due to the war with Belgium, that poor young man had had to stay in the army for nine years. That was 165 years ago. My friend the newspaperman had had a great-great-grandfather around 1820 who, according to family tradition, had skated "so fearfully fast, that he forced everyone else from the ice". He had verified it in the registers of the Leeuwarder Courant: for ten consecutive years this Hantsje Jans had indeed been unbeatable. That was 175 years ago. And Breuker had once met an old farmer who told him how, long ago during a flood, "the water had been as high as the old Middle sea dyke" — something that had indeed happened in 1825 during the same flood that Hellema described. That was 179 years ago. But he had never managed to get any further back than that.

When the French historian Emmanuel Le Roy Ladurie, by means of a series of the Inquisition's detailed case reports, attempted to reconstruct daily life in the medieval village of Montaillou, he stumbled upon exactly the same problem. "The inhabitants of Montaillou lived on a sort of island in time," is how he described that limited memory. The memory of the farmers who lived around 1320 did not appear to go back any farther than a few stories dating from the time of the previous Count who had died in 1302. Only once in the records of these conversations did Le Roy Ladurie find a vague allusion to an event that had taken place around 1240. Or, as one of the then farmers said: "The only time that exists is our own."

The Polish anthropologist Kazimierz Dobrowolki noticed a marked lack of collective memory in "his" villages too — only wars, famines and floods tended to stick in the memory. He felt that it was due to the fact that everything had to be passed on by word of mouth – there was hardly any writing done in the villages – and the generations succeeded one another too rapidly for the old stories to be passed on properly. Historical events were usually recounted in a jumbled up way, not chronologically, causing facts that were in reality far apart to be compressed into a single frame – the Iliad, the Odyssey and other heroic sagas probably originated in this way too. Besides which, the old times had frequently been so poor and desolate that later generations often preferred to forget that "uncivilised" past.

Villages suffer from amnesia, and we will just have to accept it, was Phillippus Breuker's assessment of the matter. In the end you are reliant upon archives and other written sources. And look at this: two clay dishes, early seventeenth century. Found here in the orchard, less than a foot under the ground, directly under a tree, possibly used for the chickens and left out and forgotten come autumn. I was allowed to hold them for a moment – elegant brown bowls with three little supporting feet, as perfect as though they had just come from the shop. Aren't they splendid?

But do village communities really possess such limited powers of memory? Is it possible that the joys and sorrows of generations of farmers, that such a treasure-trove of knowledge and experience, can melt away like snow in summer?

Until recently the classic method of passing on life's lessons was storytelling, the dissemination of experiences by word of mouth, the handing on from generation to generation. Whereas in the city there had been writing and printing for a long time, the countryside went on telling stories for centuries. Anyone who has ever seen a true village storyteller at work can hardly believe his eyes (and ears): the stories tumble over one another, tensions are built in, there is acting and imitation, the evening flies by and nobody is bothered about books or television any more. Real storytelling is a gift, an almost forgotten talent.

In his book about Montaillou, Le Roy Ladurie reproduced a page-long report of a conversation between two men eating in a kitchen. It was exclusively concerned with the quality of the cheese, the bread, the fish, and the woman who is operating the oil press. It bore a strong resemblance to the pattern of conversation that generally dominated the

Jorwerter pub, and that was generally referred to as "gassing": jumping from association to association; repetition of little anecdotes that give a feeling of security precisely because they are so familiar; mutual nourishing and grooming of one another's pelts, rather like apes in the sun.

It was the repetition of the story about the solicitor, how "barking" he was where cars were concerned. That once, on a warm summer's afternoon, they had seen him in a field driving around in circles for hours and hours under a sprinkler installation. "Well," he said, "I wanted to see whether my windscreen wipers were still working." Or the time he had phoned the pub all the way from Luxembourg, for Beerenburg liqueur, and the teacher had promptly climbed into his deux-chevaux to bring him two bottles of Beerenburg and a bottle of mature Dutch gin.

Folkert told a story about Hitler: "In the village of Baard there lived a certain Dijkstra, who fought for the SS on the Eastern Front. He fought so well that he was invited to meet Adolf Hitler. He was allowed to make a wish. 'I would like to go fishing with you.' Well, the very next day Dijkstra from Baard went fishing on the Volga with Hitler." This is roughly what the pub stories were like. But real storytelling takes a little bit more.

Storytelling is the literature of the poor and the unseen. Aided by props like rhythm and poetry to jog the memory, it is the best way of piloting important experiences through time, while keeping them relatively intact. But it also contains within it, like literature, deeper layers of wisdom, beauty and poetry. In this way a folk tale is sometimes reminiscent of a cathedral, a work of art that has been constructed over generations.

The stories that Ype Poortinga rescued from old people's homes in the nick of time with his tape recorder, were sometimes cathedrals. As were those that another great collector, the chaplain Adam Jaarsma, managed to unearth in the Frisian countryside between 1965 and 1980 (he found more than 16,000 stories). But it is questionable whether the story of the collapse of the Jorwerter church tower will be passed on in this way; or the story of the vicar who hid from the Germans between the church rafters; or the winter of 1979, when the snow was as high as the roof guttering.

With all the changes, the transference of history and of life's experiences by word of mouth had also come under pressure. That was not merely due to the telling itself. The storytelling moments had decreased significantly as well. In modern Jorwert there were far fewer opportunities than there had previously been to refresh the collective memory.

An alteration in the concept of "time" played an important role here. At the beginning of the twentieth century, "time" had a completely different connotation to that which it had at the close: there was a great deal of long-drawn-out and monotonous work; travelling took longer; farm work was very much linked to the seasons; for the most part, time and life coincided. Besides which a lot of work had to be performed collectively. And then there were those dark, endlessly long winter evenings on the farm. In short, the good old days were full of boring hours in which a good yarn was highly valued. Had not Steven de Bruin as a young boy, picked up the best stories when his father was hanging around waiting for a load, or was inching his way, almost becalmed, through a long fenland canal?

So that the oral tradition was not only smothered by modern methods of communication, but it also wasted away because the humus layer on which it thrived had disappeared: those long, boring days together, in which the hands of the clock seemed to turn ever more slowly.

But even when stories were told, there was still the question of just how far back memory stretched during their telling. And again: what proportion of the stories passed down in this way belonged to the village and its people? Closer inspection revealed that by no means all the folktales were genuine.

Legends and fairy tales fall into different categories depending on the way in which they were handed down. There is even an international system of classification of all the well-known fairy tales and folk tales, a sort of barcode of the mysterious. The divisions run to dozens of categories and sub-categories: animal stories, legends, fairy stories, funny stories, and so on. Hansel and Gretel, for example, fall into category AT 327A (miraculous tales, sub-category supernatural foes). Steven de Bruin's story of the peeing woman and the bewitched snake is registered as AT 285B. Orpheus and Euridice count as a variant of the AT 306 type of story.

Some years ago the man of letters Jurjen van der Kooi carried out a detailed inventory of the stories that Poortinga and others had collected, and he came to the surprising conclusion that in one in eight of these stories passed down by word of mouth, it was purely and simply a question of bogus antiquity: they were stories that had only begun to circulate after they had appeared in a newspaper, an almanac or other written source. In the case of some of the stories told to Poortinga by one elderly farmer's wife, he found the almost literal text on a wall calendar dating from the previous century.

According to Van Der Kooi, most folktales were not remnants of a rich oral tradition that had gradually been subverted by reading, but in actual fact rather the opposite: the so-called fairy tale was itself the result of literacy and a consequent increase in reading.

All of this did not detract from the fact that there were stories – told by an old farmer or elderly skipper – that came from inexplicably far away, as perfect and unexpected as Philippus Breuker's dishes. Stories that were so harsh, erotic or bizarre that they could not possibly belong to the romantic nineteenth-century tradition of storytelling. Stories that were so numerous they could not all have been plucked from almanacs or newspapers.

There really must have been a very extensive oral tradition in the Netherlands. It can hardly have been otherwise. Before the arrival of the book and the written word all historical accounts relied upon stories being repeatedly passed on, a continuous reconstruction of former times based on memory. It is what the Greek epic poems were based on, as well as parts of Jewish religious rules, and some people still adhere to the discipline of collective memory, learned and passed on by word of mouth, a verbal method of history-telling that has gone on for centuries.

It was really more or less the same with storytellers like Steven de Bruin: they almost always came from villages and families where an established tradition of storytelling already existed. Following the example of an Irish colleague, Ype Poortinga spoke of veritable "dynasties of storytellers" that were found especially among "footloose" folk – skippers, traders, migrating seasonal labourers – and in districts – like the barren heathland – where there was a large variety of people. But he too acknowledged that the idea of the "collective story" lying waiting to be discovered under a hedge was romantic nonsense.

Storytelling is an artistic achievement, Portinga wrote, and that is why an old tale can never be separated from the teller: "When Uncle Haring teetered on the edge of his chair, impatient to trump his predecessor's story, that tale sounded decidedly different to how it would have done had we read it out loud from a book."

By the time Poortinga wrote this, in 1976, that situation was almost impossible to reconstruct. It was Poortinga's experience that: "The greatest storytellers are by now often isolated figures," and in his heart he was convinced that he had in fact got hold of the last generation of great storytellers.

In Jorwert storytelling was a daily occurrence up until the 1950s. Every day groups of men and young lads would hang around by the bridge or by the inn. A lot of gassing went on, but there were also evenings when there was some real storytelling.

The Tuesday Evening Rainbow Train, an extremely popular radio programme around 1955, made the first inroads into that habit. Then television arrived, with stories that no longer required any imagination. And then came the young people who knew everything better.

Ids Meinsma and Willem Dijkstra remembered that up until the 1980s after fives matches traditional stories were told, and they had loved it, although they were only about 16. That tradition had ended with the next generation of village youth.

So the storyteller disappeared from Jorwert. And with it one of the most important means by which the village community could pass on something of itself, independent of books, television and other forms of urban media. In this way the village not only lost its heart, but, as time went on, its memory too.

On a summer afternoon in 1994 I watched the vicar, together with Gais and the bricklayer, restoring something that had been broken centuries ago. The rest of the village was celebrating the merke, but the three of them were heedless of that. The vicar had retrieved the old church altar stone, the stone that, somewhere around the time of Wattie van Hania, had been hurled from the church during the Reformation and had lain for centuries since in front of the backdoor of the vicarage. He had cleaned it up a bit, and that afternoon he carried it carefully into the church again. He had constructed a simple elevation of Roman bricks and thus, after more than 400 years, the old altar stone was returned to its rightful place once more.

Gais had lit a candle in an alcove, the flame flickered gently in the silent church, outside the villagers sang and danced, nobody else had any idea this historical event was taking place, but all the same we did feel a little solemn.

Around us lay the churchyard. The small wooden posts for the children's graves that had stood there in 1973, the verse for Eelkje Oene Hoogenbrug — *She died resigned to her fate* — the headstone belonging to Antje Kalma (1856−84) − *Her life on earth gave strength / to husband and children / But God called her from this place / That, no person can prevent* − they had all disappeared, for life goes on even in a churchyard.

But the daisies were flowering around the grave of Wiepke Algera, the farmer with the first chugging milking machine. And around Riemer de Groot's parents − *My time is in your hands*. And Tjitse Tijssen lay there, with his wife. And Fopma, the farmer who gave Oebele van Zuiden the chance of a lifetime. And Lamkje and her husband. And Hendrik Meinsma. And Aaltsje Siesling; Aaltsje lay in a permanent sea of flowers, summer and winter; Durk was forever occupied with it. That is how he told his story.

All the Joys of My Life

All the joys of my life are in the cherry tree, in the shaking
    of a single yellow leaf,
In the clouds from the south that come scudding along on
    the open air,
In hydrangea blooms that the sun shines on:
It is the slight sheen on the water in the channel,
The opulent scent of the muck heap in spring,
The sing-song calling of the Brent geese on the mudflats.

But it is also mother's carefree youth as they skate along the
    waterway together in the moonlight,
It is father's joy when the verses of one of the poets
    gladden his heart.
It is the fragile happiness of grandpa and grandma as, hand
    in hand, they welcome spring.

Oh, and perhaps it is partly the dream of the devout one
When he sees the angels open wide their white wings.

OBE POSTMA

Chapter Twelve

Epilogue

 PERHAPS, I THOUGHT MUCH LATER, PERHAPS IT was not the school conflict after all that had brought the good old times to an end in Jorwert, nor was it the quarrel between the pub and the community centre, or all that new import. Perhaps it was first and foremost the death of Hendrik Meinsma that had started it all.

"The human mind," wrote Leo Tolstoy, "is unable to conceive of the accumulation of causes that go to make up a phenomenon. But the urge to discover causes is implicit in the human soul. And if the human mind cannot discover a cause among the countless jumbled-up circumstances of life, it will pick out the first one, the most plausible one, and say: that is the cause."

In the summer of 1978, when Hendrik Meinsma became gloomier and gloomier, some people said: "He cannot accept that he has got to wind up his business." Others said: "He always was a worrier." And there was some truth in that. In summer he would walk through the village almost every evening with Gais, and if he was doing a painting job somewhere and had burned off the old layers of paint that day, then they invariably had to go and make sure a smouldering patch had not been left behind. Otherwise he could not sleep. He could never leave well alone.

That same worrier was also a cheerful man. He was always in search of good company, enjoyed himself at home, and was always playing his accordion. He loved the new openness in the village, but at the same time he began to feel that things were slipping away from him, as if his work and his craft no longer counted, as if the old family firm was gradually sliding into the canal. At least, that is how it appears to our human mind in retrospect.

His only joy during that period was a small sailing boat that he sandpapered and varnished and cherished like a child. One day he decided to make a present of it to his best friend, the teacher. "Are you kidding?" his friend had responded.

When it was time to launch the boat the whole family had to put in an appearance for a group photograph: wife, children, himself and the boat. An absolute must.

After that it was as if all the stuffing went out of him. One Sunday morning when they were going boating, Hendrik could not start the outboard motor. It upset him for the rest of the day. The following Saturday the Iepenloftspul company were due to make a farewell trip to Zeist. At the last minute he did not want to go – but they eventually managed to persuade him. That night he could not sleep. He woke Gais up time after time in order to talk, until towards morning she had fallen asleep.

At about nine o'clock when she had made coffee and called out to him in his workshop there was no reply. She walked inside and then all she wanted, as she said later on, "was a hole into which I could disappear – but there was only concrete".

For Gais they had been days of utter confusion. Everything was spinning, in her head, but also in the village around her as well. There were people who had absolutely no idea how to respond. There were neighbours who were afraid to call on her to say goodbye to Hendrik. And as for the children. "It was a disaster for us," said Gais. "But it was also a disaster for the community." It made it all doubly difficult. "Who was supposed to be helping who?"

The evening before the funeral, a sort of farewell get-together had been held, with the teacher and a few other good friends. The next day, Hendrik had been carried out of his house to the churchyard on the other side of the street, flanked by just a handful of people. Afterwards there was tea. In the evening there were memories.

After that, the daily round of ordinary life began again, step by step, a long journey, dogged by glances and stares and sometimes a question. People supported Gais. "But," she told me, "the village also required something of me. It was a sort of test. They watched how I coped with it, how I managed it."

She talked about it with anyone who cared to listen, and that had helped. She always said: "All of you find it difficult. I find it very difficult. But we must go on." And there was always the land, and the skies, and the comfort of a country fence.

The months had passed in my Jorwerter house, and an interim period had dawned, a no man's land between winter and spring. A cold wind blew across the fields. The sky was clear. The trees were still bare, the reeds yellow, the ditches grey with mud. The ducks on the meadow flattened their heads against the chill winds from the North. Between golden clouds, one shower after another rolled towards the village, wave after wave, sometimes black as pitch, hail and rain pelted down, and then the sun shone again, harsh and bright.

The farmers said that there was a vigour to the earth, though there was little sign of it. Twittering starlings circled the church tower, the solicitor's garden was full of snowdrops flattened by the wind, and on the wall near Our House someone had written in English: FUCK ME BABY and LICK MY DICK and I LOVE YOU, ALIE TERPSTRA.

I sat by the stove and read how the sociologist A. J. Wichers had viewed the basic pattern of Dutch rural culture in 1965.

The rural population has completely adjusted to the fact that they have to rely upon the earth and must labour over its cultivation, he wrote. They have even grown to love this fate, grown to love the earth and the cattle, while labour, soberness and even poverty have come to be regarded as virtues.

Marriage, family and sex are governed by the strictest of rules, he continued. This is because the means of existence used to be scarce, and this necessitates firm tenets in order to survive. Female coquetry for example is strongly frowned upon, marriage is monogamous and an extremely businesslike arrangement. Once people are married, the marriage functions primarily as a working partnership to which they are fiercely loyal.

According to Wichers, the village community forms a fairly natural whole, due to the fact that everyone is involved in the same activity — namely cattle-rearing and arable farming. Its borders often form the intellectual borders of the inhabitants so that they know little of the outside world. At the same time the village community functions as a social support network, and also as a means of control. After all, too much individuality poses a threat to the social order.

The outside world is composed of a different, unknown order: that of gentlemen, city-dwellers and drifters. The farmer's attitude to the first two is a mixture of awe and mistrust, and he vigorously opposes the latter. He would like to do that with the gentlemen and the city-dwellers too, but the experience of centuries has taught him that he will be the one who eventually has to foot the bill in such a conflict.

With regard to the future, Wichers believed, the farmer views it in the same way that he views the present and the past. So bringing up youngsters consists for the most part in disciplining them. The older generation has complete authority – which is logical, for in a society that hardly ever changes they have the most experience. What is more, an unequivocal "repayment relationship" exists: youngsters have to do something for the elderly in return. Rural culture is not something one abandons lightly: the circle remains closed – according to Wicher's analysis in 1965.

So, this is broadly what the intellectual world of generations of farmers and villagers looked like, and the older Jorwerters too had been brought up more or less according to these values. Wichers knew that he was just in time, that he was describing an ancient culture that was in the process of disappearing from the Netherlands, but he never imagined just how rapidly that disintegration would take place.

Thirty years later, 3,000 farming businesses were being abandoned annually in the Netherlands. According to EEC estimates, half the agriculture in northern Europe would disappear within a single generation. Over a third of cattle-breeding businesses had been wound-up in the previous decade.

Thirty years later, there were special "seduction courses" to help young farmers find a wife, because hardly any young girl wanted to be a farmer's wife any more. Women were advertised in farming magazines: *Ladies from Poland and Russia would gladly lend support to a serious bachelor farmer. Free brochure with photographs . . .*

Thirty years later, an advertising campaign was launched in English

agricultural magazines under the motto: *Stop the killing fields. Take it seriously.*
There was a photograph of a young mother with two children, sitting
in the back of a hearse. *Every week someone on the farm leaves his family.* In the
Netherlands, suicides were not registered by profession, but the signals
coming from churches and social workers were disturbing enough. The
dioceses in Brabant in particular drew attention to the noticeably high
number of suicides among pig farmers. English farmers had the highest
percentage of suicides of all the professions.

Thirty years later, farmer's sons and daughters no longer regarded
succession as automatic, but as something to be very seriously discussed.
The farmers' wives discovered that they were able to make choices, and
indeed had to make them. There were more farms with a female at the
helm — 1 in 30 businesses were run by a woman. But divorce also began
to occur among farming families.

"Oh yes, we do get that type of call," Hanneke Meester from the helpline
said. "Farmers who can no longer see any way out, who are looking into
a black hole. A man like that will say: 'If I do away with myself there
is a decent life insurance policy.'"

I visited the SOS Telephone Helpline for Agriculturists: a national
switchboard run by volunteers, where farmers and their wives could
pour out their hearts anonymously. The mere existence of such a helpline
would have surprised Wichers: farmers are used to fending for themselves, even more so when there are problems. Most farming families
have an irresistible urge to draw in their horns at such times. Employees
are fired, the family becomes a bulwark and the farmer feels ashamed
and no longer shows his face. If hundreds of farmers and farmers' wives
a year are using that helpline, then something really must be up.

"Only recently I had a farmer's wife on the line who was dreadfully
concerned about her husband," Hanneke Meester told me. "She said he
lay in bed all day, wouldn't talk to her any more, wouldn't answer the
phone, wouldn't seek any kind of help. She said: 'When he goes out
the back I get the urge to go after him, because I'm so scared he's going
to harm himself.' We regularly get that sort of call."

Many of the conversations were about shame. A true farmer feels
responsible for all sides of the business, including the things that go
wrong. Because of this, farmers who stopped were frequently regarded

as bad farmers – especially by themselves. There were so many other businesses failing that their reason told them it was more than a matter of bad management. But nonetheless, that is how they experienced it emotionally. They had to bid farewell to the farming organisations to which they – like their fathers and grandfathers before them – had belonged all their life. They received some additional help to wind-up the financial side of things, and that was that. But for the farmer it had only just begun. Some ex-farmers attempted to retain a bit of the old atmosphere by keeping a few sheep and horses. But the others landed unceremoniously in a terraced house in the village.

"Farming is not a profession, it is a way of life," said Hanneke Meester. "It is wedded to the earth, nature, beasts, to everything. A farmer always pays his cattle a quick visit of an evening, just to make sure everything is all right. If you lose them, you lose your life. And you start feeling: this is the end of everything."

There were courses for those who had to wind-up their businesses, and it was often only then that farmers realised they were not alone. "It's like a dam bursting," Hanneke Meester told me. "And once they start talking they just can't stop: about their emotions, how guilty they feel, how they think that others point to them in the street, how they've been let down."

That was also the general complaint of many ex-farmers about the farming bodies. They entirely ignored the mental uprooting of the farmers. The only thing that counted for them was the figures.

What is more, the men had to keep up appearances. It was primarily the women who opened up about that sort of thing, but to their surprise, right from the start, Hanneke Meester and her colleagues had had almost as many men as women on the telephone. "Sometimes we ask them during these sessions: 'Why don't you confide in your neighbour? He is saddled with the same problems after all.' 'That's impossible,' a farmer will reply, 'he's my colleague, but he's also my competitor. As soon as I enter his farmhouse I can see him thinking: Is he here for me, or is he here to relieve me of my land?'"

Hanneke Meester told me that she was once phoned by a man who was the only remaining farmer in his district. "He was terrified. He had watched all the farmers disappearing before his very eyes. Farmers feel very involved with all the basic things of life: the land, nature, provision of food. They ask themselves each day 'What on earth is going on?'"

The environmental lobby should have been a natural ally of the farmers, but the opposite was usually true. Many of the farmers who phoned had nothing but criticism for them. "Who are the ones who live close to nature? Who are the ones who have always been involved with it?" They felt that the environmentalists were ruining everything and were only concerned with their own salaries. In the Achterhoek, east of the Netherlands, there was even an eco-freak who lodged a formal objection (under the Nuisance Act) to every licence for which farmers applied. The farmers could cheerfully have murdered him.

The telephone calls received by Hanneke Meester and her colleagues indicated a clear division between the younger ones and those over 40. "Younger people are more enterprising, they have often seen a bit of the world before they entered the business, they have done work placement and sometimes they have done entirely different work previously, in the building trade, or as a teacher, or whatever. It used to be the case that a son worked for his father and stayed put until he took over the farm himself. It was the only way you knew. After the war it was a case of 'Produce! Produce!' – people were hungry and the economy had to be patched up. The older ones really do feel that they are entirely victims of circumstance."

Each day she listened to one desperate story after another. About the couple forced to stop for health reasons. Their business was doing nicely, but in the present climate no one could be found to take it over. Two-and-a-half years later the farm was still for sale and the farmer was almost bankrupt due to all the interest and repayment. "Soon they will have nothing left."

Or the young farmer who phoned, and who had a girlfriend. "We're mad about each other, but she has a permanent job, and in the present circumstances she doesn't want to become a farmer's wife. What are we to do?"

Or about the problem of succession. A childless farmer who wanted to hand on the business to a nephew who had worked hard on the farm for years. And how the rest of the family were doing everything in their power to prevent this, because it threatened their portion of the inheritance.

And, on the other hand, the farmers who wore themselves out with hard work because the decision to stop kept being postponed – they were often prevented by members of the family acting out of financial motives.

Or about banks and farmers, who frequently clung to one another like drowning men, because they both had too much money tied up in a half-bankrupt concern. "Often the bank eventually draws a line in the sand. Farmers regard the bank as the villain of the piece, but the bank is usually only taking a decision that must be taken in the end.

"It is very important that the farmer takes the decision to stop," Hanneke Meester felt. "There is often precious little time for this, but it is vitally important. Otherwise you can never come to terms with it, then it always remains something that was done to you by others."

Farmers' wives voiced it sooner and more honestly. "We regularly get calls from women who say: 'I've had enough! It's affecting our marriage. We've no money left. It's destroying us. And now my husband wants to talk to the bank one more time.' Women are more inclined to invest their last remaining energy in the future, instead of in a past which is irretrievably lost."

When a society goes through a period of rapid change parents and children quarrel. The fact is that the older generation does have a different view of life to the younger one, and that is how it should be, for they have to survive in different worlds. These sorts of divisions can occur within one's own life, and then one comes into conflict with oneself.

In a world in which everything is permanent – and that was Jorwert until 1945 – there is a good chance that what someone expects to happen will actually also take place. A woman like Lamkje knew more or less what the pattern of her life would be, and that was indeed how it turned out. There was not a very great gap between expectation and reality.

One's expectations were a reflection of what one had already experienced, or had seen happen to others. History repeated itself, and dreams, expectations and reality were not all that far removed from one another – barring a few exceptions, of course.

In societies that are going through big changes the predictability of individual lives is lost. Raised expectations are suddenly dashed, people can better themselves too, sometimes to a great extent, but they can also just as easily fall, hard and fast. The objectives one set oneself in one's youth turn out not always to be feasible in later life. More seriously still: a farmer may have to put the family ideals of mutual help and sacrifice to one side, in order to survive in today's world.

In those March weeks I ended up one morning at a public auction somewhere out in the country, near a waterway.

In a single morning the complete inventory of three generations of farmers was auctioned off: tractors, cranes, trucks, electric-fencing apparatus, milk churns, shakers, mowing machines, spray-guns, gates, barbed wire, Aukje 15, Cornelia 73, Janna 31, Marijke 128, screwdrivers, a Singer sewing machine – it was all dealt with in no time.

"And everything cash down, please. Dutch banknotes!" the auctioneer shouted. "Lot number one. The milk container behind the shed – what am I bid for the milk container?" He stood on a trailer in the middle of the farmyard: "10, 10, 15, 15, 25, 25, 40, 40, 40, 40, 40!" Behind him, tall grey and silent, stood the solicitor in a long black raincoat. Coffee was on sale in one of the sheds; the estate agent had set up office in a cowshed, between bales of straw; in the front garden a stall selling chips was doing good business.

It was a clear spring day and the air was full of birds. The name of the farm was Ebanezer, and a dog was barking in an empty cowshed, with long drawn-out howls. The furniture had already been removed from the rooms, the house had been sold to the neighbours opposite and the farmyard was now full of hundreds of farmers from near and far.

The family did not show themselves. The son, the owner of the business, had been admitted to a psychiatric hospital and, according to the neighbours, he just sat there staring straight ahead. The young man had taken over the farm from his father, had invested like mad in the newest machinery, had then devised wild plans to emigrate to Canada, and after that it had all gone wrong.

Dealers always look just that little bit more frivolous than farmers, and this was true at the auction: they wore scarves, or strange hats, or they sported blue, three-piece suits above their green wellington boots. As the morning progressed, a small market in tips, networks and business contacts developed in the farmyard, and hardly any attention was paid any more to the piercing voice of the auctioneer. The public were reminiscent of an American film: weathered faces, strange lumps and bumps, ash-tipped cigars, caps, brilliantined hair, the women with trays and long dresses.

"During the past two weeks I have visited at least 25 businesses that were winding things up," a dealer near the stall with coffee and biscuits told me. "The causes are always the same: the environmental demands and the succession. And if they require you to invest hundreds of thousands of guilders in a manure storage facility, and you are also well aware that tomorrow they will be demanding something else again, and at the same time you can make a few million – well, then it does become very tempting."

The single reason many farmers refused to make that simple choice had to do with a factor that you could not put a price on: the family. Anyone who studies Jolt Oostra's list of Jorwerter farms can see how the family relationships spring back and forth. The farms were passed on to sons or sons-in-law, then there was a widow, who in her turn married a farmhand, then a nephew came into the business, then a grandson, whole strings of four, five, sometimes 13 generations. And even at the close of the twentieth century the family was still regarded by many farmers as a sort of basic unit within which economic relations were narrowly interwoven with ties of the blood.

For farmers the phenomenon of "time" had traditionally never been a straight line linking the present to the future, but rather a circular course. That is why children belonged on a farm, they were vital pairs of hands, they functioned as an insurance policy for one's old age and they provided assurance that the world would carry on turning in the same way. Childlessness was a downright disaster for survivors. In the countryside sexual relations before marriage were often regarded as a pregnancy test in reverse. While nineteenth-century cities grew ever more prudish, on Frisian farms enamoured couples were still deliberately left alone when the parents retired to bed. The possible consequences were bravely born; often they were actively welcomed, as it was the sole way of ensuring the farmyard would never fall silent.

In modern times, too, agriculture could not exist without strong family ties. In 1995, 95 per cent of the work was still carried out by the farmer and his family in four out of five businesses. One third of the agricultural labour force was still composed of wife, children and other family members who lived in. According to calculations made by the Institute for Agricultural Economics, most farming businesses would incur severe losses if they had to pay for the work done by family members at the normal commercial rates. Only by dint of the cheap labour the family unit provided were they able to hold on to enough money to keep up with the investment race.

There were shifts, but they happened slowly. Since 1970 for example the women's share of the work had decreased by roughly a quarter, and that of the children had halved. But not to take over, to simply give up the business because of the money and the inheritance, that broke with a hundred years of family tradition and a thousand-year-old culture.

"An obstetric speculum? 10, 10, 30, 30, 50, 50, 50, going once, 70, 70 . . ." I was suddenly reminded of Jos de Putter's film, the part where his father talks about the lack of a successor. "The knowledge that you have a successor drives you on, it's the reason you do everything after all," he said. And I thought of Sake Castelein, who was saddled with the same problem, and the Wiedijks, who did it all for those little boys in their pyjamas. The family involved in the auction had been through that phase. Their son had taken over the business, albeit with difficulty. He had been full of grand ideas, but just six months later the neighbours observed that he no longer even got out of bed.

With most other businesses it did not even get to the succession stage. In 1995 two thirds of Dutch farmers over the age of 50 said they had no successor. The market value of a healthy business was so high it was virtually impossible for a son or daughter to take it over at that price. So they paid less, but that meant the other children had to forego a sizeable portion of their inheritance. The emotions this unleashed ran deep: on the one hand they had everything to do with the farming tradition of continuity from generation to generation, and on the other hand with the modern tendency towards individualisation and "putting your own interests first". Even when the other children were prepared to sacrifice their financial gain for the good of the continuity of the family business – and that often happened – even then, the successor had to carry a very heavy moral burden. For it was now up to him to pilot the family inheritance through the stormy seas of time. Many farmers' sons and daughters felt unable to risk that uncertain future. Others were broken by it.

On farms where things went wrong, family culture played a key role too, but an inverse one. In Hanneke Meester's experience, "If a business is doing badly, then the children usually get sucked into the downfall too." She told me about a vocational school nearby, specialising in agriculture, where five children had been removed from school within a single week because they had to work at home – often on farms that in the long term were past saving anyway. At her helpline they received more and more complaints about child labour. Not the informal helping out there used to be, but essential work involving children from about the age of eight upwards: driving the tractor, harvesting, helping with milking, cleaning the cowsheds, just everything. It is sheer desperation, said Hanneke Meester, and they are ashamed, and that is why they never mention it. "Sometimes we get calls from farmer's wives who say: 'I'm leaving and I'm taking the children with me. I can't bear to watch the downfall of my husband and his business any longer.' And leave they do, you hear that more and more."

So the farming profession fell noiselessly between two stools: the family and the market, tradition and modernity.

Ebanezer, thus far the Lord has guided us. Outside the lambs were bleating. The auctioneer's calls echoed across the fields – "The cheese press? 15, 30, 40, 40, 40, 40 ... going once, twice ... " – and they were carried by the wind, to the villas and the English gardens on the other side of the water.

In 1995, the turn of the year was silent and lonely in Jorwert. There were no youngsters carting loads of kindling and agricultural leftovers, which had been the custom until recently. The streets were deserted. Almost everyone was at home, keeping themselves (and the television) company. The *Leeuwarder Courant* reported that in St Nicolaasga a new vandal-proof Christmas crib was installed. Too many sculptures had been removed and destroyed in previous years. Baby Jesus had been broken in two.

Everywhere in the villages there were complaints about how icy the pavements were – many people no longer scattered salt on their own doorsteps. In their opinion that was a job for the council.

The Baarderadeel Arms had remained empty. It was said that Eef had stood behind the bar, crying.

The previous night Wietse Blanke's farm had gone up in flames, without anyone in the village noticing. He had only barely managed to escape across the frozen meadow with his wife and two toddlers. By the time the fire brigade arrived the whole place had been burned to the ground. Practically everything Wietse and his wife possessed had been lost, including two ponies, two bull calves, a few cats and the dog that Wietse was so fond of. The family was taken care of by the village, and by next morning a collection of clothes and toys was already underway. But Wietse was still to be found at the spot where his house had stood, searching among the rubble and the thin covering of snow, and calling for his lost dog.

I had been away for a while, but had come back (it was impossible not to, with a village like Jorwert). I once lived quite nearby, in Leeuwarden and in the neighbouring village of Hardegarijp. The sun never shone in Leeuwarden (this was during the 1950s); the mayor's name was Adriaan and he kept his bicycle in the front room; the people smelled of stewing steak, righteousness and wet raincoats; the rain dripped from the bare branches in Hardegarijp; the girl in the sub-post office – it was somewhere in an old villa – sat at the counter crying, and all the walls had ears. "Get away! I have to get the hell out of here!" was the only thing I could think of during those years.

I still don't know exactly when things changed. Over the years Adriaan and the wet raincoats disappeared, and I began to remember the intimacy of the old village station. The winter mornings in the waiting room when we all sat around a big coal fire waiting for the "clog express", a diesel locomotive pulling a series of worn-out coaches that had seen all Europe in their better days. The neighbours – what an incredibly good-natured, kindly lot they were. The dreamy journeys through the frozen, snow-covered pastures. The landscape.

I gradually began to accept the Frisian side of myself. I allowed my grandparents and my great-grandparents to take up residence. I gave them the best chair, and I let them tell their story: my great-grandfather, who was a baker in Drachster Compagnie, had gone bankrupt round about 1890, at the time of the great famine, because he could not bear to see his neighbours go hungry; my great uncle, a teacher, out canvassing every evening on behalf of the Social Democratic Workers Party (SDAP) and the temperance movement; my grandfather, a teacher in Gaasterland; my grandmother, daughter of a permanently drunk rural constable in Balk; my mother with her Frisian pride and clear blue eyes.

I let them tell their story, and I began to understand their language once again, their sing-song Frisian that you hardly ever hear any more; the way they talked in understatements, the subtle signals that were part of the village way of doing things; their slowness that was not sluggishness but harmony.

At the same time that sense of rediscovery was mixed with something resembling wistfulness. Just as is it does with all emigrants, the countryside in my head had in fact long since disappeared. The villages, too, had grown with the times and kept pace with progress.

When I returned and went to live in Jorwert I expected to be able to describe the results of a silent revolution, something that had already taken place and had only to be committed to paper. But the longer I remained in the village the more I realised that it was actually all still to come. Only, nobody knew just what was about to begin, or where it was heading.

With the disappearance of the farming class it seemed as though the stability of this province had been replaced by a discreet sort of panic. Every evening the *Leeuwarder Courant* was pushed through the letterbox, every evening I saw the front pages and the regional sections, and I have never seen so many sweeping plans launched amid so much furore, only to stray off course and be abandoned soon afterwards.

It caused a great hubbub when an American company settled on the Balkster industrial estate. It built brand new premises, promised to provide work for 200 people within one and a half years, and went bust within the year.

In Harlingen, a project developer presented a plan for the construction of 160 bungalows, and the upgrading of the swimming pool to a "spa with warm salt and mineral baths" – but after a tumultuous start, nothing more was heard from him.

There was a plan for a sizeable waste disposal complex near Leeuwarden — but instead of 15 jobs per hectare the complex in fact only provided a tenth of that — one-and-a-half jobs per hectare. Millions were spent in Wolvega, constructing the best sulky-racing course in the Netherlands — but because the Frisians were fond of horses but not of gambling, there was so little interest the business folded within a few years. Such things happen everywhere, but it was happening a bit too often here.

Even Aqualutra — the otter park in Leeuwarden which the city had wanted to promote throughout Holland with the slogan "Take a Ducking in Leeuwarden: Otter City" — was not a success. Within a few months of it opening the provincial press was bulging with reports of rows within the "otter team". The ten remaining otters, the one beaver, the eight storks, the polecat, the ducks and the geese in the park were soon left in the hands of a few volunteers. It eventually transpired that the director had tamed one of the otters and kept it, kitted out with a small pair of reins, at home in the attic, for his own pleasure.

It was as though the province was no longer able to strike the right balance between itself and the future. The type of yuppie that had long since disappeared from the Western conurbations popped up all over the place, eager to capitalise on the problems of a countryside going through a period of rapid change.

They wanted to create a 400 metre-long beach on the Rjochte Grou, in the meadows between Jirnsum and Friens. In Bozum the "Big-West" plan had been thought up for the "Middle Sea navigational route". Near Lemmer the "Port Lemmer" plan was developed for no fewer than 1,000 bungalows. In Gaasterland there were plans for a big recreational project that took as its theme "actively experienced silence" — but the nearby grass-drying factory stank so badly that the idea was abandoned. In Stavoren they wanted to build 80 "Hanseatic-houses", complete with two "watchtowers" on the harbour side.

After hundreds of years of cattle-breeding and crop growing the departing farmers left behind a vacuum that nobody was quite sure how to deal with. One project after the other was dreamed up, mature and naïve, useful and absurd, all mixed together. When you added it all up, it was just that little bit too much; the language was just a bit too bombastic, and in almost every case the prognoses were so optimistic that even outsiders could smell a rat.

In Grouw, for example, they wanted to create a "Waterfront Project" on the Pikmeer, modelled on San Franciso. On the other side of the water they envisaged a villa-park, but of such proportions that just about all the wealthy inhabitants of Friesland could be housed there.

In the area between Oudemirdum and Rijs a plan existed for the construction of a large bungalow park, as well as a yachting marina on the IJsselmeer, a beach, an adventure-canoeing course, a restaurant and a nature reserve of almost 500 acres – but it was scuppered by the district council. At Kollum the Kollumeroord recreation plan was developed, a "unique plan" for 175 bungalows – the only trouble was that no one could explain just what was so unique about it.

In Beetgum and Beetgumermolen we met up with our old friend Johan de Jong again, now toting a "Masterplan Menaldumadeel": a "top location" for 200 spacious villas, a fully-dredged recreational lake – "Hemmemma's Lake" – and eleven mini-castles that were to be sold as flats.

There was indeed every reason for concern – which is not the same thing as making panicky plans. In the 1980s, agriculture and everything connected with it provided a quarter of total employment in the province. Ten years later a significant part of that had disappeared. The economic growth of the province was the lowest in the Netherlands, and the forecasts were not promising. The EEC had designated a large part of Friesland a "structurally underdeveloped area" – which produced attractive subsidies, but also said something about the seriousness of the problem.

In an attempt to promote Friesland as an attractive place to set up business there were widespread advertising campaigns – although, after interviewing more than 500 "Dutch" concerns from outside the province, a research bureau came to the conclusion that the campaigns had no influence whatsoever on any possible plans to move. New businesses still preferred the environs of Schipol airport, and they steered clear of the northern wastes.

As for the companies that did apply, too often they had such a whiff about them – figuratively or sometimes literally – that there was no longer any place for them in the conurbations of the West. If businesses like this were allowed to set up shop it meant that in the long term the charm of the countryside was being sacrificed. And this clashed with recreational interests – which actually only provided jobs for about four months a year, for the Netherlands does not have a lot going for it as far as climate is concerned.

So the province was faced with a number of difficult dilemmas. Should the countryside wait for better times, as a sort of farming ghetto, a green spare lung, the Northern Ireland of the Western conurbations? Should the province throw caution to the wind and take the plunge with dubious businesses, because holiday nostalgia did not provide enough bread and butter? Should it put all its hope in the construction of the magnetic train (Schiphol–Hamburg–Berlin) which would bring the north within arm's reach of the western conurbations and northern Germany?

Or should the Frisians rely on the (frequently underestimated) possibilities of their own business community. Should they accept that young people move away and the elderly come flocking in, with all that it implies for the long-term make-up of the population? Should Friesland become the Florida of the Netherlands after all, a green recreation and residential province with employment increasingly provided by housing, feeding and caring for the elderly refugees from the western conurbations?

In the Hague meanwhile, the problems of the countryside were regarded as marginal. The fifth Governmental Amendment on Environmental Planning focused all attention on the western conurbations, on the hotbeds – Amsterdam, Schiphol and the Ruhr area – and on the so-called "development axis" in the direction of the east and south of the country.

There was talk of the Los Angeles model for the Holland of 2030 (leave the cities to sort it out themselves), or the Hong Kong model (make the city more city-like and the countryside more counrified), or the Zaanstad model (restrict growth to the ring of cities formed by Eindhoven, Rotterdam, The Hague, Amsterdam, Utrecht and Arnhem). There was also a notion of sacrificing the countryside between Alphen on the Rhine, Gouda and Woerden to the construction of Holland City, an entirely new city the size of the Hague. Others still felt the solution lay in the regions of Ede-Veenendaal, Arnhem-Nijmegen, Tilburg-Eindhoven or even in an artificial island off the beaches of Zuid-Holland.

But all the plans had one thing in common: within the coming decades no large-scale development was expected north of the Zwolle-Enchede line. "The northern provinces will be the place for anyone wanting to live quietly in the twenty-first century," noted the NRC *Handelsblad* in the summer of 1995, a message that had already got through to those people advertising villas and bungalows in the paper. The countryside was dismissed as "a peripheral zone" in internal government memorandums, where the problem of unemployment would eventually "evaporate", due to the permanent migration of the young, clever and skilled to the western conurbations.

They were difficult years for rural administrators. A great deal of serious hard work was devoted to matters that were anything but nonsense: further development of the infrastructure, improving waterways, constructing cycle-paths and recreational areas, building new schools and training centres, improving the quality of people's lives, and creating new employment.

But at the same time the mayor of every district council had to have his own ring road. District councils tried to tempt newcomers by permitting everything that was (quite rightly) forbidden elsewhere: maximum heights, locations, environmental requirements, they could always come to some agreement – despite the fact that there were already more than 1,700 acres of empty industrial sites within the province, and another 2,200 acres being developed, and that in reality only about 135 acres a year were sold.

In some villages the attitude seemed to be: anything goes, as long as building continues and as long as it provides subsidies.

During those last years the Frisian countryside sometimes reminded me of the girl in the sub-post office who was so afraid of being left alone she gave herself to anyone and everyone, quite forgetting just how nice she was in her own right.

On a clear March day I accompanied Frans Gerritsma again on his daily round through the Gaasterland landscape. Frans had a rosy complexion and always sparkled with a contagious happiness. The back of his car was inhabited by the offspring of Sunny Boy, Buster, Delta Cleitus Jabot and La Belle, all packed in dozens of thin straws, in a cooling tank with liquid nitrogen, 200 degrees below zero.

Frans was one of the 65 inseminators of the Frisian Cattle Syndicate, who together were responsible for the impregnation of about 400,000 cows a year. Choose straw, defrost, warm up insemination syringe, stick straw in back pocket to keep warm, pull on gloves, enter cow shed, grab chart, find cow, one arm up the bum, search for opening of womb with syringe – cow now arches back, gazes ahead with nonplussed expression – inject, enter details in mini-computer, and all that about 35 times a day, for the last 21 years.

"Antje 47," mumbled Frans. "Difficult animal." Antje thundered through the shed, snorting, slithering on the smooth concrete floor. He manoeuvered her into a corner with difficulty. "I already know I'll have to make a return visit. An impregnation never works when the beast concerned is so full of adrenaline."

The Frisians were still regarded as the best cattle-breeders in the world, but the famous Ademas, Gerards, and Sietskes Keimpes who modelled for the statue of "Us Mem" (Our Mother), no longer counted for much. The bull chart, which lists the rankings of the AI-station's best bulls, made that brutally obvious. In an average cow, the sperm of the American bull Jabot apparently produced offspring whose milk production was more than 1,400 litres higher. Sunny Boy improved milk production by almost 1,000 litres. The first Frisian–Dutch bull, Lodder 48, was right at the bottom of the list. Whoever made use of this bull circa 1995 to cover an average cow, lowered the milk production by at least 1,000 litres. The bull was only really kept on for hobby-farmers, for appearance's sake, as a sort of living museum piece.

Meanwhile the pumps in the milk-pit hummed, the railings rattled, and the indefinable aroma of fresh milk mixed with hay filled the air. The steamy breath of the cattle as they ate. Tractors with feed drove slowly along the gangway of the loosebox cowshed. "More and more farmers nowadays keep their cattle more or less permanently inside. It's more efficient," Frans told me. "If they roam loose they graze in different places, and that causes fluctuations in the milk yield."

The morning light fell in broad stripes through the window. The cats stretched on the hay bales. But the cowsheds were no longer full by any means, and more and more often we had to disinfect ourselves and put on special wellingtons at the door. Some sheds even contained a complete sluice, like you see in hospitals. The modern cow may be a milk factory on four legs, but she is no match for a few germs.

We passed a farm camping site — "There's no farming done here any more." A bit further up they had constructed an eel-fattening unit in the cowshed. And another farm had been sold to a butcher from Brabant. "Here, Runia State, there's a spiv from Noord-Holland living there now. At that farm they cultivate chicory nowadays. And last year, over there on the far side, the farmer was discovered lying dead among his cows."

Just in the area where Frans did his rounds, more than 70 farmers had stopped within the past few years, mostly small farmers but some bigger ones too. "The smaller farmers get squeezed by their debts. Their children come home from Agricultural college: 'Heit, we have to buy quota, otherwise we'll be in trouble.' That's where the road to the bank begins."

He told me about the stress with which his customers lived; about a farmer who tried to kill his dog because the animal had gnawed at a cow while she was calving. "When it didn't work he tied the beast to a tractor and just kept on clubbing it until it was dead. So then he'd lost both his cow and his dog."

Or about the farmer's wife who had suddenly burst into tears in the farmyard one Saturday morning. "He flogs my children dreadfully because they don't work hard enough, and he hits me too." Frans did not know where to look.

A year later when he was there again, the farmer told him that his wife had had an accident just an hour before. She was up a ladder in the barn and she had fallen backwards, onto the concrete floor. Now she lay in the vestibule. "Shouldn't you stay with her then?" Frans had enquired. "No, I have to see to the cattle." The cow that was to be covered was quite a long way off in the meadow. "Look, I'll come back another time," Frans had said, "you can't come with me now." No, it had to be now, and he was determined to go. While they were at work in the meadow, they saw the ambulance arrive and depart, and the farmer's wife was taken off to hospital, without so much as a goodbye. "In the end that farmer had his cows spread out all over the place in tiny pens, he went totally round the bend. He stopped only last year, at the age of 70.

The farm has been sold. None of his children wanted to succeed him."

As we drove through the countryside – a countryside in transition – I asked myself why farmers had accepted all these changes so resignedly. Was it because they were too busy keeping their own businesses going, and had no energy left for the interests of the farming community as a whole? Or were their subsidies at risk? Or were their interests too diverse?

Everyone in Jorwert had an opinion about it. Oebele van Zuiden felt that any farmer worth his salt should have seen the enforced increases in size coming. Bonne Hijlkema said that when it came down to it every farmer was on his own. "Some of them have more or less cracked it, and others not quite. And you always remain competitors."

I remembered a conversation with Cor Wiedijk. "Of course it's our own stupid fault," he had said. "We've allowed ourselves to be goaded into things, and afterwards we didn't have the nerve to put our foot down any more. A farmer always has his own land, his own livestock and property. And you know that you have too much to lose if you start contesting everything. It costs you too much time, there's too much at stake. So you buckle down again."

But perhaps the lack of fighting spirit among farmers also had to do with their manner of dealing with misfortune: it was fate, nature, the weather. In a way, political whim was interpreted in the same manner as a flood or an outbreak of swine fever. It was important to protect yourself, by your own means, as best you could, but apart from that it could not be helped.

There had been a farmer in the district who had wanted to start again, not bother about milk quotas and other rules, just do his own thing. Everyone warned him, Cor Wiedijk told me, but still, he purchased a farm and started milking. The factory soon stopped taking his milk because he did not have a quota. Other farmers in difficult circumstances quite often received some extra quota in those early days, but there was not a single farmer prepared to sacrifice something for this newcomer.

"Why didn't we help him?" Cor asked himself.

"Now he works for a cleaning company," added Lies Wiedijk.

"He was warned by everybody," said Cor.

"But he had the heart and soul of a farmer," said Lies, "and we let him get bogged down in the mire."

Frans had brought a lunch box full of sandwiches, and he had favourite spots where he liked to eat them. He took me to Mirns, a tiny harbour on the IJsselmeer.

"In the old days I used to sit next to my uncle on a bench in the cowshed," he said. "I thought it was wonderful, all of it. The milking, the feeding, the calving, somehow you could feel how they cherished it all. My uncle milked about 30 cows, and they provided him with a good living. Nowadays it's only the strongest and most business-like farmers who survive. Now it's all about fat content and proteins, to within a fraction of a percentage, and with entire computer systems to keep tabs on it all."

He complained that the culture of business efficiency was smothering the culture of trust. "Nowadays the margins are very narrow for farmers as well. I rush in and out, there's no time for a chat any more. In the old days, if you made a mistake with the type of semen – which happens to every inseminator – nobody was too bothered. Now they get on their high horse and come demanding compensation."

He told me about his uncle, who always used the same people: the same cattle-dealer, the same blacksmith, the same animal-feed factory. It was a relationship of trust between regular customers and regular suppliers. The family member who took over the farm had a whole succession of new people on the premises: he paid attention first and foremost to the price and was extremely calculating, sometimes playing them off against each other.

Many cowsheds now had a computerised registration system and that made it possible to plan everything precisely: the amount of feed per cow, the milk yield, everything. But it all relied on subsidies and grants whose financing was less and less certain.

One in five Dutch farmers was, perhaps not surprisingly, considering emigrating. Trade journals were full of advertisements placed by emigration agencies: Canada, and also France, Belgium and Germany. Some farmers wanted to devote themselves entirely to cattle-breeding – the great speciality of the Frisians – or to vegetables and market gardening. Others put their faith in small-scale camping sites, in "bed-and-breakfast on the farm" and in the sale of locally produced vegetables, fruit, cheese and milk.

Other farmers hoped they could stay on as sort of park wardens in the environmentally protected areas that were to be formed. In this way a new dependence on subsidies was created, only now they were nature and environmental subsidies, instead of agricultural moneys. And the question remained: who is paying for it all, and for how long, and how much? – especially if those new environmentally protected areas continue to increase and the natural maintenance provided by the farmers has disappeared.

But there was one thing everyone was certain about: what had happened was irreversible.

"Every time the farmers sell their property, they sell a bit of the country-side too," my friend the newspaperman opined. "They sell it for madcap recreational projects, for enormous factory farms, for increases in business size, for nothing." He himself was the son of a farmer. Of his brothers one became a teacher, the other a pilot, he became a journalist, and they had always been rather concerned about the one brother who stayed in farming. "He was the one who had to work the hardest for the least money. But in the last few years that has all completely changed. Now he's the one with money, and what's more, if he sells his cattle and his farm and more especially his land and his milk quota he'll be a millionaire five times over."

The socio-economic development that I came across in the Frisian countryside was particularly unusual because it was not detrimental to the income of those primarily affected. It was raining while the sun shone.

Agriculture died wealthy. Due to all the EEC subsidies, the difference between the cost price and the actual price of milk was so great that the bigger dairy farmers made a fortune. One litre of milk quota (the right to produce one litre of subsidised milk a year) cost around four guilders in 1995, and big farmers willingly paid it. That says something about their revenue, but it also says something about the lack of any real alternative to farming on blindly just to keep going. The future itself was also on sale, for four guilders a litre.

We had coffee at Frans' home. He linked his pocket computer to the centre's telephone line. "Thirty years ago farmers hung a sack outside, by the road, when they required AI. Now the fertilisation results are worked out to within a tenth of a per cent. And in Leeuwarden they can also see, at a glance, exactly what time I arrived at which farmer's this morning, and what results I achieve. That's fine by me, but some of my less handy colleagues find that sort of computer print-out very stressful." The printer began to rattle: a new roll of assignments for the rest of the day.

We called on an old farmer, stooped with hard work, who still did almost everything by hand. We saw a traditional cowshed with 13 cows, where everything was spotless, the straw yellow and abundant, the cattle sleek, the smell of manure sweet. We visited his neighbour, where the whole shed seemed to be covered in a thin layer of shit, and where the flanks of the cows were caked with thick globs of dung.

A little later we were standing in an enormous loose box cowshed, with American-style quantities of cattle, everything fully automatic. We coincided with a team from some sort of agricultural magazine, that had already spent half the afternoon preparing two cows for a photograph: they had been showered with a special cow-shampoo, the udders had been made darker with rouge, the black markings had been touched up with spray paint, the white with flour, the tassel on the tail made fuller with a piece of rope, and now the last remaining bits of hair were being shaved off.

The sun was shining. On the muckheap lay a dead, newborn calf. A woman was hanging winter clothing over the washing line. "What's this, full of the joys of spring already?" shouted Frans. Above the land birds were twittering.

"There is an assurance that labour is not futile; that nature, or God, has some part in it," wrote Robert Redfield. "There is a story or a proverb to assure one that some human frailty is just what one ought to expect; there are in many cases more serious myths to explain the suffering of the innocent or to prepare the mind for death."

So although farmers quarrelled, gossiped, hated and feared just like the rest of us, their way of life alone provided a structure, and the depth of even their simplest experience could sometimes make the world about them bearable and explicable again for a while.

When Lamkje's, Hendrik's, Oebele van Zuiden's and Tjitse Tijssen's village embraced the city and no longer had any need of farmers, butchers and hauliers, it caused this small community to gradually break loose from the old system of values. It was a process hastened still further by the influence of television and the new multimedia systems.

By 1995 almost the whole district had cable television, there was a choice of 20 television stations and in most villages even the NRC and de Volkskrant, both national dailies, dropped through the letterbox no later than they did in the Apollolaan in Amsterdam. Everyone, even on the most far-flung farms, was confronted with a storm of sounds and impulses, with people and events a long way from home, with actions that were separated from their causes and consequences, with experiences that we could only partially identify with, because they were not actually seen or experienced.

All the children of Jorwert used to believe in ghosts, and many of the grown-ups too. That was a thing of the past. Ghosts symbolised the unexpected, the untamed in nature. In that sense too, the countryside had become the city: everything was under control, they had everything in hand. But religion still played an important role in this village, just like neighbourliness, a different form of association between young people and their elders, and several other village values. And it was noticeable how quickly newcomers from the city adapted to this – had quite possibly been looking for it.

In the summer of 1996 the Jorwerter merke was celebrated once again. Jan Dijktra was almost 65, and rumours that the pub might be closing became stronger and stronger. Eef and Jan's daughter wanted to set up a big riding stables and the upstairs room could then be converted into a flat.

By now the Iepenloftspul in the solicitor's garden had become a desirable attraction for the fashion-conscious city-dweller. There were now eight telephone lines available for bookings, and the total of 6,000 tickets were sold out within two days. There were plans to construct a car park on Sake's land, complete with tiling and street lights, especially for this sort of event. An expensive evening had been organised for the sponsors, with half the village parading around in fancy dress.

Sije Hogerhuis had died at the age of 101. To the last, Akke van Zuiden had visited him every day, even in the old people's home, since, according to her, they had no time there to cut up his bread properly, and they had also mislaid his false teeth. In the churchyard he lay a few feet away from Tjitse Tijssen, under a long, narrow mound of earth, for the gravestone was not yet in place.

A stone's throw away from the ruins of Groot Hesens castle, two enormous wind turbines were now turning. There had been a few burglaries in the village, and most Jorwerters now kept their doors locked. Oebele and Akke van Zuiden were seriously considering moving. There had been a healthy crop of newcomers, and there were even plans to build four new houses.

Wietse Blanke's farm had already been half rebuilt, and he himself drove around the merke in a sleigh made from a converted car chassis, "pulled" by a strange sort of horse that, by means of an ingenious system of pneumatic piping, spewed out unexpected jets of foaming water, to the hilarity of the onlookers.

The rest of the fair, too, was an unprecedented success. It seemed as though the village had come through the worst. Douwe de Bildt acted in a play (supposedly dating from about 1949) about a man who had to take over the housekeeping from "the wife" for a day. The children had organised their own circus performance, with Nina Sieslinga – Durk's granddaughter Nienke Siesling – as the star of the elephant show.

Ids Meinsma had moved back to Mantgum. By now he was the father of a son. Wiepkje Castelein was pregnant and had also left the city behind. She was living in Weidum again. Gais Meinsma was doing voluntary work in a hostel for tramps and drug addicts in Leeuwarden. "You can't change the way you are," she said. "There's no getting around it."

In the upstairs room of the Baarderadeel Arms young and old drank and danced with one another: Gais and the bank manager, Sake, Yke, Bonne Hijlkema, even Oebele and Akke got to their feet when the band played the polka. They danced together there in that room, a little stiffly and formally, everything was exactly the same as it had always been, people came and went, and everything just kept repeating itself.

There is an assurance that labour is not futile; that nature, or God, has some part in it.

And so the village lived on, in the dream of the devout one, in the slow dance of the elderly, in a lightness formerly unknown to it.

Afterword to the 2010 Edition

And now?

IT IS ALMOST FIFTEEN YEARS LATER. I AM SEATED AT THE BIG TABLE IN THE café with the church warden and the teacher. It is autumn, the pouring rain beats against the dark windows. Not a great deal has changed in here. Jan and Eef have left, there are more volunteers working behind the bar now, there is a little more dancing and a few more parties, but the plush tablecloths, the tap, the red rafters and the old clock are still the same. Every Wednesday evening is still draughts night, once a year there is the local theatre company production, and on the Saturday before Christmas we still dance to music of The Two Left Feet.

The teacher's curls have turned grey. His cozy little school has been swallowed up by a huge administrative body, run by overly ambitious managers over whom neither the parents nor he have any sway. "They come into the classroom and don't give the children a second look," he complains. "They just stare at their laptops, scanning through the results of the written examinations. We don't teach the children anything anymore; all we do is train them to perform." He had come home half an hour late that afternoon. "Afke's rabbit died. So of course the teacher had to go along to see the grave." His bosses haven't the slightest idea what he does; in fact, they don't even want to know.

"We'll have to make an early start tomorrow," the church warden says to the man behind the bar. "It's choked full of roots over there, it'll take a fair while to dig the hole."

Conversation flags. A few days ago old Folkert was still sitting here, well into his nineties, with his Frisian gin bitters and his roll-ups. Now he is dead. He "did himself in", as they say around here, during an icy cold night with snow on the ground, in the ditch behind his house. "I can't keep it up anymore," he had written, in a few long, solemn sentences. In Dutch, not in his native Frisian. He didn't want to be a burden to his neighbours any longer. "You'll find my clogs, that's where you'll find me."

Folkert was the last of the generation that had lived through all the big changes in the village: from the oil lamp to the electric light, from the horse and wagon to the car and the tractor, from the simple performance by the village drama club to the popular song festival on German TV. "Man oh man, wasn't that a treat!" he would say when he came into the café afterwards. He was also the last of a breed of villagers who almost never went further than Mantgum. On occasion someone would take him to Leeuwarden, to buy a shirt or a few towels. In the department store he would look around in amazement: "Take a gander at this, would you! My Lord, and you can pull down whatever you want off the shelf!"

He never had grown completely accustomed to modern life, and that estrangement became more pronounced as he grew older. He turned ninety, and older, and at the same time he viewed the world through the eyes of the fifteen-year-old village boy he had once been. Towards the end of his life it was fascinating to talk to him. His observations came more and more to resemble those of someone from 1929 who had suddenly been rocketed by magic into the year 2009. "It's amazing that I'm still here, isn't it, it's already 2009! My Lord! Gjalt's car can do 160! And now they've even elected a black man president in America, I saw it on TV with my own eyes, straight from America! You wouldn't believe it otherwise, would you?"

Modernity didn't irritate him, nostalgia was not part of his makeup – the misery of bygone years was still too fresh in his memory. But he was amazed.

On the outside, Jorwert – just like the café – has barely changed since the 1990s. A handful of new houses have been built, sprightly constructions with lots of glass, square roofs and a front garden with a fence. The vicar has left, the vicarage is now inhabited by an estate agent with a hot tub in the attic. The congregation – a merger of four former parishes – comprises about a hundred and fifty souls, no more than thirty of whom actually attend Sunday services.

There has been the requisite joy and suffering: divorces, deaths, new happiness, frauds major and minor, another man – this one without a dog – who terrorises the neighbourhood. The hasty overgeneralisation still rules supreme.

During village parties and at the annual kermis, men and women no longer sit separately, the generation that could dance the valeta in such a lovely and stately fashion has quietly slipped away, but the village parties remain popular: the children who chased each other around the upstairs room in the 1990s are themselves now the organisers and life and soul of the parties; all of that continues apace. The prettiest girls always asked Folkert to dance; last summer, when he started turning them down, we knew he didn't have long to go.

The most radical changes have taken place largely around the village perimeter. The younger farmers – and some of the older ones as well – are expanding their horizons all the time. The prospects are anything but limited. In commercial terms as well, networks with friends and family who have emigrated to America are closer than ever. People talk about upping sticks and moving to East Germany, Sake Castelein is taking part in a farming project in Tanzania. Bonne Hylkema and his neighbour recently paid a working visit to farmers in South Africa.

One evening I enter into conversation with a farmer who lives down the road. He told me he had a modern business with two milking machines, which he ran with his son who was attending university in Ottawa. I looked up in surprise. "That's right, my son does the book-keeping," he said. "He keeps an eye on everything by internet. Last night he called our farmhand, who was just cycling home. 'You have to go back, there's something wrong with Aaltje VII. She's got a problem with the teat on the third quarter.' He could tell from the milk yield on his laptop, over there in Ottawa. Yup, we pretty much keep up with the times."

By the same token, however, the closures continue. In 2001, more than half the traditional Frisian farms were still operating as such. That number is quickly dwindling, because it is precisely these traditional farmers who can no longer find a successor. Sake Castelein and Cor Wiedijk encountered the same problem; Bonne Hylkema was fortunate that one of his sons dared to take the leap at the last moment.

Scattered around the province, the first ruins of the once-proud long-house farms can be seen – a unique feature in the Netherlands. Huge chunks of melancholy, their red roofs in partial collapse; upkeep has become too expensive. It is a lost cause, even with all the wealthy retirees from the big cities. In a neighbouring village they have erected the welded steel silhouette of an old castle that once stood there; around 1900, thanks to poverty and perhaps ignorance as well, it was razed for its stones and the old beams. One century from now, artists will for the same reason erect steel Meccano-set representations of longhouse farms: yes, here is where they once stood.

Large stretches of now-unused farmland have since been declared nature reserves. The number of meadow birds, however, continues to fall alarmingly. That is probably due to all that pumping and draining of which the Dutch are so fond, to the artificial rivers that run in one direction in winter and the other in summer, to altered water levels which have literally turned Mother Nature's seasons upside-down: wet in the summer, dry in winter and spring.

No meadow bird can hold out for long on the compacted clay. In the early 1990s, while I was first working on this book, I was awakened each morning in April and May by the combined cacophony of countless godwits, lapwings, larks and oystercatchers. In the spring of 2009 I took a long walk through those same fields. The weather was glorious, but the deathly silence was eerie.

The daily paper the *Leeuwarder Courant* continues to fight the good fight. With a certain regularity, new and ambitious megaprojects are still announced on its front page: a railway straight through the province with an underground station halfway; a dual carriageway to Dokkum (population 13,500), half a dozen huge industrial estates outside Leeuwarden. The occasional plan has actually been carried out: from Jorwert one can see on the horizon a dark-grey, 115-metre-high office complex, a prestige project initiated by a local architect and a few aldermen, a sort of mini-Manhattan – though one would search in vain for a copy of the *Wall Street Journal* at news-stands for miles and miles around.

These projects remind one of nothing so much as rituals designed to win the gods' favour. Nowhere here does one encounter the kinds of urban congestion that call for a train or an underground station or a dual carriageway; no, these are symbols: if you have a railway, a dual carriageway, a little Manhattan, then you are a big city.

*

Expressions of such magical thinking can be seen everywhere in European regions in the throes of crisis. They are signs of disorientation on the part of districts in a state of fundamental transition, perhaps the most important transition in their history. The agriculture and animal husbandry that were Friesland's economic motor for at least the last two thousand years have recently lost their dominance. Industry, the service sector, tourism and also technological innovation (water, renewable energy) have become much more important. As I wrote earlier: of every ten guilders spent in the café at Jorwert in the 1960s, at least eight came – directly or indirectly – from the farmers. Today, farming accounts for no more than one Euro of every ten laid on the bar. And with that, the balance between city and countryside, even in this agrarian region, has changed deeply.

At the same time, agricultural interests remain decisive not only for town and country planning in this region but, in a broader sense, for politics as well. Within sight of Jorwert itself, and despite the farmers' problems sketched above, there appear each year at least two new mega-barns, huge hulks of ugliness completely at odds with the surroundings. In another decade or so the old farming landscape around the village will have metamorphosed into an agricultural industrial estate. The system of water management, which slowly but surely sounds the death knell for all those godwits and larks, is in the same way dictated by farmers' interests. The rest barely counts.

Where will things go from here? Two thousand years of farming tradition is not something you can obliterate in a moment, nor should you want to. It is one of the cardinal traits of these regions. But one must also not turn a blind eye or try to cover up the new dilemmas with a smattering of industrial estates, a plethora of mega-barns or a few lanes of asphalt on a road to nowhere.

We will have to face up to a few realities. Most of these regions are and will remain outlying districts, and no matter how much one fiddles with the transportation infrastructure they will never take on an urban dynamism. That means saying farewell to certain dreams. But, once those are out of the way, what a host of possibilities remain!

The hard facts, after all, also have an upside. Standing still – no matter what the prophets of growth proclaim – is not falling behind. Downscaling is no disaster. This has been proven by a region like the Belgian Ardennes, for example. Throughout history, consolidation has shown itself to be an excellent alternative: the Roman Empire survived for centuries, consolidating as it went. Besides, there are qualities to which one may become so accustomed that one no longer sees them.

A case in point: the relative tranquility of a region like Friesland forms an important part of the high quality of life in modern-day Jorwert. The spaciousness and the landscape itself have gradually become valuable assets. That is something which we, all over Europe, must learn to handle with the appropriate care, just as that is now taking place within our historic cities. In addition, language, tradition and social ties also set in motion something quite unique: a culture of one's own, which at the same time remains open to the rest of the world. And, thanks to the digital revolution, it is precisely the villages, even those in remote rural areas, that are receiving fresh impetus.

In a variety of sectors and professions we have, for the first time, become almost completely independent of the physical workplace. Such freedom of choice was unimaginable only fifteen years ago. For many professions, it no longer really matters whether one is in London or in Amsterdam, or in Jorwert. The need to leave the village therefore loses its urgency, while the opportunities to choose rural life are increasing all the time. Digital connections therefore, more than physical links such as roads and railways, are of vital importance for such areas. And when those networks are present in such almost-forgotten tracts as old Friesland, the future may hold something very special indeed: a new kind of city, spread out over thousands of villages.

It therefore remains very much the question whether or not the ever-growing complexity, the mutual intertwinement and urban centralisation we have known until now will continue apace. In the 21st century, it may very well turn out that decentralisation will again become the norm in all kinds of fields – information and energy supply foremost. In that way, the countryside could once again gain ascendancy.

The same applies to the role of the farmers. Farmers are fond of tradition, that much is true. But they have always been survivors too, men and women who in often brilliant fashion have succeeded in adapting to new conditions. That is still going on. Modern farming operations are becoming increasingly efficient and productive. Despite all the worries, the tiny Netherlands is still the world's second largest exporter of agricultural products. What's more, farmers in the near future will probably play a growing role in our energy supply. A great deal of the Netherlands' renewable energy – almost half – is today produced by the incineration, gasification or fermentation of 'biomass': agricultural and horticultural waste, wood, manure, vegetable oils but also (parts of) crops specially cultivated for this purpose. The production of these energy sources, in whatever form, will almost certainly become a new and important task for farmers. It is therefore quite possible that farming will enter a new hey-day, albeit in a very different way.

Whatever the case, it will no longer amaze old Folkert. We buried him on Tuesday, 1 December 2009. The whole village was there. The sun shone bright and cold over the houses, over the café and the church across the way. He was lying on a bier in the meeting hall, a small, somewhat crumpled wax figure of himself, dressed in a shirt and jeans, that was how he looked in his coffin. Friends and a few family members gave speeches, they spoke about his jobs as baker, carpenter and workman, we all received a glass of Frisian gin bitters and drank to him, then the bells tolled. The neighbours carried him to the grave which the church warden and the man behind the bar had dug for him, a girl stood weeping in the doorway, the men eased down the ropes under the coffin and lowered him into the soil. Afterwards there was coffee and cake.

Up on the stage, at the front, were Folkert's most important possessions: his accordion, his draughts board and his pack of rolling tobacco. Accordion music was playing, the ditties he loved so well, a few popular German Schlagers, tall stories were told, yet we were all shaken.

In the twilight outside we could hear the church warden still working his shovel. It was over, that much we knew for sure, and we had no idea what was supposed to happen next.

Justification

I WROTE PART OF THIS HISTORY IN THE HOUSE WHERE FOLKERT
was born and another part in Minne de Koe's former kitchen, and
there are, I think, worse places to be. But it would never have amounted
to anything if the village of Jorwert had not accepted me into their
community.

And that brought responsibilities with it.

It is sometimes said that country people are close-lipped, but I found
the opposite to be the case. The trust that was vested in me was overwhelming, sometimes it was almost too much. It presented me with
dilemmas similar to those of James Agee, the American writer-journalist,
who stayed with a few poor farming families in Alabama for many weeks
in the summer of 1936, stole their hearts —then walked away with them,
and exposed them to the eyes of the world.

His book, *Let Us Now Praise Famous Men*, would later become a classic. But
Agee nevertheless admitted that he had been unable to repress a slight
feeling of discomfort when it was published – despite the fact that I know
of no journalist who has dealt with his subject more conscientiously.
He wrote about his "beloved, whose poor lives I have already so betrayed,
and should you see these things so abandoned, so destroyed, I dread to
dare that I shall ever look into your dear eyes again".

It never got to that stage between me and the Jorwerters. But by
the time I had done some 20 or 30 interviews I began to experience
emotions similar to those of Agee's 60 years ago. I became aware that
my role as outsider was untenable in such a small community, and that
I was unavoidably drifting into a situation in which I was not only
observer, but also participant. I was soon no longer simply there as
a journalist (as I was in the city), but also as a neighbour, acquaintance
and friend. Moreover it was not unusual for people to share all their

joys and sorrows with me during the interviews, and that forges a bond.

So I owe a debt of gratitude to all Jorwerters, and especially to the immense trust they put in me. To my friends Armande van Ginkel and Gijs van Woudenberg who introduced me in the village, and without whose help, warmth, and hospitality this book would never have been written. To Wiebe and Willemijn Bakker who so generously offered me accommodation. To Gais Meinsma, on whom I could always rely for good advice, and who prevented me from making factual blunders during the writing of this book. And all the other Jorwerters, who allowed me to share in their lives.

I profited greatly from the Littenseradiel district archives, and the impressive research done by Jolt Oostra who – assisted by the earlier sleuthing of the former Jorwerter baker Klaas de Jong – had delved into the entire early history of the village. It was my good fortune that his *Topography of Jorwert* had just been completed when I began this project, so that I could build on Oostra's work.

Hans Maarten van den Brink, by his friendship and good advice, saw me through an impasse during the writing of this book.

Enormously supportive too, was the continuous help of Hylke Speerstra – skater, farmer's son, former editor of the *Leeuwarder Courant* and the *Agrarisch Dagblad* – who prevented me from taking too many nasty tumbles on the thin ice of the agricultural sector. I also owe a debt of gratitude to the Foundation for Special Journalistic Projects that enabled me to hang around for so long in Jorwert.

Finally there were my Frisian neighbours, Johannes and Mientje Lenis. Through them, I got to know the reality of the farming world with all its ups and downs. They were the ones who – in countless conversations – taught me, an out-and-out city type, what was happening in the countryside, what was happening to farming families, what the quiet revolution meant, what surviving was all about in our time. They were the first of a whole series of friends and companions who inspired me to write this book.

I thank them all from the bottom of my heart.

Amsterdam, Jorwert, Katlijk 1993–96

Bibliography

Agee, J. and Walker Evans, *Let Us Now Praise Famous Men* (London: Panther, 1969; Boston: Houghton Mifflin Co., 1960)

Barentsen, P. A., *Het Oude Kempenland* [The Old Kempen Country] (Groningen, 1935).

Berger, J., *Pig Earth* (London: Writers and Readers Publishing Co-operative, 1979; New York: Pantheon, 1979).

Bieleman, J., *Geschiedenis van de landbouw in Nederland, 1500–1950* [History of Dutch Agriculture, 1500–1950] (Meppel, 1992).

Bos, J. M., *Archeologie van Friesland* [Frisian archeology] (Utrecht, 1995).

Brunt, L., *Stedeling op het platteland* [City-dweller in the Country] (Meppel, 1974).

Brunt, L., *Stad* [City] (Meppel, 1996).

Burger, W., "Ontstaan, ontwikkelingsfasen en funktie van het formele organisatiewezen in een Drentse gemeente" [Emergence, phases of development and function of formal organisations in a Drentish borough], in H. M. Jolles, ed., *Verenigingsleven in Nederland* [Organised Societies in the Netherlands] (Arnhem, 1963).

Castelein, M. H., *Tuolle-prakkesaesjes* [Musings from the Milking Stool] (Leeuwarden, no date).

Castenmiller, P. and Frans Knol, *Convergentie of divergentie. Sociale en culturele ontwikkelingen in stedelijke en landelijke gebieden* [Convergence or Divergence: Social and Cultural Developments in Urban and Rural Areas], Sociaal en Cultureel Planbureau report (Rijswijk, 1989).

Chotjewitz, P. O., "Neuland – Leben in der Provinz" [New Land – Provincial Life], in Kursbuch, nr. 39, Provinz (Berlin 1995).

Critchfield, R., *The Villagers: Changed Values, Altered Lives, The Closing of the Urban-Rural Gap* (New York: Anchor, 1994).

Deursen, A. Th. van, *Een dorp in de polder* [A Polder Village] (Amsterdam, 1994).

Dijkstra, W., *Uit Frieslands Volksleven* [From Friesland's Folk Life] (Leeuwarden, 1895).

Dobrowolski, K., "Peasant traditional culture", in Shanin, 1971.

Eijk, D. van, "Hongkong aan de Noordzee" [Hongkong on the North Sea], in *NRC Handelsblad*, 15 July 1995.

Fokkinga, A., *Een land vol vee* [A Country Full of Cattle] (Doetinchem, 1995).

Gelder, B. van, *Nachtboek van een kerkuil* [Night Diary of a Barn Owl] (private edition, no date).

Giesen, K., *Crisis op de boerderij* [Crisis on the Farm] (Utrecht, 1993).

Groot, J. P., *Kleine plattelandskernen in de Nederlandse samenleving. Schaalvergroting en dorpsbinding* [Small Rural Centres in Dutch Society: Increase in Scale and Village Ties] (Wageningen, 1972).

Groot, J. P., *Het kleine dorp* [The Small Village] (Baarn, 1974).

Groot, J. P., *Groeiende en kwijnende plattelandskernen* [Growing and Declining Rural Centres] (Den Haag, 1980).

Groot, J. P., "Dorpsbinding en lokaal bewustzijn" [Village ties and local awareness], in P. P. P. Huigen and M. C. H. M. van der Velden, eds., *De achterkant van verstedelijkt Nederland* [The Reverse Side of the Urbanised Netherlands] Nederlandse Geografische Studies (Utrecht, 1989).

Guillaumin, E., *Het landelijk leven* (Paris, 1922).

Hellema, D. W., *Kroniek van een Friese boer. De aantekeningen (1821–1856) van Doeke Wijgers Hellema te Wirdum* [Chronicle of a Frisian Farmer: Notes (1821–1856) by Doeke Wijgers Hellema from Wirdum], ed. H. Algra (Franeker, 1978).

Jansen, J. C. G. M., "Ontsnappen aan economische achterstand, een bijzonder probleem" [Escaping economical deprivation, a special problem], in H. Diederiks et al., *Het platteland in een veranderende wereld* [The Countryside in a Changing World] (Hilversum, 1994).

Janszoon, D., *Aantekeningenboek van Dirck Janszoon (1604–36)* [The Notebook of Dirck Janszoon], edited by J. A. Faber, K. Fokkema and P. Gerbenzon (Hilversum, 1993).

—

Klaver, I., *Herinneringen van een Friese landarbeider* [The Recollections of a Frisian Agricultural Labourer] (Nijmegen, 1974).

Kooi, J. van der, *Volksverhalen in Friesland. Lectuur en mondelinge overlevering, een typencatalogus* [Frisian Folk Tales. Written Matter and Oral Tradition, a Catalogue of Types] (Groningen, 1984).

Kronjee, G. H., *Risico op armoede en stedelijke omgeving. Aanzet tot een kansarmoede-atlas van Nederland* [The Risk of Poverty and the Urban Environment. Initiative for an Atlas of Deprivation in the Netherlands] (Utrecht, 1994).

Le Roy Ladurie, E., *Montaillou: Cathars and Catholics in a French Village*, 1294–1324 (London: Scolar Press, 1978; New York: Vintage, 1979, under the title *Montaillou, the Promised Land of Error*).

Meulen, T. van de, *De Voorstap: Enkele verkenningen naar toekomstige ontwikkelingen, met name op ruimtelijk gebied. Provincie Friesland* [The First Step: An Exploration of Future Developments, Especially in the Field of Environmental Planning. Province of Friesland (Leeuwarden, 1989).

Meulen, T. van de, *Gruts op Lyts: Evaluatie van het kleine kernenbeleid 1988–1995 van de Provincie Friesland* [Proud of the Small-scale: Evaluation of the Policy on Small Regional Centres in the Province of Friesland, 1988–95] (Leeuwarden, 1994).

Noordam, D. J., "Modernisering in de beroepsstructuur van Holland en Friesland in de vroegmoderne tijd" [The modernisation of the professional structure of Holland and Friesland in the Early Modern Period], in Herman Diederiks et al., *Het platteland in een veranderende wereld* [The Countryside in a Changing World] (Hilversum, 1994).

Nota Landelijke Gebieden [Rural Areas Bill], Derde Nota RO, deel 3a, vergaderjaar 1976/1977, 14392, nrs. 1 and 2, Den Haag, 1977.

Oostra, Jolt, Rzn., *Uit de geschiedenis van Jorwert, Toponymy fan Jorwert* [From Jorwert History] (Franeker 1993).

Poortinga, Y., *De ring fan it ljocht. Fryske folksforhalen* [The Ring of Light: Frisian Folk Tales (Baarn/Leeuwarden, 1976).

Postma, O., *Samle Fersen* [Collected Poems] (Baarn/Leeuwarden, 1966).

Saal, C. D., "Dorp en route: waartoe en waarheen?" [Village en route:

what for and to where?], in *De Gids* 1972, pp. 279–86, quoted in Brunt 1996.

Schama, S., *Landscape and Memory* (London: HarperCollins 1995; New York: Alfred A. Knopf, 1995).

Schuyt, C. J. M., *Tegendraadse werkingen* [Contrary Effects] (Amsterdam, 1995).

Segalen, M., *Love and Power in the Peasant Family: Rural France in the Nineteenth Century* (Oxford: Blackwell, 1983; Chicago: University of Chicago Press, 1983).

Shanin, T., ed., *Peasants and Peasant Societies: Selected Readings* (Harmondsworth: Penguin Education, 1975; New York: Blackwell, 1987).

Sillevis, H. A., *De boer en zijn wereld* [The Farmer and His World] (Assen, 1959).

Slicher van Bath, B., *De agrarische geschiedenis van Europa, 500–1850* [European Agricultural History, 500–1850] (Utrecht, 1960/ 1987).

Terpstra, P., *Honderd jaar Friese landbouw* [A Hundred Years of Frisian Agriculture] (Leeuwarden, 1977).

Thomas, W. I. and Florian Znaniecki, *The Polish Peasant in Europe and America* (New York, Dover Publications, 1958).

Tolstoy, L. N., *Anna Karenina* (Oxford: Oxford University Press, 1998, trans. by Aylmer and Louise Maude).

Verrips, K., "Woont daar nog iemand? De plattelandsbevolking in 2015" [Does anybody still live there? The rural population in 2015], in *Spil* (magazine), pp. 81–2 and 83–4 (Wageningen, 1989).

Volkers, C. R., "Perspektieven voor landelijke gebieden" [Perspectives for rural areas], in P. P. P. Huigen and M. C. H. M.van der Velden, eds., *De achterkant van verstedelijkt Nederland* [The Reverse Side of the Urbanised Netherlands] Nederlandse Geografische Studies (Utrecht, 1989).

Vries, J. de, "De Boer" [The Farmer], in H. M. Beliën et al., *Gestalten van de Gouden Eeuw* [Figures of the Golden Century] (Amsterdam, 1995).

Westerloo, G. van, *Voetreiziger: Verslag van een tocht door Nederland* [Foot Traveller: An Account of a Walking Tour of the Netherlands] (Amsterdam, 1993).

Wichers, A. J., *De oude plattelandsbeschaving* [The Old Rural Civilization] (Wageningen, 1965).

Wie het kleine niet eert . . . [He that Will Not Stop for a Pin . . .],

Studiecommissie Kleine Kernen van de Vereniging van Nederlandse
Gemeenten (Den Haag, 1979).

Wielen, K. v.d., *Lusten en lasten van wonen in een landelijk gebied.Verslag van een soci-
aal-geografisch onderzoeksprojekt in Zuidwest-Friesland* [The Joys and Sorrows of
Living in a Rural Area. Report of a Social-Geographic Research Project
Conducted in South-West Friesland] (Utrecht, 1985).

World Resources 1996—97:The Urban Environment, a joint publication by the
World Resources Institute et al. (Oxford: Oxford University
Press, 1996).

Woud, A. van der, *Het lege land. De ruimtelijke orde van Nederland 1798—1848* [The
Empty Land. Environmental Planning in the Netherlands 1798—1848
(Amsterdam, 1987).

Zwier, G. J., J. J. Slauerhoff. *Alleen voor Friesland heb ik nog een zwak* [But I Still
Have a Soft Spot for Friesland] (Leeuwarden, 1992).

Most of the figures, unless stated otherwise, have been taken from
reports of the Landbouweconomisch Instituut (Institute for Agricultural
Economical Affairs), the IKC, and the magazine De Boerderij (The Farm),
especially the 13 June 1995 issue (on the cost of land and milk quota
in comparison with the rest of Europe), the 27 March 1995 issue (on
the extent of beef farming and intensive cattle farming), 22 March
1994 (about farmer's expectations for the future), and 16 November 1993
(about the future prognosis for Dutch dairy farming).

Acknowledgements
The drawing by Douwe de Bildt (page 3) is reproduced courtesy of
Gais Meinsma. The frontispiece engraving of Jorwert in the eighteenth
century, the photograph of the church (page 151), and the Jorwert stamp
illustration at the beginning of each chapter are all reproduced courtesy
of the Gemeentearchief Littenseradiel in Wommels, The Netherlands.